# INDIVIDUAL DIFFERENCES

**Ann Birch**
**and**
**Sheila Hayward**

MACMILLAN

First published 1994 by
THE MACMILLAN PRESS LTD
Houndmills, Basingstoke, Hampshire RG21 2XS
and London
Companies and representatives
throughout the world

ISBN 0–333–58813–4

A catalogue record for this book is available from the British Library.

10   9   8   7   6   5   4   3   2
03   02   01   00   99   98   97   96   95

Printed in Hong Kong

Cartoons by Sally Artz

# Individual Differences

# INTRODUCTORY PSYCHOLOGY

This series of titles is aimed at A-level psychology students in sixth forms and further education colleges and those wishing to obtain an overview of psychology. The books are easy to use, with comprehensive notes written in coherent language; clear flagging of key concepts; relevant and interesting illustrations; well-defined objectives and further reading sections to each chapter; and self-assessment questions at regular intervals throughout the text.

*Published*

INDIVIDUAL DIFFERENCES
Ann Birch and Sheila Hayward

DEVELOPMENTAL PSYCHOLOGY: From Infancy to
   Adulthood
Ann Birch and Tony Malim

COGNITIVE PROCESSES
Tony Malim

SOCIAL PSYCHOLOGY
Tony Malim and Ann Birch

PERSPECTIVES IN PSYCHOLOGY
Tony Malim, Ann Birch and Alison Wadeley

---

**Series Standing Order**

If you would like to receive future titles in this series as they are published, you can make use of our standing order facility. To place a standing order please contact your bookseller or, in case of difficulty, write to us at the address below with your name and address and the name of the series. Please state with which title you wish to begin your standing order. (If you live outside the United Kingdom we may not have the rights for your area, in which case we will forward your order to the publisher concerned.)

Customer Services Department, Macmillan Distribution Ltd, Houndmills, Basingstoke, Hampshire, RG21 2XS, England.

# Contents

# List of Figures

# Preface

The aims of this book are to highlight some of the ways in which psychologists have investigated differences between individuals and to critically examine some of their more significant findings. It focuses on three important areas of psychological functioning: intelligence, personality and abnormal behaviour.

Chapter 1 critically examines definitions of intelligence, the measurement of intelligence and the controversial nature/nurture debate. Different theoretical approaches to the study of personality are explored in Chapters 2 and 3, along with some ways in which personality can be assessed. Chapters 4 to 6 concentrate on abnormal behaviour and include a critical examination of the problems which arise when attempts are made to distinguish 'abnormal' from 'normal' behaviour, some of the characteristics and possible causes of various mental disorders, and a range of different therapies used to treat them.

In line with previous books in the series, the authors have attempted to present the text concisely in the form of comprehensive notes which are suitable either as an introduction to this area of psychology or as a revision text.

For the independent student, each chapter is prefaced with objectives to be met during the study of the chapter and each section ends with some self-assessment questions so that readers may test their understanding of the section.

The reader is advised to work through the text a section at a time and to consider the self-assessment questions following each section. The self-assessment questions should then be re-examined after further reading has been undertaken.

While the books in the series are aimed primarily at those who are studying psychology at 'A' level or GCSE, they should also prove useful for students encountering psychology for the first time at degree level or on nursing and BTEC courses.

We are confident that this book will prove as useful and popular as have the previous ones in the series. We very much hope you will enjoy it.

*Ann Birch*
*Sheila Hayward*

Every effort has been made to trace all the copyright-holders, but if any have been inadvertently overlooked the publishers will be pleased to make the necessary arrangements at the first opportunity.

THEY'RE IDENTICAL TWINS, AREN'T THEY? WE'D BETTER HAVE THEM REARED APART.

# Intelligence and Its Measurement

1

At the end of this chapter, you should be able to:

1. Discuss different definitions and theories of intelligence;
2. Appreciate the implications of different theories for intelligence testing;
3. Understand the nature and functions of intelligence tests and be aware of the controversies surrounding their use;
4. Appreciate the issues surrounding the heredity/environment controversy in intelligence and evaluate different kinds of evidence used by psychologists to reach a conclusion;
5. Discuss the interactionist approach used by psychologists in assessing the relative influence of heredity and environment on intelligence test performance.

## SECTION I DEFINITIONS AND THEORIES OF INTELLIGENCE

### What is Intelligence?

The idea of 'intelligence' or 'ability' is a far-reaching and powerful concept in everyday life. It is used freely to describe differences between people and to explain why people behave as they do. Terms such as 'bright', 'quick-thinking', 'dull' and 'slow' are frequently used to label people as being of a certain type. Despite the confidence with which these terms are used, finding a precise definition of intelligence that all psychologists can agree upon is very difficult.

In 1921, the editor of the *American Journal of Educational Psychology* invited seventeen leading psychologists to write about 'What I consider "intelligence" to be. . .'. So diverse were their views that later commentators attempted to group them into a few main categories. Vernon (1960), for example, classified descriptions as biological, psychological or operational. Freeman (1962) divided them into those emphasising (a) power of adaptation to the environment (b) capacity for learning and (c) ability for abstract thinking.

Some of the better known definitions of intelligence are:

'The ability to carry on abstract thinking' (Terman, 1921)
'Innate general cognitive ability' (Burt, 1955)
'To judge well, to comprehend well, to reason well . . ' (Binet and Simon, 1905)
'Intelligent activity consists in grasping the essentials in a situation and responding appropriately to them' (Heim, 1970a)

These definitions demonstrate that the term 'intelligence' means different things to different people. Some early definitions implied that intelligence is an entity – something one has a lot or a little of. Others prefer to stress purposeful activity and successful adaptation to the environment. Estes (1982) suggests that intelligence is a property of behaviour, jointly determined by cognitive functioning and motives.

Vernon (1969) and Sternberg (1984) argue that any definition of intelligence must recognise the cultural context in which the definition is being applied. What is classed as intelligent behaviour in one culture may not be so highly regarded in another. Also, the opportunity to develop or acquire particular behaviours varies from one culture to another. This view contrasts with Burt's use of the word 'innate' in defining intelligence, implying something which is fixed and unchangeable rather than varying according to the influence of a particular environment. There has been much controversy over the relative merit of these two views (see Section III).

Finally, the definition of intelligence is closely linked to the notion of **intelligence quotient (IQ)**, which is the score derived from an intelligence test (see Section II). Since intelligence is often defined in relation to the ability to do intelligence tests, some psychologists have suggested that intelligence is what the tests measure.

### The Use of Factor Analysis in the Study of Intelligence

The statistical technique of factor analysis has been used by many researchers in their efforts to describe the nature of intelligence. Principally, it has been used to identify the specific abilities that make up what we know as intelligence.

Based on the statistical technique of **correlation**, factor analysis involves a complex process which may take a number of different forms. However, the underlying ideas are quite easy to follow; a brief summary of the most important points is shown in Figure 1.1.

---

### FIGURE 1.1

**The Use of Correlation and Factor Analysis in the Study of Intelligence**

1. Factor analysis makes use of the statistical technique of **correlation**. Correlation is a measure of the extent to which two things are related to each other. For example, as children grow older their feet tend to grow larger. This would be called a **positive correlation** since both measures are moving in the same direction. Where high scores on one measure are related to low scores on the other, such as the number of miles travelled at various points on a journey and the amount of petrol remaining in the car, then a **negative correlation** between the two measures is indicated.

   The degree of relationship between two measures is expressed as a **correlation coefficient**, which varies from a value of $+1.00$ (a perfect positive correlation) or $-1.00$ (a perfect negative correlation) to zero (no relationship). For example, a correlation coefficient of 0.8 would indicate a strong positive relationship between two measures, where 0.03 would indicate almost no relationship

2. The aim of factor analysis is to find factors (hypothetical entities such as numerical ability, verbal ability, etc.) which are common to a number of different tests or in some cases sub-sections within one test.

3. If a number of tests, say intelligence tests, are administered to a large sample of people, their scores on each test can be correlated with their scores on each of the other tests to produce a correlation matrix. An example is given in the hypothetical correlation matrix relating to four tests shown overleaf:

FIG. 1.1 *cont.*

| Tests | 2 | 3 | 4 |
|---|---|---|---|
| 1   (Numerical) | 0.39 | 0.58 | 0.12 |
| 2   (Verbal) | | 0.38 | 0.40 |
| 3   (Spatial) | | | 0.06 |
| 4   (Memory) | | | |

   The assumption is made that the higher the correlation between two or more tests (that is, the closer the correlation coefficient is to 1.00), the more similar are the scores and the more likely it is that the tests are measuring the same ability, or factor (note that the strongest relationship exists between the scores on Test 1 and Test 3 and the weakest relationship between those on Test 3 and Test 4). Using the technique of factor analysis, the matrix is scanned to identify clusters of high correlations, indicating groups of tests which are attributable to one factor. So, for example, if all tests were measuring the same ability, only one factor would emerge from the analysis. This would suggest that the structure of intelligence was dominated by one major ability. If, however, the tests were measuring a number of different and independent abilities, then several factors would emerge from the analysis.

4.   Let us assume that a factor analysis of the correlation co-efficients in the matrix above has yielded three underlying factors (in this case abilities). A further analysis would then be carried out to show which tests are most highly correlated with each of the three factors. For example, if a test correlated 0.05 with factor I, 0.75 with factor II and 0.21 with factor III, it would be assumed to be most heavily loaded on (influenced by) factor II. The factors identified would then be interpreted by examining the content of the tests most heavily weighted on each factor.

5.   It is important to note, that whilst factor analysis is a precise mathematical technique for analysing the common factors underlying a number of different tests or sub-tests, the interpretation and naming of the factors rests with the researcher and must be carefully justified. In some cases, the somewhat arbitrary nature of the labels attached to the various factors has been questioned (see criticisms of factor analysis later in this section).

---

Factor analysis has allowed researchers to investigate the possible structure of intelligence. For example, the method has been used to explore the question of whether intelligence should be conceived of as a single dimension along which all individuals can be placed, or whether there is more than one dimension indicating that an individual may excel in one area of intelligence and not in another.

   The reader should note that the technique of factor analysis has also been used to identify attributes underlying other psychological characteristics such as personality (see Chapter 2).

## General Intelligence or Specific Abilities

When we talk about 'intelligence', we imply that there is one kind of intellectual ability. Thus the term 'general intelligence', or *g* as it became known, suggests one overriding capacity which affects every activity in life from doing mental arithmetic to wiring a plug. This could be contrasted with the possibility that individuals possess a number of separate, independent capacities, for example mathematical ability or verbal ability.

The debate about whether we possess one intelligence or a number of separate abilities is centuries old. This debate can be seen in some of the theories about the nature of intelligence discussed below.

## Theories of Intelligence

Below is an account of some theoretical approaches which aim to clarify the nature of intelligence, starting with some which have made use of factor analysis to arrive at a description of the structure of intelligence.

### *The Factor Analytical Approach*

SPEARMAN'S TWO-FACTOR THEORY **Charles Spearman** (1863–1945) was the pioneer both of tests of mental abilities and of the technique of factor analysis. After analysing the scores from children's performance on a number of tests, he found a strong correlation between all the tests. He therefore proposed that all the tests were measuring a common factor which he called *g* (**general intelligence**) He also found that an individual's performance on one test, for example one of verbal ability, did not exactly match their performance on another, for example mathematical ability, so the *g* factor could not account for *all* the variation between individuals. Spearman therefore proposed the existence of another factor specific to each test which he labelled *s* (**specific factor**). Thus a person's measured intelligence would be made up mainly of *g*, which he saw as roughly equivalent to the ability to see relationships between things. Individuals differed according to how much *g* they possessed with 'bright' people having a lot and 'duller' people having less. Yet, they would vary also according to their specific abilities (*s*) in that one person might be better mathematically where another would excel verbally.

HIERARCHICAL THEORY   During the 1940s and 1950s, factor analytical techniques were extended further by **Cyril Burt** and **Philip Vernon**. Though in broad agreement with Spearman's model of intelligence, they considered that to conceive of intelligence as composed of *g* and *s* factors alone was too simple. Using test scores drawn from school children, they elaborated Spearman's two-factor model by proposing the existence of a series of group factors between the *g* and *s* levels. Figure 1.2 shows how this model was conceived. A major division exists between verbal/educational abilities (v:ed) and spatial/mechanical abilities (k:m). Vernon believed that the v:ed factor represents largely verbal skills such as reading, spelling and so on together with some aspects of mathematical ability and of creative ability. The k:m factor reflects the more practical spatial, mechanical and some mathematical abilities.

**FIGURE 1.2**

**Vernon's Hierarchical Theory** (after Vernon, 1950)

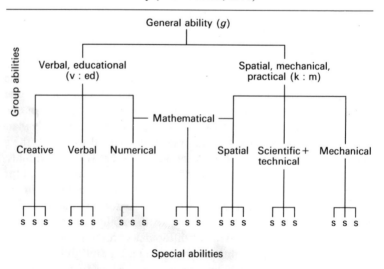

Burt and Spearman were agreed that *g* was inherited and unchangeable whereas *s* resulted from training. Burt and Vernon believed that the group factors also were a function of education.

THURSTONE'S MULTI-FACTOR THEORY   Spearman, Burt and Vernon (sometimes known as the 'London Line') postulated a model of intelligence based on the existence of a general factor which affected all aspects of human functioning. However, in the United States, other researchers were developing models which proposed that intelligence consisted of a number of different and basically unrelated skills. The most notable of these models was that of **Thurstone** (1938) who proposed seven **Primary Mental Abilities** (PMAs). The abilities, he believed formed the basis of human intellectual functioning. All were equally important and none correlated highly with any other.

The Primary Mental Abilities are as follows:

Verbal ability
Perceptual speed
Numerical reasoning
Rote memory
Word fluency
Spatial ability
Inductive reasoning

Since this model denies the existence of a *g* factor which affects all areas of functioning, each PMA is assessed by a different test. Performance yields a profile of seven scores, rather than a single *g* score.

Later researchers questioned Thurstone's model pointing out that there was similarity between people's scores on the seven tests, which suggested that a *g* factor did exist. Following a second-order factor analysis (carrying out a further analysis on the first set of results), Thurstone conceded the possible existence of a *g* factor in all the PMAs. So, it seems that hierarchical theory could be valid.

Gould (1981) discussed the political and educational implications of the debate. He strongly criticised Burt's insistence on a hierarchical model of intelligence with its assumption of a dominating 'innate' *g* factor. The influence of this model in the 1940s on the development of the eleven plus examination to select children for grammar school education was not supportable, especially given the lack of evidence for an innate basis for intelligence. Thurstone's PMAs, he believed, whilst still open to criticism, represented a less entrenched and rigid view of a child's abilities.

### Criticisms of Factor-analytical Theories of Intelligence

1. First, some points on the technique of factor analysis:

   (a) As already noted, factors emerging statistically must be interpreted and labelled by the investigator. Therefore, it can be claimed that the process of identifying the factors is subjective.

   (b) Gould (1981) draws attention to the fallacy of **reification** (the tendency to see abstract concepts such as 'verbal ability' as concrete entities). A factor is just a statistic. Because it has been given a label such as, for example, 'spatial ability', does not 'prove' its objective existence.

   (c) There is more than one method of factor analysis. The number of factors revealed in an investigation may depend upon which method is used, as well as the number and variety of tests analysed and the kind of sample used. Spearman and Thurstone used different forms of factor analysis and where Spearman tested mainly samples of school children, Thurstone used college students. This could in part account for some of the differences in their analyses.

2. Fundamental to factor-analytical models is the notion that intelligence is measurable and that it is possible to describe a person's intellectual ability at a given time. These are highly controversial issues. A more complete discussion of them can be found in the next section under 'Criticisms of intelligence testing'.

### The Systems Approach

Whereas factor-analytical theories attempt to identify the structure of abilities which make up intelligence, a number of more recent theories seek to explore the working of the abilities themselves. The theories of Gardner (1983) and Sternberg (1985, 1988) attempt to understand intelligence in terms of a complex interaction of various cognitive and other systems. Each theory will be briefly discussed below.

GARDNER'S THEORY OF MULTIPLE INTELLIGENCES   **Gardner** (1983) has put forward a theory based partly upon the results of tests and partly on research from neuropsychology. The theory has three fundamental principles:

1.  There exists seven distinct intelligences as follows:

    **linguistic** (language skills such as reading, writing, speaking and listening)
    **logical-mathematical** (numerical skills)
    **spatial** (understanding relationships in space as in driving or playing chess)
    **musical** (skills such as singing or playing an instrument)
    **bodily kinaesthetic** (using the body as in dance or athletics)
    **interpersonal** (understanding and relating to others)
    **intrapersonal** (understanding oneself)

2.  The intelligences are independent of each other. They operate as modular systems without a 'central control' to co-ordinate them. In other words, a person's abilities as assessed under one intelligence should in theory be uncorrelated with the person's abilities as assessed under another intelligence.

3.  Though they are separate and independent of each other, the intelligences interact and work together whenever the need arises; for example solving a mathematical word problem would require linguistic and logical-mathematical intelligence to work together.

Gardner believes that each intelligence resides in a separate portion of the brain and that a particular intelligence could be isolated by studying brain-damaged patients. Damage in one area of the brain could impair one intelligence leaving the others intact. The phenomenon of severely retarded individuals who have one exceptional skill such as playing a musical instrument or manipulating numbers provides evidence for the independent existence of one particular intelligence.

The first three intelligences proposed by Gardner are very much in line with those measured in conventional IQ tests. However, Gardner's inclusion of the other abilities as part of intelligence represents a new and interesting approach as does his attempt to explore the roles of physiological and cognitive processes in intelligence.

Among criticisms made of Gardner's theory is that the kinds of intelligences he proposes are not measurable in the way that factor analytical theories are. However, Gardner replies that the intelligences he proposes may not be measurable by conventional IQ tests but can be assessed through the activities engaged in by children at school, such as composition or athletic activities (Gardner and Feldman, 1985).

Sternberg (1990) suggests that whilst Gardner's theory is at present too vague to be substantiated in detail, it represents an important contribution to understanding the human mind and intelligence.

STERNBERG'S TRIARCHIC THEORY OF INTELLIGENCE    Sternberg's triarchic (governed by three systems) theory of intelligence (Sternberg, 1985, 1988) seeks to explain the relationship between

1.  intelligence and the internal world of the individual, that is the mental mechanisms that underlie intelligent behaviour (the **componential sub-theory**);
2.  intelligence and the external world of the individual, that is the use of these mental mechanisms in everyday life in order to adapt to the environment in an intelligent way (the **contextual sub-theory**); and
3.  intelligence and experience or the role played by life experience in linking the individual's internal and external worlds (the **experiential sub-theory**).

THE COMPONENTIAL SUB-THEORY
Sternberg proposes that intelligent functioning, for instance trying to solve a mathematical problem, involves three basic information-processing mechanisms or components. These are:

**Metacomponents** which include higher order processes involved in identifying the nature of the problem, developing a strategy for its solution and evaluating the success of the solution;
**Performance components** which include lower order processes involved in actually solving the problem according to the plans laid down by the metacomponents;

**Knowledge-acquisition components** which include processes involved in learning new material, such as sifting out relevant from irrelevant information.

Other components have been considered by Sternberg. These include **retention components** – processes involved in retrieval of information from memory – and **transfer components** – processes involved in generalising (transferring information from one situation to another).

The components function together in a highly interactive way and are not easy to study in isolation from each other. Metacomponents activate performance and knowledge components, which in turn provide feedback to the metacomponents.

Understanding the nature of the components, Sternberg argues, is not sufficient to allow an understanding of the nature of intelligence, as there is more to intelligence than a number of information-processing components. Nor is it sufficient to assess an individual's intelligence solely through IQ tests. The other two aspects of the triarchic theory go some way to explaining the other elements of intelligence which contribute to individual differences in intelligent behaviour – outside of testing situations as well as within them.

THE EXPERIENTIAL SUB-THEORY

The information-processing components discussed above are always applied to tasks and situations where the person has some level of previous experience. The essence of the experiential aspect of the triarchic theory is that an individual's intelligence can only be understood if account is taken not just of the components but of his/her level of experience.

Intelligence is measured most effectively where the tasks being undertaken are either relatively novel (not totally outside the individual's understanding, but close to the limits) or in the process of becoming automised (performed automatically).

**Novelty**. Different sources of evidence suggest that assessing the ability to deal with relative novelty is a good way of measuring intelligence. In studies with children, Davidson and Sternberg (1984) found that those who were intellectually gifted had the ability to deal with novelty in a problem-solving situation without being given helpful cues, whereas less gifted children benefited from help. Sternberg contends that the various components of intelligence that are involved in dealing with novelty in particular situations provide apt measures of intellectual ability.

**Automisation**. Equally, Sternberg believes that the ability to automise information, as in skilled reading, is a key aspect of intelligence. Poor comprehenders are often those who have not automised the elementary processes of reading and therefore have not the resources to allocate to more complex comprehension processes. Thus, the ability to automise allows more resources to be devoted to novelty. Similarly, if one is able to deal effectively with novelty, more resources are available for automisation.

THE CONTEXTUAL SUB-THEORY

According to this aspect of the theory, intelligence is not a random mental activity that happens to involve certain information-processing components. Rather, it is purposely directed towards one or more of three behavioural goals – adaptation to an environment; shaping of an environment and selection of an environment.

**Adaptation**. The components of information-processing and the importance of dealing with novelty and automisation of information-processing are seen by Sternberg as universal in that they operate in the same way for individuals in one culture as they do for those in all other cultures. However, the way these components show themselves in the experience and behaviour of individuals will vary from culture to culture. What is intelligent in one culture may be seen as unintelligent in another.

**Shaping**. This involves adapting the environment to one's own preferred style of operating rather than the other way round. Sternberg sees this as a key feature of intelligent thought and behaviour: 'In science, the greatest scientists are those who set the paradigms (shaping) rather than those who merely follow them (adaptation)' (Sternberg, 1990, p. 281).

**Selection**. This involves renouncing one environment in favour of another. It sometimes occurs when both adaptation and shaping fail. For example, if one has failed to adapt to the demands of a particular job or to shape the nature of those demands to make them fit in with one's needs, the intelligent thing to do may be to select a new environment by changing one's job.

It can be seen that a major feature of Sternberg's theory is his emphasis upon the need to go further than studying intelligent behaviour as represented by typical problems in IQ tests. Bee (1989) argues that standard IQ tests have failed to assess many of the kinds of abilities featured in Sternberg's contextual and experiential sub-theories and which are so relevant to intelligent functioning in the 'real world'. However, Sternberg himself (in press) is developing a test based on his triarchic theory of intelligence. In addition to providing scores for componential skills, it will also assess coping with novelty skills, automisation skills and practical intellectual skills.

## Biological Intelligence

The biological approach to intelligence attempts to understand intelligence by studying the brain and the operation of the central nervous system. It involves relating various physiological measures to psychological functioning, such as completing IQ tests. Eysenck (1986) holds that if the study of intelligence is to be fully scientific, it is necessary to include an investigation of the biological character-istics that underlie intelligent behaviour.

REACTION TIME One of the first physiological measures to be investigated was that of reaction time. This was first studied by Galton as long ago as the 1800s. More recently, researchers have attempted to demonstrate a correlation between people's reaction times to various stimuli and their IQs. Eysenck (1986) reports correlations of 0.60 between reaction times and the results of standard intelligence tests. Eysenck claims that speed of informa-tion processing is a basic quality of biological intelligence.

ELECTROPHYSIOLOGICAL MEASURES Some researchers have cho-sen to relate intelligence to measures of electrical activity in the brain. Early studies used **electroencephalogram (EEG)** measurement (see p. 133) and attempted to relate different patterns of EEG activity to intelligence or other cognitive functions. For example, Galin and Ornstein (1972) showed a link between the amount of EEG activity in each of the brain's two hemispheres and the type of tasks performed by the individual.

More recent studies have used **evoked potentials**, a more sophisticated electrophysiological measure of the brain's wave-forms. Early research in this field was carried out by Ertl and his co-workers (Ertl and Schafer, 1969; Ertl, 1971). These investigators found consistent correlations between averaged evoked potentials and IQ though subsequent studies did not always replicate these results (Eysenck, 1986). More recently, Hendrickson and Hendrickson (1980) obtained high correlations between an evoked potential measure and scores on a standard IQ test. These findings have been replicated by Blinkhorn and Hendrickson (1982) using a variety of IQ tests.

The biological approach has generated a great deal of research which relates the functioning of the brain to intelligent activity. However, Gazzaniga (1985) points out that the interpretation of this research is by no means straightforward. For example, what does it mean to show a relationship between evoked potentials and IQ test scores? Does intelligent behaviour lead to certain patterns of evoked potential or do the evoked potentials somehow cause intelligent behaviour? Equally plausible is the possibility that intelligent activity and the evoked potentials depend upon some as yet little understood aspect of the brain. Nonetheless, researchers in this field claim that psychophysiological measures may provide a 'purer' measure of intelligence which is 'culture-free', that is uncontaminated by an individual's culture or education (see Section II for a discussion of culture and IQ tests).

### A Developmental Approach to Intelligence

Brief mention should be made of a totally different approach to the study of intelligence that of **Piaget**. Piaget carried out a monumental investigation into the development of the intellect. This approach is concerned not with the ways in which individuals differ, but with the intellectual structures and processes common to all individuals.

Piaget proposed that the intellect develops through the systematic formation of schemata – internal representations of physical or mental actions. Central to the theory is his account of how the child develops logical thinking in a number of distinct stages from birth to adolescence.

A detailed consideration of Piaget's theory is beyond the scope of this text. However, a more complete account can be found in the first book in this series (Birch and Malim, 1988).

**Self-assessment Questions**

1. How would you define 'intelligence'?
2. What is 'factor analysis'? How has factor analysis been used in attempts to clarify the nature of intelligence?
3. Contrast the hierarchical view of intelligence with Thurstone's multi-factor theory. What are the implications of these two approaches for the measurement of intelligence?
4. Briefly discuss some of the limitations of factor analysis in the study of intelligence.
5. Indicate what has been added by more recent theories to our understanding of the nature of intelligence.


## SECTION II   MEASURING INTELLIGENCE

**Psychometric Testing**

Psychometry is concerned with the measurement of psychological characteristics such as intelligence or personality through the use of standardised tests, which will be explained later in this section. The essence of psychometric testing so far as intelligence is concerned is the measurement of differences in individuals' ability to solve problems and answer questions. The form such problems and questions take depends partly upon the researcher's definition of intelligence and partly upon the results of practical investigations into the sorts of tasks which do discriminate between individuals.

Fundamental to psychometrics is the belief that psychological differences between individuals can be **quantified** (assigned a numerical value) in the way that characteristics such as height or weight might be. This assumption is implicit in factor analytical theories of intelligence discussed in the last section.

Tests designed to measure differences between people have been in existence since the beginning of this century. The use of ability tests to assign children to different kinds of education and to select individuals for vocational training or jobs has caused much debate and controversy. Many people claim that such tests are narrow and inflexible and fail to account for important characteristics such as motivation and social skills and for cultural influences on behaviour; others contend that the use of ability tests provides an objective and scientific means of identifying talent and providing information to help with educational and career choices.

Below is a consideration of the nature and uses of ability tests together with a discussion of some of the controversial issues which surround their use.

The main focus will be on tests of general intellectual ability, often referred to as 'intelligence tests'. However, when using this term, it should be borne in mind that there is no generally agreed definition of intelligence and that, at best, tests are likely to measure only a part of what could be regarded as intelligent behaviour.

### Intelligence Tests – a Historical Sketch

The earliest examples of intelligence tests were provided at the end of the last century by **Sir Francis Galton** in England and **J. McK. Cattell** in America. These early tests which were based on the measurement of simple sensory processes such as the speed of reaction times and judging the difference between two weights did not prove useful as measures of intelligence.

**Simon–Binet**. The first tests to resemble modern intelligence tests were devised by the French psychologist **Alfred Binet** and his co-researcher, **Theodore Simon**. In 1905, Binet was requested by the French government to devise tests which would identify children who needed special educational help. Using the judgements of school teachers on what constituted 'average' performance on a range of tasks involving reasoning and judgement, Binet first undertook to identify the 'mental level' of the 'normal' child in various different age groups. From this work, a number of age-related scales were devised based on the concept of **Mental Age**. Thus, a seven-year-old child who satisfactorily completed all those items normally completed by the average eight-year-old was said to have a mental age of eight; the ten-year-old who was able to complete only those tasks expected of eight-year-olds would also be assigned a mental age of eight.

The result of this work was the Simon–Binet (1905) test, which is generally regarded as the first intelligence test.

**Intelligence Quotient**. Later researchers contended that in order for a more complete assessment to be made of the ability levels of children of different age groups who exhibit the same mental age, some account should be taken of the child's chronological, or actual age. In 1912, **Stern** introduced the idea of an **intelligence quotient** (IQ) which could be calculated as follows:

$$IQ = \frac{\text{Mental Age (MA)}}{\text{Chronological Age (CA)}} \times 100$$

It can be seen that when MA and CA are the same, using this calculation, IQ is 100, that is, average.

**Stanford–Binet**. In 1916, the Simon-Binet test was revised by **Lewis Terman** of Stanford University. The Stanford–Binet test as it became known was originally designed for children but was later extended to measure IQ in adults. The Stanford–Binet Intelligence Scale was revised many times, the most recent revision being in 1986. Before the 1986 revision, the IQ score was derived from an amalgam of all the items and would not reflect differences between a child's performance in for example numerical ability compared to verbal ability.

**Wechsler**. The most widely used test of adult intelligence, the Wechsler Adult Intelligence Scale was devised in 1939 and this was followed later by the Wechsler Intelligence Scale for Children. Both these tests have subsequently been revised. Because it was felt that the Stanford–Binet scales relied too heavily on language ability, the Wechsler scales provide measures not just on a verbal scale but also a non-verbal performance scale, which requires the manipulation or arrangement of blocks, pictures and other displays.

**British Ability Scales**. The Stanford–Binet and Wechsler tests were designed mainly for use with American populations. An important milestone so far as Britain is concerned is the British Ability Scales designed for 2 to 17-year-olds (Elliott *et al.*, 1983). This test, in addition to using traditional items concerned with reasoning, short-term memory and so on, measures aspects of development and moral reasoning.

### Interpreting IQ Scores

There are a number of important factors to be considered when interpreting IQ scores:

1. **Ratio and Deviation IQs**. Intelligence quotients which simply express the ratio of MA to CA are known as **ratio IQs**. It

follows that, in order for IQ to be consistent over time, the MA must increase at the same rate as the CA. However, since the majority of tests assume that the intellect is fully developed by around 16–20 years (depending upon the test used), the concept of MA is not meaningful beyond that age. For this and other 'technical' reasons, which need not be discussed here, a growing number of psychologists have abandoned the concepts of MA and ratio IQ. Instead, greater reliance is now placed on a **deviation IQ**. Deviation IQs express the test result in relation to its deviation from the norm – or average score – for the relevant age group. Specifically, it yields a standard score based on how many **standard deviations** (SDs) above or below the mean of the test-taker's age-group the score falls. (A standard deviation is a measure of the average distance of scores around the mean.)

2.  **Differences between Tests**. All tests are designed so as to provide a **normal distribution** with a mean of 100. A normal distribution is arrived at when a large number of measures of some human characteristic, such as height or weight are plotted into a histogram. It is bell-shaped and symmetrical. Approximately 68 per cent of all scores fall between 1 SD above and 1 SD below the mean. A problem arises because, although the majority of intelligence tests are developed to a SD of 15, this measure may be different on some tests. Thus, an individual completing two tests – one with a SD of 15 and one with a SD of 20 – would be assigned two different IQ scores. Figure 1.3 shows the normal curve of distribution for two hypothetical tests, one with a standard deviation of 15 and the other with a SD of 20. Based on a deviation IQ, an individual scoring 115 on Test 1 would score an IQ of 120 on Test 2. Therefore, when interpreting an IQ score, careful note should be taken of the SD quoted by the test constructors.

3.  **The Relationship between 'Intelligence' and IQ**. Though IQ scores purport to be a measure of intelligence, the relationship between 'intelligence' and 'IQ' cannot be considered in the same way as, for example, that between 'weight' and 'pounds and ounces'. Whilst we accept a numerical value expressed in pounds and ounces as an objective and exact indication of the weight of something, because of the complexity and uncertainty surrounding definitions of intelligence, the same cannot be said for an IQ score in relation to intelligence.

Continuing the analogy between weight and intelligence, claiming that someone who weighs 60 lbs is half as heavy as someone who weighs 120 lbs is legitimate; arguing that a person with an IQ of 70 is only half as intelligent as someone with an IQ of 140 cannot be supported.

---

**FIGURE 1.3**

**The Normal Curve of Distribution for Test 1 with a Standard Deviation of 15 and Test 2 with a Standard Deviation of 20**

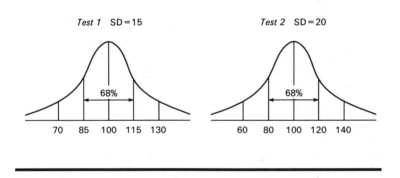

---

**Some Kinds of Intelligence Tests**

Tests of intelligence can be classified in many ways. Some of the ways they might be divided, for example, are:

(a) those that are given to one individual at a time and those that are administered to groups
(b) 'pencil and paper' tests (verbal and non-verbal) and performance tests
(c) tests designed for children and tests designed for adults
(d) tests that provide a single measure of general intelligence and those that yield a profile of scores relating to particular abilities.

In the comments which follow, the main distinction made is that between **individual** and **group** tests. During this discussion, some of the other distinctions referred to above should become clearer.

*Individual Tests*

The Stanford–Binet and the Wechsler scales (referred to above) are examples of the most widely used tests which are administered to one individual at a time:

**The Stanford–Binet** uses a variety of different types of task to assess intelligence. Figure 1.4 gives some examples of typical tasks used in the 1986 Stanford–Binet Intelligence Scales for 6 to 8-year-olds. Before the 1986 revision, the test yielded a single IQ score, each item contributing equally to the final score, which did not reflect a child's possible strengths and weaknesses in different sections of the test. The 1986 test yields a profile of scores reflecting four broad areas of intellectual ability: verbal reasoning, quantitative reasoning, short-term memory and abstract/visual reasoning. This change reflects the current notion of intelligence as being composed of different, but interrelated abilities (see Section I).

**Wechsler Intelligence Scales.** The Wechsler was one of the first tests to measure and record separate abilities. It is divided into two main sections – a **verbal** scale and a **performance** scale – each with a number of sub-sections. The performance scale, as, the name suggests, does not rely heavily on language ability and requires the testee to solve problems involving blocks, pictures or other materials. For example:

Block design   Pictured designs must be copied with blocks; tests ability to perceive and analyse patterns

The Wechsler scales yield a profile of scores which illustrates a person's strengths and weaknesses in different areas of intellectual functioning. A mismatch between verbal and performance scores may alert the tester to investigate particular learning difficulties, perhaps associated with language problems.

*Group Tests*

Group tests, which are usually in paper and pencil form, are used whenever large numbers of people have to be assessed. Group tests have been used extensively in the 11 plus examinations which were designed to select children to receive different kinds of schooling

**FIGURE 1.4**

**Some Typical Items from the 1986 Stanford–Binet Intelligence Scale for 6–8-year-olds**

## VERBAL REASONING

**Vocabulary** Defines words, such as 'dollar' and 'envelope.'

**Comprehension** Answers questions, such as 'Where do people buy food?' and 'Why do people comb their hair?'

**Absurdities** Identifies the 'funny' aspect of a picture, such as a girl riding a bicycle in a lake or a bald man combing his head.

**Verbal Relations** Tells how the first three items in a sequence are alike and how they differ from the fourth: scarf, tie, muffler, shirt.

## QUANTITATIVE REASONING

**Quantitative** Performs simple arithmetic tasks, such as selecting a die with six spots because the number of spots equals the combination of a two-spot and a four-spot die.

**Number Series** Gives the next two numbers in a series, such as

$$20 \quad 16 \quad 12 \quad 8 \quad \_\_ \quad \_\_.$$

**Equation Building** Builds an equation from the following array:
2   3   5 + =. One correct response would be $2 + 3 = 5$.

## ABSTRACT/VISUAL REASONING

**Pattern Analysis** Copies a simple design with blocks.

**Copying** Copies a geometrical drawing demonstrated by the examiner, such as a rectangle intersected by two diagonals.

## SHORT-TERM MEMORY

**Bead Memory** Shown a picture of different-shaped beads stacked on a stick. Reproduces the sequence from memory by placing real beads on a stick.

**Memory for Sentences** Repeats after the examiner sentences such as 'It is time to go to sleep' and 'Ken painted a picture for his mother's birthday.'

**Memory for Digits** Repeats after the examiner a series of digits, such as 5-7-8-3, forward and backward.

**Memory for Objects** Shown pictures of individual objects, such as a clock and an elephant, one at a time. Identifies the objects in the correct order of their appearance in a picture that also includes extraneous objects; for example, a bus, a clown, an *elephant*, eggs and a *clock*.

*Source*: Atkinson, R. L., Atkinson, R. C., Smith, E. E. and Bem, D. J., *Introduction to Psychology*, Harcourt Brace Jovanovich Inc.

and in the Civil Service and armed forces to select personnel. Group tests may be verbal, relying entirely on the use and comprehension of language, or non-verbal, emphasising the ability to detect relationships in patterns or shapes. A brief description of some commonly used group tests follows.

The **AH series**, devised by Alice Heim, is a widely used series of group tests which are used to assess general ability, from school-leaving age upwards. **AH2/3 and AH4** are designed for apprentice and clerical/general staff selection. AH2/3 are two parallel tests, each with three parts – verbal, numerical and perceptual. AH4 is primarily a test of deductive reasoning arranged in two sections which assess an individual's ability to solve verbal, numerical and diagrammatic problems. **AH5** consists of two parts, each of 36 items, one being verbal and numerical, the other mainly diagrammatic. Alice Heim describes it as a test of general intelligence designed for use with selected, highly intelligent people. It is intended for adults such as students and research workers and potential entrants to higher education and the professions. The **AH6** is often used in selecting amongst groups for managerial posts (Heim, 1970b). It is available in two forms, one designed for use with scientists, engineers and mathematicians and the other for arts specialists and other non-scientists.

**Raven's Progressive Matrices**, first published in 1938, has been revised several times since then. It is a non-verbal test designed to measure abstract reasoning ability by asking testees to solve problems posed through geometric patterns. It is designed for use with people of all ages and nationalities.

The test has been widely praised by some psychologists; both Spearman and Vernon believed the first version to be the purest available tests of intelligence, uncontaminated by educational and cultural influences. However, this view may have been over-optimistic. (See comments on Culture and IQ later in this section.)

*A Comparison of Individual and Group Tests*

1.  Individual tests tend to be used whenever it is necessary to have a detailed picture of a person's intellectual abilities. This occurs most often in a clinical situation to aid the **diagnosis** of learning difficulties in children. By comparison, group tests are most often used for the purposes of **selection**, as in the 11 plus

examination referred to above, or where a large group of people are to be assessed as part of a research project.

2. An individual test is more informative than a group test. The tester can observe the person's approaches to various tasks and is more likely to be able to assess his or her level of motivation. On the other hand, individual tests involve interaction between tester and testee and the tester's approach may vary a little from individual to individual. Therefore, group tests, where each person receives exactly the same instructions and answers are interpreted in the same way for everyone, can be regarded as more objective.

3. Administering individual tests is more time-consuming and requires greater training and expertise than group testing.

## What Makes a Good Test?

Psychometric tests are widely used in our society. Whatever the purpose of a test, be it to aid diagnosis of learning difficulties or to select individuals for jobs or entry to different kinds of educational institution, there are certain criteria which must be fulfilled before the test can be used with confidence in a practical situation. Some of these criteria are outlined below.

### *Reliability*

In order for it to be considered **reliable**, a test given to the same individual on two or more occasions should yield the same or nearly the same score. Reliability, then, relates to how **consistent** a test is. Two kinds of reliability need to be established.

(a) **Consistency over time**, which is assessed using the **test-retest** method. The test is given to the same group of people on two different occasions, with a suitable time-lag to prevent them from remembering the test. The technique of correlation (See Section I) is applied to the two sets of scores to examine the degree of similarity between them. The resulting correlation coefficient, known as a **reliability coefficient**, should be in the region of 0.90 (the Wechsler Intelligence Scale has a reliability coefficient of 0.91). An alternative technique often used is to administer the test in two different but equivalent forms. This is known as **parallel-forms** test of reliability.

(b) The **internal consistency** of the test, which is measured using the **split-half** method. This involves splitting the test into two halves, usually by taking scores from odd-numbered items on the test and comparing them to scores for even-numbered items again using the technique of correlation. A high degree of correlation would be expected.

*Validity*

Establishing the reliability of a test is not enough. It is necessary also to demonstrate that the test is measuring what it claims to measure. This is its **validity**. The main types of validity are as follows:

(a) **Face Validity**. This simply refers to whether the test *looks* as though it is measuring what it claims to. Given the disagreements surrounding the nature of intelligence, having confidence in the face validity of an intelligence test is more problematical than with, say, a test of mathematics.

(b) **External Validity**. This can involve two practices, both concerned with correlating test results with some external measure of the characteristic being measured. For example:

   (1) Pupils scores on an IQ test might be correlated with their teacher's assessment of how intelligent they are. This is **concurrent validity** since the test results were compared to some present measure of behaviour. Another measure of concurrent validity involves correlating people's scores on a new test with their scores on another well-established test. This assumes, of course, that the well-established test is itself effectively measuring the relevant attribute.

   (2) If pupil's scores on an IQ test are correlated with some *future* measure of intelligence, such as later school achievement, this is an example of **predictive validity**. Many studies have demonstrated the success in predicting performance in a wide variety of settings both in education (at all levels ranging from school to university) and in the workplace (Jensen, 1981; Minton and Schneider, 1980).

(c) **Construct Validity**. This refers to the accuracy with which a test measures the psychological construct indicated by the theory that underlies it. This is difficult to achieve, particularly where there is disagreement among test constructors about the definitions and theories in existence. The methods of validity described so far, though useful, do not strictly demonstrate that tests of intelligence are in fact measuring intelligence as distinct from other constructs such as, for example, motivation or ability to carry out instructions. What is needed is an established **theory** of intelligence which can be investigated using a range of criteria (including measures of concurrent and predictive validity) to answer questions such as 'How does intelligence relate to other constructs, such as motivation?' 'How stable are test scores over time' 'How strong is the correlation between test scores and criteria such as school achievement?' 'What does neuropsychological evidence tell us about intelligence?'

*Standardisation*

Before a test can be used effectively in a practical situation, it is necessary to **standardise** it on the population for whom it is intended. The process of standardisation involves 'trying out' the test on large samples of this population and then making a number of adjustments, which include:

(1) Eliminating items which are either too difficult or too easy and therefore do not effectively **discriminate** between individuals.
(2) Ensuring that the pattern of scores produced by the test approximates to a **normal distribution** (see Figure 1.3). The main reason for this is that since biological characteristics such as height and weight are normally distributed in the population, it is assumed that a psychological attribute such as intelligence is also normally distributed. This assumption has been criticised on the grounds that it lacks scientific support and produces an artificial view of intelligence.
(3) Producing a table of **norms** or average scores for the particular population aimed at. When the test is later used, individuals' scores can then be compared to the norm for a particular age

group or professional group, or whatever categories of people have been investigated.

## Controversies Surrounding the Use of IQ Tests

Advocates of psychometric tests have drawn attention to the great value of IQ testing as a reliable and standard means of comparing individuals to others. The results of tests, it is claimed, can be a valuable source of information in a wide range of situations from diagnosing learning difficulties to helping individuals to make educational and career choices. However, there have been a number of criticisms associated with their use:

1. **Achievement or Aptitude**. It is claimed that IQ tests do not measure knowledge and skills acquired through learning but are measures of actual or potential 'brightness' and intellectual capacity. Indeed, some theorists, for example Burt, see this capacity as largely innate and inherited. As such, IQ tests are referred to as **aptitude tests** and are viewed as qualitatively different from the sorts of tests used in schools (such as those of reading, mathematics and so on) and referred to as **achievement** (or attainment) **tests**. However, many researchers (Ginsburg, 1972; Stott, 1978) argue that questions in IQ tests are learned (though not necessarily in the formal sense) in the same way that answers to achievement tests are. Like achievement tests, they should be seen as measures of *present* performance, rather than as measures of capacity or future performance. As with other measures of present performance, levels of success are likely to be affected by numerous factors both within and external to the test taker.

2. **Culture and IQ Tests**. One of the most controversial issues in IQ testing is the question of whether tests are biased in favour of white, middle-class people. If so, their use with groups whose social or cultural experience is very different would seem to be unfair. This is a particularly important issue with verbal tests that require competence in a particular language. A child whose first language was not English could not be expected to score as highly on verbal items as a child from a solely English-speaking home. And even where English is the first language, the

vocabulary used may differ significantly between middle-class and working-class homes. One of the most widely used tests thought to be relatively culture-free is Raven's Progressive Matrices (referred to previously) which uses non-verbal items in the form of shapes and symbols. However, cultural factors, it has been claimed, can also influence performance on non-verbal items depending upon the particular experiences of test-takers and how familiar they are with the materials and content of the tests (Irvine, 1966; Simon, 1971). Vernon (1969) reflects the view of many psychologists when he argues that there can be no such thing as a truly culture-fair test.

The importance of social and cultural influences on IQ testing is illustrated by Warburton (1951) who described some of the difficulties encountered in devising ability tests for Gurkha recruits. Brought up in a less competitive society than our own, they were not motivated to succeed in what appeared to be irrelevant, abstract tasks and they were unaccustomed to working within a set time limit. Consequently, their achievement, even on 'performance' tests was thought not to be a reflection of true ability. The messages from this study are still relevant today.

3.   **Labelling and the Self-fulfilling Prophecy**. One area in which the concept of intelligence has been and still is influential is that of education. The most significant example of the use of IQ tests to select pupils to receive different kinds of schooling can be seen in the 11 plus examinations, which still exist but are much less common than in the 1950s and 1960s. And within the education system, teachers sometimes make use of intelligence tests to make decisions about the allocation of pupils to particular classes or to groups within classes. Such a tendency to select, to categorize and to label is thought by many psychologists to be potentially harmful (Gould, 1981). Studies have illustrated the possible effects of a **self-fulfilling prophecy**, where people who are treated in a particular way because of some label that is applied tend to develop behaviour and characteristics generally associated with the label. Thus, if teachers, parents and child form certain expectations about school performance based on an IQ score, this might lead the child to do as well or as badly as everyone expects. An

intriguing example of the self-fulfilling prophecy can be seen in Rosenthal and Jacobson's (1968) study. At the beginning of a school year, a group of teachers were told that 20 children joining their classes had high IQ scores and were expected to do well in the coming year. In fact, the children were of average IQ. In line with teachers' expectations, all the children performed very well and scored highly in school tests a year later. This is held as a classic study of the possible effects of teacher expectation, though it should be noted that some psychologists have criticised the design of the study and the ambiguity of the results (Shackleton and Fletcher, 1984). Others have condemned the study on ethical grounds

4. **Definition of Intelligence?** Given that there is as yet no general agreement on what constitutes intelligent behaviour and bearing in mind the range and diversity of theories about the nature of intelligence (see in particular the theories of Gardner and Sternberg in Section I), the question might be asked 'Should we be attempting to measure it?' Though mindful of the complexities of this issue, Heim (1970a) concludes that a well-established test is still the best means of measuring a person's intelligence. Houghton and Wigdor (1989) argue that despite their limitations, ability tests are still the most useful aids available for judging what job or kind of training is suitable for a particular individual.

## Self-assessment Questions

1. What do you understand by 'mental age'? How has this concept been used to determine IQ in children?
2. Outline some of the factors which should be taken into account when IQ scores are interpreted.
3. Briefly compare the relative strengths and weaknesses of group and individual tests.
4. Explain the processes of reliability, validity and standardisation in relation to IQ testing.
5. What are thought to be the main benefits of IQ testing? Discuss some of the controversies arising from the use of IQ tests.

## SECTION III   THE HEREDITY/ENVIRONMENT ISSUE

**Nature or Nurture?**

During the last century, Francis Galton (1869) studied the relative effects of heredity (**nature**) and environment (**nurture**) on the development of intelligence. Subsequently, this issue developed into probably the most controversial and divisive debate to be encountered in the field of psychology. The question that concerned psychologists was 'Which is the more important influence on the development of differences in intelligence: heredity (that is, genetic inheritance) or environment (usually defined as all the experiences an individual is exposed to from the time of conception)? Before discussing this issue a number of points must be made:

1.   The heredity/environment issue was considered both in relation to differences between individuals and (controversially) in relation to differences between groups, such as different social, cultural and racial groups.
2.   It should be borne in mind when considering the research evidence which follows, that 'intelligence' is equated with the results of IQ tests, with all their limitations as noted in Section II.
3.   The knowledge that differences in intelligence are the result of an **interaction** between heredity and environment is now more than well established. However, the question remains 'What is the *relative* importance of each?' A number of sources of evidence have been used to answer this question. Some of them are discussed below.

*Family and Twin Studies*

An important source of evidence relating to the inheritance of intelligence came from studies which correlated IQ scores between people of varying degrees of genetic relationship, for example parents paired with children, siblings (including twins) paired with each other, cousins paired with each other. Figure 1.5 shows the correlation coefficients arrived at from three individual studies (Newman *et al.*, 1937; Shields, 1962; Burt, 1966) and from a survey

**FIGURE 1.5**

**Family Studies of Intelligence Showing IQ Correlation Coefficients**

| | Name of Study | | | |
|---|---|---|---|---|
| | Newman et al. (1937) | Shields (1962) | Burt (1966) | Bouchard and McGue (1981)* |
| *Relationship:* | | | | |
| Monozygotic twins | | | | |
|    Reared together | 0.91 | 0.76 | 0.94 | 0.86 |
|    Reared apart | 0.67 | 0.77 | 0.77 | 0.72 |
| Dizygotic twins | | | | |
|    Reared together | 0.64 | 0.51 | 0.55 | 0.60 |
| Siblings | | | | |
|    Reared together | | | | 0.47 |
|    Reared apart | | | | 0.24 |
| Single parent-offspring | | | | |
|    Reared together | | | | 0.42 |
|    Reared apart | | | | 0.22 |
| Cousins | | | | 0.15 |

*Median correlation.

which examined 111 studies on familial resemblances in measured intelligence (Bouchard and McGue, 1981).

Of particular interest is the data relating to **twin studies**. But first some facts about twins. Twins are of two different kinds: monozygotic (MZ) or 'identical' twins and dizygotic (DZ) or 'fraternal' twins. DZ twins have developed from two separately fertilised ova and are no more alike genetically than any two children of the same parents. MZ twins have developed from a single fertilised ovum and are thought to start life genetically identical. Differences in behaviour between identical twins must, it is thought, be attributed almost entirely to the effects of the environment.

Examining the data in Figure 1.5 a number of points can be made:

1. Overall the data clearly shows that the closer the family relationship, the higher is the average correlation-coefficient between IQ scores and therefore the more similar are the IQ scores. It also shows of course that correlation coefficients rise as the *environments* become more similar.
2. The highest correlation coefficients relate to MZ twins, indicating that they have more similar IQs than any other pairs. Hereditarians would attribute this to the greater degree of genetic similarity between MZ twins. However, it is probable that they were also *treated* more similarly than DZ twins.
3. Even MZ twins **reared apart** have more similar IQ's than DZ twins **reared together**. Hereditarians claimed this as powerful support for genetic influences on intelligence.

EVALUATION OF TWIN STUDIES  As noted above, hereditarians claimed that the evidence from twin studies overwhelmingly supported the role of genetic inheritance in intelligence. However, environmentalists have made a number of criticisms of twin studies:

1. Different studies used different intelligence tests; it is therefore difficult to make a valid comparison between them.
2. Many of the MZ twins reared apart were in fact brought up in very similar homes and in some cases were raised by members of the same family. This suggests that their environments may have been quite similar (Kamin, 1974). An example in one study (Newman *et al.*, 1937) where a MZ pair were brought up in very different environments revealed an IQ difference between the twins of 24 points.
3. Some of the early studies are likely to have suffered from sampling inaccuracies because at that time, there was no reliable method of identifying true MZ twins.
4. Herman (1984) pointed out that families who produce twins may not be typical of the general population. Therefore, generalisations from twin studies should not be made.
5. The data produced by Burt is open to doubt since the results of at least some of his twin studies are thought to have been faked.

(Burt's data are not included in the Bouchard and McGue review.)

## Heritability

Using data taken from twin studies, researchers attempted to estimate what proportion of the variance in measured intelligence was due to heredity and what proportion to environment. **Heritability** (H) refers to the proportion of a trait's variance *within a particular population* that can be attributed to genetic differences.

Estimates of H in relation to IQ scores have varied widely between different researchers. For example, Burt (1966) and Jensen (1969) proposed an H of 80 per cent. Chipeur *et al*. (1989) estimated H at 46 per cent using summary data from the Bouchard and McGue (1981) survey of familial resemblances in measured intelligence. A number of important points should be noted in relation to H:

1. H relates to differences *within a population* and not to a particular individual. There have been occasions when H has been incorrectly used to suggest that, say, 80 per cent of a person's IQ is due to heredity.
2. H calculated from data drawn from a particular population, for example white, middle-class Americans, should not then be used to make inferences about a totally *different* population, for example black, working-class people.
3. Given the problems associated with the data drawn from twin studies, noted above, and that heritability research has tended to yield such varied estimates, it seems clear that a reliable estimate of H is not possible in relation to IQ.

## Adoption Studies

A large number of studies have compared the IQs of adopted children with that of both their adoptive parents and their natural parents. The assumption is that if heredity is the more important influence the correlation between children's IQ scores and those of their natural parents will be higher than the correlation with their adoptive parents.

Two early adoption studies (Burks, 1928; Leahy, 1935) found very low correlations of 0.13 and 0.18, respectively, between the IQs of children and their adoptive parents. The correlation for children and natural parents living together is about 0.50. It seems from these figures that environment is important though less so than heredity.

Hereditarians claimed that foster/adoption studies offer powerful support for a high heritability component to IQ. However, environmentalists argued that there are major flaws in the early studies cited by hereditarians. For example, Kamin (1977) drew attention to the process of **selective placement** practised by adoption agencies. Selective placement involves placing children in homes which resemble as closely as possible the home environment of their natural parents. Thus the children of 'bright' mothers may be placed in homes with high-IQ adoptive parents, whereas the children of less 'bright' mothers may be placed in homes where the adoptive parents' IQs resemble that of the natural parents. Therefore, selective placement could account for the similarity between the IQ of adopted children and their natural parents even if they have not lived together. Kamin also pointed out that the correlation between the IQ of children and adoptive parents is likely to be artificially lowered because of the nature of adoptive parents as a group relative to parents in general. Because of the conditions laid down by adoption agencies, adoptive parents are likely to be emotionally stable, financially secure, not alcoholic, etc. Also, there is likely to be less variance in their IQs than that of the children they adopt. This could artificially reduce the correlations between the IQs of the two groups.

More recent studies have attempted to avoid some of the problems in the early adoption studies and have concentrated on parents who have brought up both adopted and natural children (Scarr and Weinberg, 1977; Horn *et al.*, 1979). In both studies, the correlation of mother–natural child IQs was very similar to the correlation of mother–adoptive child IQs (0.22 and 0.20, respectively in the Scarr study). This provides no support for the high heritability of intelligence since the second relationship did not involve similar genes.

A study which supported the environmentalist case in highlighting the effects of a 'good' environment on IQ was carried out by Schiff *et al.* (1978) in France. They studied 32 children born to parents of low socio-economic status who were adopted before they were 6 months by parents of high socio-economic status. A comparison was made between the children's IQs and those of their biological siblings who had been reared by their natural mothers. The average IQ of the adopted group was 111 while that of the 'naturally-reared' group was 95.

*Environmental Influences*

After much research, there appears to be a general consensus on the environmental conditions that enhance the development of an individual's intellectual potential: these conditions include good prenatal and postnatal nutrition and health care; intellectual stimulation; a stable emotional climate in the home; parental encouragement and support. There follows an outline of some of the studies which have contributed to this view:

1. A classic longitudinal study carried out by **Skeels** (1966) studied a group of children brought up in an unstimulating orphanage environment. At 19 months, their mean IQ score was 64. Some of the children were removed from the orphanage and given individual attention. At age six, the latter group showed a mean IQ of 96, compared to 60–70 in the institutionalised group.
2. Studying 12 year old children, **Fraser** (1959) found a strong, positive correlation between high IQ and factors such as the level of parental encouragement, general family atmosphere and the amount of book-reading in the home.
3. **Wiseman** (1964) found a strong correlation between the standard of child care and IQ.
4. **Bayley** (1970) contended that IQ differences between children of low and high socio-economic status become progressively greater between birth and entrance to school, suggesting that the quality of the environment amplifies any genetic differences present at birth.

*Environmental Enrichment*

Because children from underprivileged homes tend to be at a disadvantage intellectually, a number of programmes were mounted which aimed to provide greater intellectual stimulation for these children. The first and best known of these programmes is **Project Headstart**.

**Headstart**. In 1965, funds were allocated in the USA to provide enriched learning experiences for preschool children from deprived homes. A variety of approaches was used. In some, teachers visited children and their parents at home to provide intellectually stimulating activities of the kind that children from 'better-off' homes tend to receive from their parents. In other programmes, the children attended classes where they took part in special learning activities.

Early follow-up studies showed that the project had not been as successful as had been hoped in that no lasting IQ gains were found in children who had participated compared to those who had not. However, later follow-up studies highlighted some lasting benefits. Compared to a control group of children who had not received pre-school enrichment, participants in Headstart at age 15 were a full grade ahead, scored higher on tests of reading, arithmetic and language use and exhibited less antisocial behaviour (Zigler and Berman, 1983; Lee *et al.*, 1988) Significantly, programmes that actively involved parents in stimulating their child's intellectual development have tended to produce the greatest benefits (Darlington, 1986)

### Race and IQ

A lively and often bitter debate developed over the years. The question arose as to whether or not genetically determined differences in intelligence existed between different racial groups. It is an undisputed fact that using standard IQ tests, black Americans score on average approximately 15 points below the average of the white population (Shuey, 1966); the controversy arose from how this information was interpreted.

The debate began in 1969 with the publication of an article by Arthur Jensen in the USA in which he claimed that genetic factors were strongly implicated in the average Negro–white intelligence differences found. He based this view on an 80 per cent heritability estimate, which was calculated from studies of the white population. He added that the evidence did not support the possibility of strong environmental influences. In view of the implications of this view for social policy and in particular the allocation of resources for such enrichment projects as Headstart, a heated exchange began between hereditarians and environmentalists. There follows a summary of some of the more important points made:

1. Jensen's use of an 80 per cent heritability estimate is based on *within-group* differences, i.e. differences within the white population. It does not follow that conclusions can be drawn about *between-group* differences, ie differences between black and white populations (Mackenzie, 1984).

2. Tobias (1974) pointed out Jensen's failure to take account of the possible cumulative effects of generations of environmental deprivation suffered by American blacks in the form of poverty, malnutrition, prejudice and lack of educational opportunity. It is well known that the effects of poverty and malnutrition can persist for at least two generations after improvements in conditions have taken place.

3. Kamin (1977) argued that the complex interaction between genetic factors and environmental influences is not well understood. No study has yet been able to estimate the extent to which different environments can affect intellectual development.

4. Fontana (1988) argues that a starting point for the debate must be the difficulties in defining and measuring intelligence (See Sections I and II). Concepts of intelligence and the methods for measuring it in western white societies are **culture bound**, that is, they may not be valid for other cultures.

5. Race, like intelligence, has no agreed definition though most commonly it refers to a group sharing a common gene pool. However, known differences in gene structure are greater *within* a racial population than *between* such populations (Bodmer, 1972).

6. Where black or mixed-race children are adopted before they are a year old and reared by well-educated, high income white families, they score an average of 15 IQ points higher than underprivileged black children reared in their biological families (Scarr and Weinberg, 1977).

7. Fontana (1988) suggests that ' . . . there are no conclusive grounds for supposing genetic differences in intelligence exist between races. Such measurable differences as do exist would

seem to be far too strongly contaminated by environmental variables to allow us to explain their origins with any confidence' (p. 102).

## Nature/Nurture: An Interactionist Approach

As we have seen, the nature/nurture debate in intelligence was concerned with the role of genes and environment in determining measured intelligence. Much of the research discussed has served to highlight the complexity, and some would argue the futility, of trying to unravel the relative contributions of each.

In a classic paper in 1958, Anastasi argued that the only fruitful course for psychologists is to ask how the two **interact** rather than which has the greater influence. Both genes and environment influence behaviour. Different environments acting on the same genetic structure would produce different behaviours. Conversely, individuals who were genetically different but sharing the same environment would also exhibit different behaviours. It is therefore more logical to accept that heredity and environment interact and to consider the question of how changes in one may affect the influence of the other.

**Norm of Reaction**. Anastasi and others have used the concept of 'norm of reaction' in relation to the question of how heredity and environment may interact. Genetic structure is seen as imposing a top and bottom limit on an individual's potential behaviour. Where within this range the individual's behaviour (in this case IQ) will fall is determined by the kind of environment experienced. Thus, individuals who are exposed to a rich stimulating and emotionally supportive environment would be expected to develop to their full intellectual potential. Scarr-Salapatek (1971) maintained that individuals have a reaction range of 20–25 points. Thus an IQ score can vary within this range depending upon the kind of environment encountered.

A classic theory proposed by Hebb (1949) illustrates the concept of 'norm of reaction'. Hebb distinguished two kinds of intelligence which he called **Intelligence A** and **Intelligence B**. Intelligence A is seen as the individual's genetic potential or the basic given qualities of the central nervous system; intelligence B relates to the amount of Intelligence A that is realised as a result of experience, learning and other environmental factors. However, there is no way of observing Intelligence A or B, much less comparing them between individuals. In 1969, Vernon added the term **Intelligence C** as being that portion of Intelligence B which is measurable by IQ tests.

Because of the difficulty of assessing genetic potential and the interaction with various environments, the usefulness of 'norm of reaction' is at present limited. Moreover, recent developments in genetics suggest that genetic structure is more flexible than had been thought. Rigid upper and lower limits may not exist. Nonetheless, until more conclusive evidence is available, it serves to remind educationists and social policy makers of the complex interaction between heredity and environment and the need to ensure that all individuals receive the best possible environmental conditions. It may also encourage researchers to develop more searching studies of the social and educational practices which might reduce IQ differences between groups.

Note that a more detailed account of the nature/nurture debate in psychology can be found in Malim *et al.* (1992).

### Self-assessment Questions

1. What do you understand by the 'nature/nurture debate' in relation to intelligence?
2. Explain and evaluate the contribution of twin studies to the debate.
3. Briefly define 'heritability'.
4. Referring to supporting evidence, discuss some environmental factors which are likely to enhance the development of the intellect.
5. Briefly discuss the main issues arising from the controversy surrounding race and IQ.
6. Referring to the concept 'norm of reaction', discuss the interactionist approach to the nature/nurture debate in intelligence.

### FURTHER READING

H. J. Butcher, *Human Intelligence: Its Nature and Assessment* (London: Methuen, 1968).

S. J. Gould, *The Mismeasure of Man* (London: Pelican, 1984).

V. Shackleton and C. Fletcher, *Individual Differences: Theories and Applications* (London: Methuen, 1984).

R. J. Sternberg, *Metaphors of Mind: Conceptions of the Nature of Intelligence* (Cambridge University Press, 1990).

SHE'S NOT REALLY AGGRESSIVE, YOU KNOW, IT'S
JUST THE SITUATION SHE'S ALWAYS FINDING
HERSELF IN.

# Personality    2

At the end of this chapter you should:

1. Have an appreciation of the diversity of definitions of personality and some of the issues relevant to personality theory.
2. Be able to critically evaluate the following approaches to personality:

   — Multi-trait
   — Idiographic
   — Situationist and interactionist
   — Single-trait

3. Have examined and made an assessment of some of the ways in which personality has been assessed.

## SECTION I   INTRODUCTION: DEFINITIONS, ISSUES AND ASSUMPTIONS IN PERSONALITY THEORY

Describing and making assumptions about the personalities of others is something we all do in everyday life. Phrases such as 'She has lots of personality' and 'He has no personality' are typically used. In a psychological sense, however, these phrases are meaningless. All people have a personality and they differ not in the *amount*, but in the *kind* of personality they have.

Separately studying psychological processes such as perception, thinking, motivation and emotions makes it very difficult to describe the person as a whole. The concept of personality attempts to encompass all the different psychological processes and present a coherent picture of the individual's characteristic ways of thinking, feeling and behaving. Like intelligence, person-

41

ality is notoriously difficult to define and there is no one definition that all psychologists would subscribe to. For example, some psychologists use the term 'personality' to refer to all the various ways in which individuals differ from each other, including social behaviour, emotions, intellectual functioning, and so on, where others limit the term to account only for social and emotional aspects of behaviour. Hall and Lindzey (1978) carried out a review of personality theories and concluded that: '. . . no substantive definition can be applied with any generality. . . . the way in which given individuals will define personality will depend completely upon their particular theoretical preference' (p. 9). Hampson (1988) suggests that the following definition of personality by Child (1968) is one which is considered acceptable by many psychologists: ' . . . more or less stable, internal factors that make one person's behaviour consistent from one time to another, and different from the behaviour other people would manifest in comparable situations' (p. 83).

Theories of personality vary in terms of the assumptions made about psychological functioning in humans and about appropriate methods used to study personality. Below is a brief indication of some of the issues and controversies which concern psychologists who study personality. From this the reader should begin to appreciate the complexity of this field where many theories exist relatively independently of each other and offer diverse and often contradictory viewpoints. The remaining sections of this chapter will attempt to explore some of these theories in greater depth, along with a number of different ways in which personality is assessed. It should be noted that the concepts of **reliability** and **validity** (discussed in Chapter 1, Section II) are as important a consideration in personality assessment as they are in intelligence testing.

**Issues and Controversies in Personality Research**

*Idiographic versus Nomothetic Approaches*

A major difference between personality theories is the way in which they emphasise the uniqueness of the individual – an **idiographic** approach – as compared to the similarities which exist between people – a **nomothetic** approach.

*— Mischel*

Idiographic theorists aim to build up a detailed picture of each individual's personality and generally believe that the study of similarities between people is of limited value. **Gordon Allport** is probably the main advocate of this approach, though paradoxically in addition to studying **individual traits** (unique personal character-istics) he also considered the existence of **common traits** (basic characteristics which apply to all members of a particular social or cultural group)

The humanistic psychologist, Carl Rogers also represents the idiographic approach as does George Kelly with his Personal Construct Theory. The theories of Allport, Rogers and Kelly will be examined in Section IV of this chapter.

**Nomothetic** approaches to the study of personality have been carried out by **Cattell** and **Eysenck**, both of whom have attempted to discover the major dimensions of personality which are present to some extent in everyone but on which individuals will differ. The work of these two theorists will be examined in Section II.

**Freud's** psychoanalytic theory was developed from clinical case studies of his patients. To this extent, his theory is idiographic. For Freud, personality structure consisted of three interrelated systems – the id, ego and superego. A key element of his theory rests in his notion of an unconscious mind harbouring repressed ('forgotten') memories which influence conscious thoughts and behaviour. Freud's theory together with those of post-Freudians **Jung** and **Erikson** are considered in Chapter 3.

*Type and Trait Approaches*

Many theorists make use of the concept of **traits**, as referred to above, in describing personality. Traits are considered to be stable and enduring aspects of personality which are reflected in people's behaviour. Examples might be 'liveliness' or 'even-temperedness'. Cattell is considered to be a trait theorist. Other theorists subscribe to the view that individuals may be categorised into distinct personality types. Probably the earliest type theory was the Greek physician Hippocrates' division of human beings into sanguine, phlegmatic, melancholic and choleric temperamental **types**. It was thought that the personality was dominated by a particular body fluid for example, blood, phlegm, black or yellow bile.

Types differ from traits in that a person cannot be said to possess a type to varying degrees; the person either is or is not categorised as a particular type. Traits, on the other hand are factors that are thought to be normally distributed throughout the population and are therefore represented in everyone but to varying degrees.

By far and away the most famous and prolific personality theorist is H. J. Eysenck. Eysenck's theory proposes two major dimensions of personality as continuums along which each individual can be placed. These dimensions are **Introversion–Extraversion** and **Neuroticism–Stability**. Both Cattell and Eysenck arrived at their theories through analysing the scores from large numbers of personality questionnaires and other data such as direct observations of behaviour. They both used the statistical technique of **Factor Analysis** (see Chapter 1, Section I). These two theories will be examined in greater depth in Section II of this chapter along with more recent multi-trait theories.

*Consistency versus Situational-Specificity*

Trait approaches view the individual's personality as being generally consistent. Thus, it is thought that people will usually react in similar ways in many different situations: the person who is honest at work will also be honest in dealing with friends; the aggressive person may be expected to behave aggressively in a number of different settings. The notion of personality traits as consistent has been challenged by Mischel who argued that behaviour is more likely to be influenced by the situation a person is in than by that person's temperament.

Mischel criticised traditional personality theories which use the concept of trait both on conceptual and statistical issues. His challenge led to the **situationist** approach which holds that behaviour is largely determined by the situation in which it occurs. More recent research, not surprisingly, has concentrated on the interaction between a person's temperament and characteristics of the situation in which s/he is operating. Thus, the **interactionist** approach provides a compromise between the trait and situationist stances. The issue of consistency of personality will be examined in Section III of this chapter and will include a discussion of both situationist and interactionist positions.

**What Makes a Good Theory?**

Bearing in mind the controversies and disagreements which exist between personality theorists, is it possible to say what should be expected of a good personality theory? Most theorists would agree that a good personality theory should

— be consistent and logical and put forward assertions which are capable of being tested empirically;
— be supported by valid scientific evidence;
— be able to describe and explain human behaviour in terms which make 'real world' sense. For example, how far is the theory useful in terms of predicting suitable career choices or understanding possible causes of psychological disorder?

The reader may wish to keep these criteria in mind while considering the personality theories which follow.

**Self-assessment Questions**

1. Briefly explain some ways in which psychologists have defined personality.
2. Distinguish between idiographic and nomothetic approaches to the study of personality, referring to the work of one theorist who exemplifies each approach.
3. What do you understand by type and trait approaches to the study of personality?
4. What issues arise in relation to the consistency of personality?
5. What might be the characteristics of a good theory of personality?

## SECTION II  MULTI-TRAIT APPROACHES

**Traits versus Types**

As was noted in Section I of this chapter, some personality theorists have categorised people into distinct personality types. Reference has already been made to the Greek physician Hippocrates who assigned individuals to one of four types of temperament on the basis of a predominance of particular body fluids. Other type theories have centred around proposed links between temperament and body physique, the most noteworthy by **William Sheldon** (1942). Such theories have intuitive appeal, as witness the popular tendency to describe fat people as 'jolly' and thin people as 'sensitive'. However, little empirical evidence can be found in support of the links between body type and temperament. Other type theories have categorised people into purely psychological categories. For example, **Jung** (1923) the psychoanalytic theorist (see Chapter 3) proposed that people are predominantly either 'introverts' or 'extraverts', the introvert being shy and withdrawn and the extravert confident and outgoing.

The notion of types is tempting because of its simplicity. However, research evidence suggests that people differ in the *degree* to which they exhibit a particular characteristic or dimension of behaviour rather than slotting neatly into a distinct type. Hampson (1988) argues that individual differences cannot be adequately captured by placing people into a few all-or-none categories. Much recent research in personality has centred on the concept of traits.

Though there are many definitions of traits which differ in detail, in general they are seen as 'broad, enduring, relatively stable characteristics used to assess and explain behaviour' (Hirshberg, 1978, p. 45). Thus, one person's personality may characteristically reveal dominant traits such as thoughtfulness and friendliness; another may typically display greater shyness and sensitivity.

Multi-trait theories are designed to convey a picture of the whole personality. They aim to identify the range of traits that are central to the human personality and to produce tests of these traits which will indicate the extent to which people differ. They assume that individuals all share the same basic personality structure but will differ from each other in the extent to which they exhibit particular traits.

The two best known multi-trait theorists are Eysenck (1947) and Cattell (1965) and their theories will be discussed in this section. The personality tests produced by Eysenck and Cattell are widely used today and it is useful to understand something of the theories which led to their development. First, however, it would be helpful to note in Figure 2.1 some similarities and differences between the two theorists.

## Figure 2.1

**Similarities and Differences between Eysenck and Cattell**

1. Both received their training in psychology in Britain and both worked as applied psychologists, Eysenck in clinical practice and Cattell in the field of education.
2. Both were influenced by the work done by Spearman and Burt in the study of intelligence (see Chapter 1, Section I).
3. Both used the statistical technique of **factor analysis** (described in Chapter 1) to arrive at the major dimensions which characterise the human personality in the way that researchers such as Spearman and Burt identified the structure of intelligence. Factor analysis, you will recall, is a statistical technique which is used to reduce a large amount of data to a much smaller amount made up of overlapping characteristics or factors. (Eysenck and Cattell analysed people's scores on personality questionnaires or objective tests as well as assessments of their observed behaviour.) The reader is advised to re-read Figure 1.1 on factor analysis in Chapter 1, Section I before proceeding with the current chapter.
4. Because Eysenck and Cattell used different variations of the technique of factor analysis, they arrived at rather different representations of personality. Eysenck based his approach on **orthogonal** methods of factor analysis where Cattell used **oblique** methods.

   When orthogonal methods are used, the various factors which emerge are smaller in number, and are uncorrelated and therefore independent of each other; thus knowing an individual's score on one factor-dimension indicates nothing about that person's score on another factor-dimension.

   Oblique methods, on the other hand yield a larger number of factors which are likely to be correlated with each other to some extent and are therefore not independent. The correlation coefficients arising from oblique methods can be subjected to a further factor analysis which produces **second order** factors; these represent re-groupings of the original (**first-order**) factors. First order factors are often referred to as 'traits' and second-order factors as 'types'.

   Thus, Cattell's preference for stressing the first-order factors (or source traits) produced from oblique factor analysis essentially means that his theory is referred to as a 'trait' theory of personality. Eysenck's emphasis on the smaller number of independent second-order factors (Cattell calls them surface traits) arising from orthogonal analysis results in his theory sometimes being referred to as a 'type' theory of personality, though Eysenck himself prefers to use the term 'dimensional' rather than type. The concept of dimension differs from the concept of type in that people can be located at any point along a dimension, whereas being assigned to a certain type is an all-or-nothing matter.

The remainder of this section will explain the theories of Eysenck and Cattell and will conclude by referring to other more recent multi-trait approaches.

### Eysenck's Theory

Eysenck (1947) used the technique of factor analysis to analyse personality data drawn from his study of 700 battle-fatigued soldiers diagnosed as neurotic. His analysis led him to propose that personality can be sufficiently described by two dimensions: **extraversion–introversion** and **neuroticism–stability**. The two dimensions are thought to be normally distributed in that the majority of people can be placed in the middle of the dimension and relatively few at either extreme. Below are some of the characteristics Eysenck associated with the extreme positions on these dimensions:

1. **Extraversion/Introversion (E)**.   Typical EXTRAVERTS are sociable, thrive on human company, frequently seek exciting activities and are willing to take risks. They are impulsive, restless, optimistic and not always reliable.
   INTROVERTS are typically more serious and reserved individuals who prefer solitary activities to people. They are more cautious, pessimistic, orderly and restrained.
2. **Neuroticism/Stability (N)**.   Highly NEUROTIC individuals tend to be more prone to worries and anxiety and are often touchy and irritable. They are more likely to complain of headaches and to suffer from eating and sleeping difficulties.
   Highly STABLE individuals are less likely to make strong emotional responses and tend to be relatively calm, even-tempered and controlled.

Remember that these descriptions relate to the extreme ends of the dimensions and that very few people would fit them exactly. The majority of individuals would fall somewhere in the middle.

   Eysenck's later factor analytical studies led him to identify a third personality dimension, **psychoticism (P)**, which is unrelated to E and N. High scorers on the psychoticism scale tend to be solitary and lack feeling for others. They are also likely to be insensitive, aggressive and hostile. Unlike E and N, psychoticism is not normally distributed in the population. The distribution of P is highly skewed with the majority of people falling at the 'low' end of the scale (Eysenck and Eysenck, 1976). There is some evidence that criminals and schizophrenics have high psychoticism scores (Hampson, 1988).

## Measurement of Eysenck's Personality Dimensions

Initially Eysenck's dimensions were assessed using rating scales based on observer data. Later he and his colleagues devised a series of questionnaires designed to measure E and N. The present version is the **Eysenck Personality Inventory (EPI)** (Eysenck and Eysenck, 1964). This is a self-report questionnaire made up of a number of questions to which respondents are required to reply simply 'yes' or' no'. The EPI contains a **Lie Scale**, which assesses an individual's tendency to give socially-acceptable answers. More recently the **Eysenck Personality Questionnaire (EPQ)** has been produced and this contains a scale designed to measure P (Eysenck and Eysenck, 1975).

The EPI and EPQ are intended to be used primarily for research purposes rather than to make diagnoses in individual cases. On the whole, they have been found acceptable in terms of reliability and validity. Barrett and Kline (1982) found that the EPQ factors emerged with 'remarkable clarity' in three different samples of people. However, as in other studies, the P dimension was less clearly defined than E and N and this remains the most controversial of Eysenck's dimensions.

Eysenck's personality questionnaires (like those of Cattell referred to later) are further examples of psychometric tests (see Chapter 1, Section II). Like intelligence tests they have been exposed to the processes of reliability and validity.

## The Hierarchical Structure of Personality

As we have seen, Eysenck claims that the structure of personality comprises just three different dimensions. In support of this claim he offers a hierarchical model of personality (see Figure 2.2) which neatly illustrates the processes involved in factor analysis.

**FIGURE 2.2**

**An Illustration of Eysenck's Hierarchical Model of Personality in Relation to Extraversion (adapted from Eysenck, 1947)**

(Note that a similar model exists for the dimensions of neuroticism and psychoticism.)

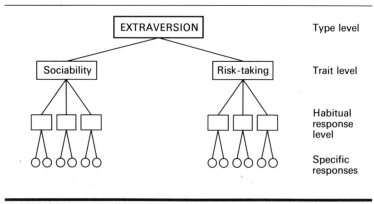

The lowest level relates to numerous specific pieces of behaviour such as talking to someone in a supermarket or reading a book on a bus. At the next level, his analysis reveals habitual responses, which are typical ways of behaving made up of clusters of specific responses. Habitual responses can be explained by the traits contained at the third level. For example, in Figure 2.2, 'sociability' includes the habitual responses of 'going to parties' and 'taking part in team games'. At the top of the hierarchy is the type level; in Figure 2.2 this is Extraversion. E contains several subcomponents, sociability and risk-taking being just two of them. (Though Eysenck refers to the top of the hierarchy as the 'type' level, remember that E, N and P are *dimensions* rather than types, since every individual possesses all three to varying degrees and are not assigned into rigid categories.)

According to Eysenck, knowing a person's score on one of the dimensions at the type level makes it possible to predict that person's traits, habitual responses and specific responses in relation to that particular dimension. Eysenck claims support for this assertion from his use of **criterion analysis**. Criterion analysis involves the use of the EPI and EPQ with groups of people who are already known to differ on the dimensions of E, N and P. The logic is that people who, for example, have been identified clinically as highly neurotic would be expected to score highly on N compared with non-neurotics.

## The Physiological Basis of Personality

Eysenck's theory offers no firm support for the biological basis of P. However, he proposes that differences in E and N between people are related to the types of nervous system they possess. Below is a summary of some of the more important points made in this aspect of his theory:

1. The concept of **cortical arousal**, or alertness, is related to E. Extraverts are considered to be less aroused than introverts and to constantly seek stimulation in order to increase their arousal level. Conversely, introverts are seen to be generally over-aroused and are therefore likely to look for strategies to avoid excessive stimulation

2. Cortical arousal is controlled by activity in a particular part of the brain known as the ascending **reticular activating system** (**ARAS**) which is easily activated in introverts, but responds more slowly in extraverts. Eysenck suggests that extraverts have 'strong' nervous systems – the ARAS is biased to **inhibit** neural impulses (chemical 'messages' within the nervous system: see Chapter 5, Figure 5.3, for a brief explanation of neural transmission) which 'dampens down' the effects of stimulation to the brain. Conversely, introverts have 'weak' nervous systems where the ARAS provides strong **excitation**, or boosting, of incoming stimulation, thereby increasing its effect. Put very simply, for introverts a little stimulation will have a relatively powerful effect, while extraverts may need a large amount of stimulation before any effect is felt (hence their tendency to seek extra stimulation).

3. Eysenck proposes that the physiological basis of N is to be found in the **autonomic nervous system** (ANS). The sympathetic division of the ANS is active when emotion is felt and it controls bodily changes associated with strong emotional reactions, for example increased pulse and heart rate, sweating and churning stomach. In neurotics, the ANS reacts more

quickly and strongly to stimulation causing them more readily to experience anxiety than their less neurotic counterparts.

CONDITIONABILITY   As we have seen, Eysenck believes that biological factors can explain differences between introverts, extraverts, neurotics and stable individuals. One of the most significant *psychological* effects, he believes, relates to the relative ease or difficulty with which individuals become conditioned. Introverts because of their sensitivity to stimulation, will condition more quickly and strongly than will extraverts. This difference was demonstrated by Franks (1956, 1957) who found that introverts could be conditioned to produce eye-blinks in response to a buzzer more quickly than could extraverts. The biological explanation suggests that since introverts produce a higher level of arousal than extraverts, their nervous systems are more likely to form the necessary associations.

This difference in conditionability also partly explains the characteristically different patterns of behaviour shown by introverts and extraverts. Shackleton and Fletcher (1984) suggest that the introvert, whose social conditioning has been more effective, is likely to be more conformist and cautious than the extravert.

IS THERE SUPPORT FOR THE BIOLOGICAL THEORY?   In looking for support for Eysenck's biological theory, four kinds of evidence have been considered: genetic evidence, laboratory studies, clinical data and 'real world' behaviour. A selection of the findings appears below:

1.  **Genetic Evidence**. Shields (1976) showed that identical twins (identical genetic structure) were significantly more similar in E and N than were non-identical twins (different genetic structure).
2.  **Laboratory Studies**. Eysenck's biological theory predicts that introverts will differ from extraverts in their levels of cortical arousal. Traditionally, cortical arousal has been assessed using the **electroencephalogram** (**EEG**) a mechanism for measuring the electrical activity of the brain. Gale (1981) reviewed 30 studies which attempted to relate EEG activity to personality measures. Only half of them showed significant differences

between introverts and extraverts with the better designed, more recent studies doing so more frequently. Gale, however, pointed out that the laboratory conditions themselves may influence cortical activity in that extraverts are less likely to be influenced by the presence of others than are introverts. Clearly, effective control must be exercised in experiments if findings are to be meaningful.

3. **Clinical Data**. Studies which have used psychiatric samples have shown that individuals scoring high in N exhibit a wide variety of physical responses such as increased sweating and heart rates. They often also fail to habituate (become accustomed to and stop responding) to external stimuli, which implies that they may have a poorly functioning ANS (Lader, 1975). Whilst these findings apply to patient groups, there is generally no evidence of links between N scores and these measures of autonomic functioning in non-patient groups. Thus, no unequivocal support exists for Eysenck's suggested association between ANS functioning and N.

4. **'Real World' Data**. The Eysenck Personality Questionnaire is quite a good predictor of behaviour outside the laboratory. In a study of participants' choices of leisure activities, Furnham (1981, 1982) found that extraverts tended to search for stimulating social situations involving competitiveness, intimacy and assertiveness. He regarded this as an indication that extraverts strive to raise their arousal level. Neurotics tended to avoid social interaction and competitiveness, while high psychoticism scorers chose situations where they were able to manipulate people.

## *Eysenck's Theory of Criminality*

Eysenck (1964) proposed that because of the poorer conditionability and thus poorer socialisation of extraverts, the incidence of crime would be higher in that group. Furthermore, a combination of high E with high N would produce a strong drive level resulting in a tendency towards anti-social behaviour. Eysenck's 'typical' criminal, therefore, would be a neurotic extravert. Later, criminality was linked also to high levels of P (Eysenck and Eysenck, 1970).

Research evidence has been equivocal. Two studies have found that delinquent boys had higher P scores than controls (Edmunds and Kendrick, 1980; Farrington *et al.*, 1982). Rushton and Crisjohn (1981) found that E and P, though not N, were related to self-reported delinquency. Many studies have produced findings which undermine Eysenck's claims. In a review of studies which compared prisoners' scores on the EPI to those of controls, Cochrane (1974) concluded that though prisoners were higher on N, they were no higher on E. In summary, there is no convincing evidence that offenders are more extraverted than non-offenders, though there is some evidence that they are more psychotic and more neurotic.

*Evaluation of Eysenck's Work*

1.  As has already been noted, there is no firm support for many aspects of Eysenck's theory. Criterion studies do seem to give validity to his dimensions of E and N and to a more limited degree, P. However, a crucial element of the theory, his proposal that introverts condition more easily than extraverts, has received only limited support. Consequently, his application of this element to social conditioning and likely differences in social behaviour between extraverts and introverts seems precarious.
2.  Kendrick (1981) suggests that clinical applications of Eysenck's theory have been limited and that few clinicians have made use of predictions arising from the theory when treating patients. Lanyon (1984) claims that the EPQ has not been sufficiently well validated on clinical samples to firmly demonstrate its practical usefulness.
3.  Critics have questioned whether such a simple instrument as the EPI with its inflexible 'Yes/No' questions is adequate to measure the complexities of human personality (Heim, 1970a).
4.  Whilst acknowledging its shortcomings, Shackleton and Fletcher (1984) pay tribute to Eysenck's theory and point out that it has generated a vast amount of research and has provided an invaluable model for personality investigations. Of Eysenck himself they say that '. . . almost every problem to which he has addressed himself has benefited from the debate his attention invariably stimulates'.

**Cattell's Theory**

The work of Cattell (1965) resulted in a complex personality theory which postulates that the basic structure of human personality is made up of at least 20 traits. His research addressed aspects of human functioning often ignored by other personality theorists (For example, ability, emotion, motivation and learning.) Like Eysenck, his work led to the development of a questionnaire designed to measure personality. A brief account of the main elements of his approach and findings follows.

*The Structure of Personality*

Cattell started by devising a technique to ensure that every possible aspect of personality would be investigated. Using a standard English dictionary, he collected 18,000 words, or traits names, which could be used in everyday language to describe personality. His aim was to reduce this vast amount of data to more manageable proportions, using the technique of factor analysis as already described. The main stages in his analysis were:

1.  Groups of individuals were observed and rated on the trait names. Factor analysis of this data revealed that 15 first-order factors (known by Cattell as **primary traits**) could encompass all the terms used to describe human personality. The 15 primary traits were referred to by Cattell as **L Data** (life data).
2.  This stage involved the construction of questionnaires based on the 15 source traits. After administering them to groups of people, the resulting scores were analysed. Sixteen factors emerged and 12 of these closely resembled the source trait derived from the earlier analysis. Thus, three of the earlier factors did not reappear but four new ones emerged. The resulting factors (known as **Q data**) form the basis of the widely used 16PF (Personality Factors) Questionnaire (see Figure 2.3) which will be discussed later. The first twelve factors lettered A to O are found in L-data and Q-data while the last four are identified from Q data only.
3.  At the third stage of the project, a number of objective tests were administered to large groups of people. These tests involved observing individuals in structured situations (a more

**Figure 2.3**

**Factors Measured by Cattell's 16PF (after Cattell, 1965)**

| Low Score Description | Factor | High Score Description |
|---|---|---|
| Reserved, cool, detached | A | Outgoing, warmhearted |
| Less intelligent, concrete thinker | B | More intelligent, abstract thinker |
| Emotionally unstable, easily upset | C | Emotionally stable, calm, mature |
| Humble, mild, submissive | E | Assertive, aggressive, stubborn |
| Sober, cautious, serious | F | Happy-go-lucky, impulsive, enthusiastic |
| Expedient, disregards rules | G | Persevering, conscientious |
| Shy, restrained, timid | H | Adventurous, socially bold |
| Tough-minded, self-reliant | I | Tender-minded, clinging |
| Trusting, adaptable | L | Suspicious, self-opinionated |
| Practical, careful | M | Imaginative, unconventional |
| Simple, natural | N | Shrewd, calculating |
| Self-assured, confident | O | Insecure, self-reproaching |
| Traditional, conservative | $Q^1$ | Experimenting, liberal |
| Group-dependent | $Q^2$ | Self-sufficient |
| Undisciplined, self-conflict | $Q^3$ | Controlled, socially precise |
| Relaxed, composed | $Q^4$ | Tense, frustrated |

unusual one was blowing up a balloon, which identifies timid people) in order to make predictions about their behaviour in different situations. Twenty-one factors emerged from this data (known as **T data**) and a number of them were found to coincide with the second-order data drawn from the questionnaire data.

Thus, Cattell used a comprehensive range of different measures of human behaviour in his search for the basic structure of human personality. Unfortunately, the three sources of data described above did not reveal exactly similar structures. Whilst there seems to be considerable agreement between the factor structure found in L and Q data, T data appears to expose a somewhat different aspect of personality. Twenty factors have emerged from T data, but Hampson (1988) points out that the relationship between these factors and those located in L and Q data is yet to be fully established.

## Integrating Cattell and Eysenck

Cattell, it will be recalled, used an oblique method of factor analysis which revealed a relatively large number of first-order factors (his source traits which form most of the factors in the 16PF). These, he believed, gave a more accurate and useful picture of the structure of human personality than did the broader second-order factors emerging from Eysenck's (orthogonal) analyses. However, Cattell further analysed his first-order factors which revealed a smaller number of second-order factors (Cattell called them '**surface**' traits). Two of them, exvia and anxiety, correspond closely to Eysenck's major dimensions of extraversion and neuroticism. Thus the two accounts of the structure of personality have more in common than would at first appear and some differences appear to be accounted for by the different techniques of factor analysis used by the two researchers.

## Cattell's Measurements of Personality

A number of questionnaires have been developed by Cattell and his colleagues; as already noted, the best known one is the 16PF (Cattell *et al.*, 1970) which is intended for adults. The 16PF measures the factors shown in Figure 2.3. Versions of the 16PF are also available to assess the structure of children's personality.

All the above tests are appropriate for normal groups. Unlike Eysenck, Cattell believes that the abnormal personality is qualitatively different from the normal personality (Cattell, 1973). Therefore, although the 16PF can distinguish between neurotics and normals, additional factors are included to distinguish psychotics who are considered to possess personality traits not found in normal groups. Twelve abnormal factors were presented by Cattell and Kline (1977). Seven of these were associated with depression.

## The Influence of Situational Factors on Behaviour

Though Cattell believed that general personality factors and abilities remain relatively constant over time, he recognised that a number of different situations and body states may temporarily influence the way people behave. For example, states such as tiredness, elation, fear or drunkenness may all cause a person to act 'out of character'. Therefore, trying to predict behaviour on the basis of trait factors without taking account of moods or states in particular situations could be deceptive.

Thus Cattell, to a greater extent than Eysenck, upheld the importance of temporary fluctuations in behaviour in the light of particular circumstances. This led him to develop the Eight State Questionnaire which measures mood and state factors such as depression, arousal, anxiety, and fatigue. These are thought of as short-term phenomena as, for example, when a usually composed individual becomes agitated after a road accident.

*Practical Applications of Cattell's Theory*

Cattell has applied aspects of his theory to many different situations, some of which are outlined below:

1.  **Abnormal psychology**. The 16PF questionnaire has been used in clinical situations, largely for research purposes as its validity is insufficiently well-established for use in individual diagnoses (Williams *et al.*, 1972). The Clinical Analysis Questionnaire has also been developed for psychiatric settings.
2.  **Occupational selection and counselling**. Cattell has provided profiles derived from personality scores for different occupational groups such as accountants and lawyers. These have been used in vocational counselling.
3.  **Education**. His tests for use with young children and adolescents, as described earlier, have been widely used in educational settings. His work on intelligence has led to the development of a 'culture fair' test which attempts to measure intelligence uncontaminated by cultural factors (see Chapter 1, Section I).

*Evaluation of Cattell's Work*

1.  While a good level of support exists for Cattell's surface traits, particularly exvia (extraversion) and anxiety, a relatively large number of studies have failed to support the validity of his source traits (for example, Eysenck and Eysenck, 1969; Vagg

and Hammond, 1976; Saville and Blinkhorn, 1976; Browne and Howarth, 1977). However, Kline (1981b) argues that this may be partly accounted for by the fact that different researchers have used different, sometimes inadequate, techniques.

2. Peck and Whitlow (1975) argue that if Cattell's theory is to be widely accepted amongst psychologists, it must be demonstrated that the data used is appropriate and is capable of producing a stable number of primary factors. Also, these factors should be seen to have psychological, as well as mathematical validity.

3. Though disagreements exist between Eysenck and Cattell about the best methods for arriving at a theory of personality structure, paradoxically, the agreements between them about some of the second order factors lend some validity to the theories and personality questionnaires of both researchers.

### Conclusions: The 'Big Five'

It has been seen from the work of Eysenck and Cattell that the former prefers to describe the structure of personality broadly in terms of his three personality dimensions (neuroticism, extraversion and psychoticism) where the latter favours a more detailed view (between 16 and 23 factors). It has been shown that despite these differences, many aspects of their theories are essentially the same. What can be concluded? A consensus seems to be emerging among trait researchers that five factors may provide a compromise between the conclusions of Eysenck and Cattell. An outline of relevant research findings and views appears below:

1. The most influential findings arose from a series of studies carried out by Tupes and Christal (1961) and Norman (1963). The researchers factor-analysed data drawn from a range of different samples using Cattell's (1947) trait rating scales. Despite differences in the samples, a common picture emerged of five factors which seemed to form the basis of personality structure. The factors were labelled extraversion, agreeableness, conscientiousness, emotional stability and culture. They have since become known as **the Big Five**. These are displayed in Figure 2.4 together with some of the trait scales which characterise each of the five factors.

**FIGURE 2.4**

**The Five Factors Forming the Basis of Personality Structure (after Norman, 1963)**

| Factor name | Representative Trait Scales |
|---|---|
| Extraversion | Talkative – silent<br>Frank, open – secretive<br>Sociable – reclusive |
| Agreeableness | Good-natured – irritable<br>Not jealous – jealous<br>Mild, gentle – headstrong |
| Conscientiousness | Fussy, tidy – careless<br>Responsible – undependable<br>Scrupulous – Unscrupulous |
| Emotional stability | Poised – nervous, tense<br>Calm – anxious<br>Composed – excitable |
| Culture | Artistically sensitive – artistically insensitive<br>Intellectual – unreflective, narrow<br>Polished, refined – crude, boorish |

2. The Big Five have now been identified in many different studies using samples of children (Digman and Inouye, 1986) and adults (McCrae and Costa, 1985, 1987). However, some disagreement exists regarding the exact nature of one of the Big Five. McCrae and Costa (1985) have proposed a new, important personality factor called **openness** which distinguishes individuals who are open to experience as indicated by their artistic and intellectual pursuits, creativity, liberal, untraditional values, independence and impracticalness. Eysenck and Eysenck (1985) disagree that openness is a new factor and argue that it is at the opposite end of the continuum to psychoticism. Hampson (1988) proposes that openness to experience could be a form of the Big Five factor called culture rather than a new factor.

3. Goldberg (1981) proposes that the Big Five can account for all the personality structures derived from trait ratings by the various multi-trait theorists.
4. Hampson (1988) concludes 'Although the debate over the definitive structure of personality ratings is far from over . . . the Big Five represents a reasonable compromise between the extreme positions offered by Eysenck and Cattell' (p. 71).

**Self-assessment Questions**

1. For what purpose did Eysenck and Cattell use the technique of factor analysis in their study of personality?
2. Briefly outline the major dimensions of personality identified by Eysenck. What techniques are used to assess them?
3. Summarise the main claims made by Eysenck about the physiological basis of personality. Is this aspect of his theory supportable?
4. Identify some of the ways in which Cattell's theory differs from that of Eysenck.
5. What are some of the practical applications of Cattell's theory?
6. Outline more recent views about human personality put forward by multi-trait theorists.

## SECTION III   IS PERSONALITY CONSISTENT?

The concept of **consistency** is central to the view of personality put forward by trait theorists. Trait theorists propose that personality is made up of a number of stable, internal factors (e.g. extraversion, neuroticism and psychoticism in the case of Eysenck's theory) which are consistent and therefore cause individuals to behave in similar ways on different occasions and in a range of different situations. Thus, it is expected that a person who is generally aggressive or very shy will be so in a wide variety of different situations. The most harmful criticism of trait theories, if it were upheld, would be to weaken their claims regarding the consistency of behaviour. Such a criticism was made by Mischel (1968), a social learning theorist. A brief explanation of social learning theory is given in Figure 2.5. (For a more explicit account, the reader is referred to Birch and Malim, 1988.)

---

**FIGURE 2.5**

**Social Learning Theory**

---

Social learning theory has received its main stimulus from theories of learning arising from laboratory experiments carried out initially with animals but later applied to human behaviour. One such theory was that of **operant conditioning**, the leading exponent of which was Skinner (1974) a highly significant and influential figure in psychology. A key principle of operant conditioning is that if people have been **reinforced** (rewarded) for particular kinds of behaviour in particular situations then they are likely to learn that behaviour and repeat it again in similar situations. Bandura (1969) extended this theory further in relation to human learning by proposing that a significant influence on human learning is the observation of what others do, known as imitation or observational learning. Thus, a social learning theory approach to human behaviour proposes that the main determinants of an individual's behaviour are not any consistent, internal characteristics or traits they may possess, but what happens to that individual in the environment, through observing the behaviour of others and receiving patterns of reinforcement. Observed behaviours may be 'stored' and only introduced when individuals feel they will be rewarded.

---

**Mischel's Attack on Traditional Personality Theories**

In a book called *Personality and Assessment*, Mischel (1968) strongly attacked the concept of personality and traits in particular. He argued that traditional personality theories, such as Freud's psychoanalytic theory (see Chapter 3) and trait theories had greatly overstated the case for behavioural consistency. He proposed instead that it is particular *situations* which may cause an individual to behave in certain ways, for example, calmly or aggressively. Consistencies in behaviour must therefore arise from similarities between situations in which people find themselves.

In reviewing the evidence for behavioural consistency, Mischel was considerably influenced by a long-standing study by Hartshorne and May (1928) which used several thousand children as participants. The aim of their investigations was to examine the concept of a trait of honesty. It was thought that someone who is basically honest will consistently behave with honesty in many different situations, regardless of whether there is any pressure upon them to be honest or dishonest. Hartshorne and May found, however, that children who were honest at home were not necessarily so at school and vice versa. They concluded that honesty is not a consistent behaviour which is determined by a personality trait, but is mainly a function of situational factors.

Despite the evidence from the honesty studies and several other investigations, Mischel conceded that behaviour may be consistent over time in *similar* situations. However, he argued that if the situations *vary*, the behaviour may also change. He did not regard consistency of behaviour in similar situations as sufficient evidence for the existence of stable personality traits.

### Situationism

Following Mischel's criticisms of traditional personality theory, interest was renewed in psychology over the long-standing issue of which has the more important effect on people's behaviour, characteristics within themselves or the situation they find themselves in. Mischel, as has been noted, subscribed to the latter view, which became known as **situationism**.

Research is available which has vividly portrayed the compelling effect of the situation on behaviour. Haney *et al.* (1973) carried out the classic 'prison' experiment in which student volunteers with no known anti-social tendencies were kept in a prison setting. Some were randomly allocated to be 'prisoners' while others became 'guards'. After only a few days, the 'guards' displayed extremely aggressive and brutal behaviour, whilst the prisoners became passive and dependent, several of them showing symptoms of severe emotional disturbance. It is important to note that all the participants had originally been judged as emotionally stable, physically healthy and 'normal to average' in relation to personality tests.

Despite evidence in support of it, intuitively people feel uncomfortable with the extreme version of situationism. Logic tells us that, in general, people are recognisably the same in different situations.

### *Criticisms of Situationism*

Bowers (1973) pointed out the weaknesses of pure situationism by drawing attention to its failure to acknowledge the ability of individuals to determine their own course of action. He argued that it is misguided to attribute the causes of behaviour either solely to situations or solely to internal traits. The foolishness of such approaches is illustrated by the ease with which it is possible to find supporting evidence for either. For example, driving in city traffic can provide support for situationism in that the majority of people comply with traffic lights. Alternatively, when driving on the motorway, individual preferences (and perhaps personality traits) may determine driving speed more so than does the situation. Bower concludes that the dispute about traits versus situations should be discontinued in favour of an **interactionist** approach which takes both into consideration.

Mischel himself moved towards an interactionist position by proposing that situations alone cannot account for people's behaviour. The same situations may have different 'meanings' for different people, depending on what he referred to as 'person variables' arising from their previous learning experiences. Person variables were seen as an alternative to traits and included such things as competence, expectancy and values. Thus, different people may respond quite differently in the same situation.

## Interactionism

Interactionism provides a compromise between the trait and situationist approaches to personality. Pervin and Lewis (1978) argue that not only should an interactionist approach address internal characteristics of people and features of the situations in which individuals operate, but it should also pay attention to the process through which one influences the other. A large amount of research has been carried out from an interactionist perspective. Examples are discussed below:

1. McCord and Wakefield (1981) tested the hypothesis that introverts would perform better in arithmetical tasks than extraverts in classes where punishment prevailed, whereas extraverts would achieve more in situations where rewards predominated. Findings indicated that this was the case indicating that personality (introversion–extraversion) inter-acts with the kind of situation (punishment-oriented or reward-oriented). It should be noted that this kind of interac-

tion is 'one-way', the situation affecting the individual rather than the other way round.

2. A study by Moos (1969) is an example of a study which attempted to estimate the extent of the influence of characteristics of the person, situation factors and their interaction on behaviour. Psychiatric patients were observed in a number of different situations (for example on the ward, in the chapel, having occupational therapy) and their behaviour (such as smoking, talking, listening) was noted. Moos found that situation factors accounted for 10 per cent of the observed differences in behaviour, characteristics of the person accounted for 12 per cent and their interaction for 21 per cent. Thus, the interaction was seen to influence behaviour to a greater extent than either person or situation factors studied alone.

Many studies have demonstrated the effects on behaviour of the interaction of person factors and situation factors. Much of it has been criticised for failing to demonstrate fully the highly complex nature of this interaction.

## *Criticisms of Interactionism*

1. Olweus (1977) suggested that a significant interaction does not reveal anything about the process underlying that interaction. Nor does it tell us much about why people *behave* as they do. He adds that a study of the way personality interacts with situations can only be meaningful in the context of a sound theory of personality dispositions.
2. Mischel (1981) stresses that the concept of 'interaction' must be clearly defined and analysed. Otherwise, interactionist research may result only in statements of the obvious.
3. Cronbach and Snow (1977) draw attention to the difficulties arising from the virtually unlimited number of possible interactions that could be studied and the number of other variables which may intervene to modify the particular interaction studied.
4. A major problem in interactionism has been in defining precisely what is meant by 'situation'. Though psychologists have tried to develop taxonomies (classifications) for different

kinds of situations, they have encountered many difficulties. For example, disagreements exist on whether situations can be defined objectively without allowing for people's perception of the situation. Thus, the word 'situation' is often used in a vague, poorly defined way.

5. Hampson (1988) argues that interactionism was a paradoxical solution to the consistency problem since it emphasised the importance of both personality traits and situational variables. Whilst it has succeeded in restoring confidence in the concept of personality, it has not resolved the fundamental problem of whether people's behaviour is consistent.

## Person-centred Approaches to Consistency

Over the last decade or so, a number of new approaches have attempted to resolve some of the issues in the consistency debate. One such approach is known as the **person-centred** approach, which centres on people's own perceptions of the consistency of some of their own personality traits. It suggests that consistency does exist but only for some kinds of people and certain kinds of behaviour in certain situations (Bem, 1983).

A study which greatly influenced the person-centred approach was carried out by Bem and Allen (1974). They investigated friendliness and conscientiousness in a group of college students. Bem and Allen found that when participants were asked to rate themselves on consistency of these two traits, those who saw themselves as *consistently* friendly did in fact behave in a friendly way in a large number of situations (supported by direct observations and by ratings from peers and parents). Students who rated themselves as *inconsistently* friendly were indeed found to be friendly in some situations and not others. Similar findings emerged for the trait of conscientiousness. Thus it seems that the traits of friendliness and conscientiousness may not be characteristic of all individuals. However, those for whom it is characteristic can be expected to act in a consistent way in a wide range of situations.

As a result of Bem and Allen's research, the importance of *self*-assessed consistency as a predictor of consistency in behaviour has been widely acknowledged.

Bem and Allen's findings have been supported by Kenrick and Stringfield (1980) though not by Chaplin and Goldberg (1984).

## Conclusions

Evidence suggests that a pure trait approach to personality does not provide sufficient support for the idea that people's behaviour is invariably consistent. However, the opposite view, situationism, has also proved inadequate. Intuition, supported by research evidence, tells us that the way we behave is influenced both by who and what we are and the situations in which we find or place ourselves.

Research goes on into the issue of the consistency of personality and new solutions continue to be sought.

## Self-assessment Questions

1. Explain Mischel's situationist view of the nature of personality. In what way does this view challenge the beliefs of trait theorists?
2. What does Bowers (1973) suggest are some of the weaknesses of a pure situationist view of personality?
3. What are the main tenets of an interactionist approach to personality? Refer to some relevant studies.
4. What insights does the study by Bem and Allen (1983) provide into the issue of consistency of personality?
5. What conclusions can you draw about the consistency of behaviour?

## SECTION IV   IDIOGRAPHIC APPROACHES TO PERSONALITY

In the introduction to this chapter, a distinction was made between **idiographic** and **nomothetic** approaches to the study of personality. The latter approach, you will recall, emphasises the similarities between people and it is exemplified by the theories of Eysenck and Cattell discussed in Section II. Idiographic approaches focus on the uniqueness of individuals and take the view that the essence of personality can only be captured by a detailed study of individual lives and experiences (see Malim *et al.* (1992) for a detailed consideration of the idiographic/nomothetic dichotomy). In this section, the work of three theorists will be discussed as examples of an idiographic approach to personality: **Gordon Allport, Carl Rogers** and **George Kelly**.

The approach of Allport, as has already been noted, was not 'purely' idiographic in that, whilst greatly emphasising the individuality and uniqueness of each personality, he also recognised the existence of some common traits that all people share to varying degrees.

Carl Rogers was a leading figure in **humanistic psychology**, a major force in psychology which gathered momentum towards the middle of this century. Humanistic psychology, with its emphasis on studying the unique and subjective experiences of individual people, provided an important balance to the two major approaches which dominated psychology during the first part of this century: **behaviourism**, which views human personality as being 'shaped' by the effects of the environment and **psychoanalysis** (discussed in Chapter 3) which emphasises the effects on the human personality of an unconscious mind (see Malim *et al.* (1992) for a discussion of the major approaches in psychology).

The third idiographic theorist, Kelly, sought to understand human personality by examining individuals' own interpretations of themselves and their social world. He used the term **personal constructs** to denote the dimensions people use in their attempts to interpret the people and events in their lives.

### Allport's Trait Approach

In 1937, Allport published a theory of personality. It was a reaction against previous theories which had been based on the study of abnormal personality and those which had been derived from the study of children or animals. He believed that the study of personality should emphasise the experience of unique, normal human adults and should aim to describe the psychological structures that determine the individual's characteristic ways of thinking and behaving. Some of the main points of Allport's theory are outlined below.

#### Personality Traits

According to Allport, traits have a very real existence. He saw them as mental structures which form a part of each person's personality and which result in that person behaving and thinking in a generally consistent manner. For example, a person who possesses the trait of 'friendliness' would tend to behave in a generally sociable way in a number of different situations, such as mixing with work colleagues or meeting a stranger.

Since Allport valued a common-sense view of human personality, be began his search for personality traits by searching through an English dictionary. He found nearly 18,000 adjectives, for example 'lazy' and 'cheerful', which are used to describe personality (Allport and Odbert, 1936). Personality traits, he believed, can take one of three forms within the individual:

1.  **Cardinal Traits**. These are the most important traits which have a great influence on an individual's personality. In a few cases, a person's behaviour may be totally dominated by a single trait; for example, extreme meanness or selfishness. Allport believed that personalities like this are relatively rare; most people do not have one single, dominant trait.
2.  **Central Traits**. These are less general traits, though Allport believed that they represent the basic dispositions which characterise an individual's usual ways of dealing with life. For example, one person's central traits might be honesty, liveliness, friendliness and conscientiousness.
3.  **Secondary Dispositions**. These are less influential and consistent traits. They represent a person's specific preferences and attitudes in particular situations.

## *The Whole Person*

Though Allport's study of personality traits emphasised individual aspects of people, he strongly believed that the study of personality should not lose sight of the *whole*, unique person. He considered that attempting to measure isolated facets of personality by using rating scales was misguided. Thus Allport's theory aims to provide a detailed and total description of individuals rather than comparing isolated elements of their personalities with those of other people.

## *Personality Assessment*

Allport proposed that people's traits could be identified in various different ways – by direct observation of their behaviour in a range of situations, by interviews to discover their views and goals and by using evidence from letters, diaries and other documents. He urged the study of individuals through detailed and long-term case studies. A famous example of one of his own case studies centred on the personality of a young woman called Jenny. Allport and his assistants identified the central traits of Jenny's personality by analysing her letters to a friend written over many years (Allport, 1965). This study epitomises the idiographic approach.

### Evaluation of Allport

Allport is generally regarded as having made a major contribution to the study of personality. His concern with the uniqueness of individuals and the need to study the whole person has provided an important balance to nomothetic approaches with their emphasis on similarities between people, usually with no consideration of individuality.

Conversely, nomothetic theorists have criticised Allport's rejection of scientific methods of studying personality. Allport believed that the scientific method with its emphasis on establishing general laws and principles was not the best route to knowledge about humans. The only meaningful approach, he believed, is to view the world from each individual's unique perspective.

Kirby and Radford (1976) argue that Allport is misguided in that he confused the study of individual differences with the art of biography, which is a descriptive science. Whilst biography makes a valuable contribution to the study of individuals, it does not by itself provide an adequate way of understanding human nature in general. They further comment that if an individual existed who was truly unique, that person would not be recognisable as human, since people are recognisably human because of their similarities.

### Carl Rogers: 'Self' Theory

Rogers's personality theory originated from his work in the fields of counselling and psychotherapy. In contrast to psychoanalysis (see Chapter 3) there is no attempt to examine the hidden meanings of people's behaviour or to look for causes in their childhood. The focus is on the *here and now* and individuals are regarded as the best experts on themselves. How individuals perceive events in their lives determines their reactions to them (Rogers, 1951).

## *The Self*

Central to Rogers's theory is the concept of the **self** (or self concept), the individual's view, acquired through life experiences, of all the perceptions, feelings, values and attitudes that define 'I' or 'me'. This **perceived self** influences both the individual's perception of the world and his or her own behaviour. The other aspect of self, according to Rogers, is the **ideal self**, one's perception of how one should or would like to be. For example, a woman might perceive herself as successful and respected in her career but with certain shortcomings as a wife and mother (which might or might not be true). Her ideal self might demand that she be equally successful in both these spheres of her life. Good psychological health exists where the perceived self and the ideal self are reasonably compatible. It is when there is a serious mismatch (Rogers refers to this as **incongruence**) between the two or between the self and the feedback received from the external world that psychological problems arise. In a study of 250 people who were assessed separately on neuroticism and congruence or genuineness (closeness to inner emotional experiences) Tausch (1978) found that individuals with high degrees of incongruence were the most likely to display neurotic symptoms.

## *Self-actualisation*

All people, Rogers believed, are born with the **actualising tendency**, a motive which drives us to grow and develop into mature and healthy human beings who will realise their full capacities.

This actualising tendency can manifest itself at different levels. At the lowest level it involves basic desires for physical requirements such as food, water and comfort. At a higher level are the needs for self-fulfilment in terms of independence, experience and creativity. This motivation for self-actualisation serves as a criterion by which the individual judges all experiences. An event is evaluated as good or bad dependent upon whether it leads to self-actualisation.

## *Positive Regard from Others*

Rogers (1959) assumes that there exists in all people a need for **positive regard** which develops as the awareness of the self emerges. Positive regard is seen as respect, acceptance and love from the important people in an individual's life. It can be clearly seen in the young child's need for approval and love from the parents. Sometimes parents' approval is conditional, that is, dependent on the child behaving in the way they would wish, or they may accept him or her unconditionally. However, the person needs positive regard not only from others but from him or herself. Where a person experiences unconditional positive regard, positive *self-*regard will also be unconditional. Rogers believes that this situation provides the individual with genuine psychological adjustment. However, most people do not achieve this. Love and approval from others is often conditional on the individual behaving in ways that are acceptable, for example, the child who strives to learn a musical instrument in order to please the parents. Thus the individual develops what Rogers refers to as 'conditions of worth', those ways of behaving which will earn positive regard from significant others. This may involve the individual suppressing spontaneous feelings and actions and behaving in ways which are intended to please others. Rogers believes that many psychological disorders arise from attempts to live our lives by other people's principles rather than our own.

Rogers's **client-centred therapy** (see Chapter 6, Section V) aims to offer the client unconditional positive regard in a warm, accepting atmosphere in order that insight may be gained into disturbing problems and possible solutions explored.

## *Personality Assessment*

**The Q-sort Technique**. This is a technique originally developed by Stephenson (1953) for describing the personality. It was later used by Rogers for examining the self-concept and as an assessment instrument to study changes in the client's perceptions of self during the course of therapy. A full description of the Q-sort technique has been produced by Block (1961/78).

Typically, the procedure for using the Q-sort is as follows:

1. The participant is given a large number of cards, each one containing a descriptive statement such as 'I am likeable', 'I am an impulsive person' or 'I am satisfied with myself'. These are sorted into nine piles with those that are least characteristic of the person in pile one and those most characteristic in pile nine with the remainder being distributed in the intervening piles.
2. The participant is instructed to sort the cards with the majority of them falling in the middle of the continuum and with relatively few falling at either extreme. Thus a rough normal distribution is formed. This makes the results easier to deal with statistically and also controls 'response sets' such as the tendency to stick to average ratings or extreme ratings.
3. In Rogers's procedure, once a profile has been obtained of the participant's perception of 'self', the cards will usually be re-sorted with the aim being to provide a profile of the 'ideal self'. The two sorts can then be correlated in order to register the degree of similarity or discrepancy between 'self' and 'ideal self'. A low correlation indicates a large discrepancy, implying maladjustment and low self-esteem.

The Q-sort is a flexible technique which can be used to assess individuals' perceptions of a number of different aspects of their lives. It is fully in line with Rogers's belief that people are themselves the best judges of their own feelings and attitudes. However, there is some evidence that individuals may respond in ways which they feel are socially acceptable or in line with the expectations of the investigator.

Studies which have attempted to assess the validity of Q-sort techniques have been equivocal. Truax *et al.* (1968) found the results of Q-sorts to be in agreement with other psychological measures of adjustment and change in delinquents and neurotics. However, Garfield *et al.* (1971) found little agreement between eight different measures of outcome in therapy, one of which was the Q-sort. No firm evidence exists in support of the reliability of the Q-sort.

## Evaluation of Rogers's Theory

Rogers's theory, along with those of other humanistic theorists, has served the valuable purpose of encouraging psychologists to consider the subjective experience of the individual and appreciate the importance of self-regard in human functioning. His approach has had its greatest impact in the fields of psychotherapy and counselling and has provided a welcome alternative to psycho-analytic and learning theory approaches to therapy (see Chapter 6).

As a theory of personality, Rogers' approach has a number of shortcomings, which include the following:

1.  It has been suggested that his reliance on self-report is misguided, since people are rarely fully aware of the truth about themselves and in addition may be influenced by the expectations of the investigator.
2.  His concepts of self and the actualising tendency are not sufficiently well-defined to be adequately measured and tested. However, Rogers has made available tape-recordings of his therapy sessions in order that other psychologists may investigate his ideas. Some empirical studies have been carried out using the Personal Orientation Inventory (Shostrum *et al.*, 1976) which claims to be a measure of self-actualisation.

### Kelly's Personal Construct Theory

Kelly (1955) believed that in dealing with the world, people act like scientists. Scientists, he claimed, begin by putting forward theories and hypotheses about what the world is like and then proceed to test them out through research. Thus, Kelly considered each person formulates hypotheses or predictions about the world, tests them out and when necessary, revises them in the light of the 'experi-mental' (interactions with others and with the environment) results. The unique view of the world formed by each individual becomes that individual's idiosyncratic framework which is used to govern his or her behaviour and to interpret further experiences and events. Thus, Kelly maintained, people interpret or **construe** the world rather than observing it directly.

At any given time, the particular hypotheses an individual holds about the world are called personal constructs.

### *Personal Constructs*

To understand the individual, Kelly believed, one must know something about that person's personal constructs. In turn, understanding the person's personal constructs involves finding out also about his or her behaviour. For example, one cannot know what a woman truly means when she says 'I am in love' without looking at some examples of her behaviour.

Kelly viewed personal constructs as pairs of opposing dimensions which individuals use to describe and make sense of the people and events around them. For example, one person may tend to see others as being either friendly or reserved, either warm or cold; another individual may typically use the constructs of intelligent or dull, honest or dishonest. Kelly believed that an individual's personality was made up of the construct system, used to construe (make sense) of the people and events in that individual's life

Kelly devised a method of gaining access to an individual's constructs known as the role construct repertory grid, usually known simply as the repertory grid.

## The Repertory Grid

Kelly mainly used the repertory grid to discover how individuals construe the world in terms of the other people in their lives. However, the technique can also be used to explore other aspects of the person's life such as 'subjects studied at school' in the case of a child or for adults, 'occupations'.

Figure 2.4 illustrates an extract from a repertory grid which has been arrived at to determine the way a fictitious individual, referred to here as James, construes the most important people (**significant others**) in his life. The procedure would be as follows:

1. The roles played by these significant others, for example, mother, father, sister, are listed across the top of the grid. James would be asked to fill in the actual names of the people who play these roles in his life. These are known as the **elements** of the grid.
2. The purpose of the grid is to find the main constructs James uses to interpret and understand the behaviour of the elements (that is, the named people in his life). These are listed in the right-hand column of the grid. To arrive at these, James would be asked to consider the similarities and differences between the elements. These would be considered in threes; for example, typically he would be asked to state how his mother, father and

**FIGURE 2.6**

**An Extract from a Fictitious Repertory Grid**

A tick indicates that the first pole of the construct is applied to the element and a cross that the second pole is applicable.

| ELEMENTS | | | | | CONSTRUCTS |
|---|---|---|---|---|---|
| Mother | Father | Sister | Girl-friend | College tutor | |
| ✓ | ✓ | ✗ | ✓ | ✗ | Understanding – Unsympathetic |
| | | | | | Gentle – Aggressive |
| | | | | | Warm – Cold |
| | | | | | Intelligent – Unintelligent |

sister are alike, and also how they are different. If James thought of his mother and father as being alike in that they are both understanding and his sister being different in that she is unsympathetic, the construct to emerge would be *understanding–unsympathetic*. The constructs are said to be expressed in a bipolar way (showing opposite extremes) with the 'similar' pole placed first. By the time James had worked through all the people in the grid, he would have revealed his own idiosyncratic framework showing the particular constructs he uses to understand the actions of the people in his life. This procedure would be repeated many times until all the possible constructs had been revealed. James would then be asked to go through the grid rating each of the people named against all the constructs arrived at. For example, he would consider whether number 4 (girlfriend) was understanding or unsympathetic, and so on. (A tick would indicate the first of the poles and a cross the second.)

When a repertory grid has been completed, it will contain a large amount of information about the individual's ways of viewing the world. This can be extremely helpful in the treatment of mental disorder (see Chapter 6) where the ability to make changes in personal constructs is seen as crucial to the individual's well-being.

## Criticisms of Personal Construct Theory (PCT)

1. PCT is seen by many as an imaginative and comprehensive theory which emphasises the cognitive aspects of human personality. However, it has been criticised because of its failure to allow for other aspects of human functioning. For example, Bruner (1956) argues that the theory does not deal adequately with the possible effect of strong emotions such as love or anger on an individual's construct system.
2. Thomas (1978) argues that it is difficult to think about PCT in isolation from the repertory grid techniques devised by Kelly and his colleagues. The very act of eliciting constructs from individuals imposes limits on their thought processes which constrains the kind of data that is collected. Thus, the theory could be seen as self-validating in the sense that so long as Kelly's techniques are used, no evidence against the theory could be revealed.

## Idiographic Approaches: Some Conclusions

Idiographic approaches to personality emphasise the uniqueness of the individual. Therefore they represent an important balance to nomothetic approaches in that they could be said to have brought the person back into psychology. However, if the aim of personality theories is to predict human behaviour, idiographic approaches would allow predictions to be made for only one person at a time.

In 1962, Allport and Holt debated the relative virtues of idiographic and nomothetic approaches. Holt argued that only nomothetic approaches satisfy the rigorous scientific methods demanded if psychology is to be considered a science. Allport's response was that idiographic and nomothetic approaches must work together since neither is adequate on its own: idiographic approaches give too isolated a picture of someone while nomothetic ones are too general.

Lamiell (1981) proposes that **idiothetics** provides a compromise. This is an approach which attempts to capture the best of both worlds. As Pervin (1983) says: 'there is an effort to bring the person back into personality research without, however, relinquishing the goal of systematic, general principles of psychological functioning' (p. 268)

### Self-assessment Questions

1. Outline Allport's view of the nature of personality traits. Refer to cardinal traits and central traits.
2. Outline and evaluate Rogers's 'self theory'.
3. Evaluate the use of the Q-sort technique as an assessment of personality.
4. What does Kelly mean by 'personal constructs'? How are they important to an understanding of an individual's personality?
5. What do you believe is the main contribution made by idiographic theories to our understanding of human personality?

## SECTION V   SINGLE-TRAIT THEORIES

The major personality theories considered so far have attempted to describe the whole of personality and to predict behaviour in a wide range of situations. Single-trait theories emphasise the role played by one particular aspect of the personality in influencing behaviour. Some examples are as follows:

### Internal–External Locus of Control (Rotter, 1954)

Research has focused on the extent to which people perceive themselves as being able to influence and control their own lives (internality) or, in contrast, to attribute what happens to them with regard to such factors as luck, fate, other people, etc. (externality).

## *Need for Achievement* (*n Ach*) (McClelland, 1953)

This area of research has examined influences on people's need to attain success or some standard of excellence. It was developed further by Atkinson (1966), who added the related motive **fear of failure**.

## *Type A Personality* (Friedman and Rosenman, 1974)

This deals with a particular pattern of behaviour and the likely consequences. Type A behaviour is characterised by impatience, aggression, competitiveness and a sense of 'deadline urgency'. A large amount of research evidence has revealed a link between Type A behaviour and coronary heart disease.

Though single-trait theories are generally less comprehensive than their multi-trait counterparts in that they address more limited aspects of human personality, increasingly, they are becoming an important focus for research into personality.

The single-trait theory to be discussed here focuses on the trait of field dependence–field independence. This has been chosen because of the vast amount of research it has generated over the past 40 years or so. Reviews of this and other single-trait theories can be found in London and Exner (1978).

## Field Dependence–Field Independence (FD-I)

### *Cognitive Styles*

FD-I is an example of a **cognitive style**. Cognitive styles relate to the *manner* in which people think, remember, perceive and generally process information. It relates not only to the sorts of tasks generally thought of as 'cognitive' such as solving problems or remembering factual information, but also to how people deal with their social worlds. Thus the study of cognitive styles has its roots in both cognitive psychology and personality theory. Messick *et al.* (1976) described 19 separate cognitive styles that have been the focus of research, of which field dependence–field independence has been the most widely studied.

*Origins of FD-I*

FD-I has the distinction of being discovered accidentally by Herman Witkin in 1949. Witkin and his colleagues were investigating perceptual processes in human beings and in particular the use of internal (within the body) and external (in the outside world) cues when perceiving and judging whether a straight rod was vertical when set in different positions. Two imaginative tests were devised to separate out these external and internal cues: the rod and frame test and the body adjustment test.

**Rod and Frame Test (RFT)**. Participants were seated in a completely darkened room facing a tilting luminous frame within which was a luminous rod. They were required to adjust the rod to a vertical position when the rod and frame were tilted, sometimes in the same, sometimes in the opposite directions. The degree of difference of the rod setting from the true upright constituted the participant's score. Those who relied heavily on external cues tended to set the rod in line with the frame; those who relied on internal cues set the rod more closely to the true vertical. The former were described as field dependent and the latter as field independent

**Body Adjustment Test (BAT)**. This took place in a small tilted room. Participants, who were seated, were required to adjust their body to the upright position while the room remained tilted. Field dependent people, relying on external cues, tended to misjudge the situation and adjust their bodies to the angle of the room, whilst field independent people, relying on internal cues were able to make a more accurate judgement and adjust their bodies to the true vertical.

Witkin's hope of separating out the relative importance of internal and external cues in perceiving the vertical was never achieved, since he found wide individual differences between people. Some consistently depended upon internal cues while others relied on external cues. Consequently he abandoned his research into perception of the vertical and concentrated instead on investigating individual differences in a range of tasks and exploring the possible psychological basis for them. The most extensively studied of these tasks was the embedded figures task:

**Embedded Figures Test (EFT)**. In this, participants are required to pick out simple figures which were embedded within more

**FIGURE 2.7**

**An Item Similar to those in the Embedded Figures Test (Witkin, 1950)**

The simple figure on the left can be identified within the more complex design on the right.

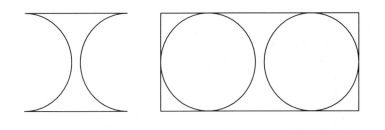

complex designs. Figure 2.7 contains a likely example. Those described as field independent were found to locate the figures quickly and easily while field dependent people were distracted by the complexity of the

surrounding 'field'. A group version of the EFT, the Concealed Shapes Test, devised by Gardner, Jackson and Messick (1960) has also been widely used to assess FD-I.

Witkin found that there was a high correlation between participants' scores on the RFT, BAT and EFT.

What all three measures of FD-I have in common, it seems is that they each require the participant to disembed an item from its context, or 'field'. For some people the field exerts a strong influence making it difficult for them to extract and interpret the constituent parts. Others can more easily analyse and interpret the constituent parts of the whole field. It is important to note that many people are neither extremely field dependent nor highly field independent, but fall somewhere on the continuum between these two extremes.

*Individual Differences in FD-I*

Witkin maintains that there is a close relationship between FD-I and personality: 'Field dependence–independence is a manifestation in the perceptual sphere of a broad dimension of personal functioning which extends into the sphere of social behaviour and into the sphere of personality as well' (Witkin, 1976, p. 44). A large amount of research has been carried out into differences between field dependent and field independent people. This has explored links between FD-I and such diverse areas as problem-solving skills, career choices and social sensitivity among others. A sample of some of this research is described below.

## Cognitive Skills

Studies of cognitive skills have tended to investigate people's performance in problem-solving tasks. The field independent person is usually found to be more successful in such tasks than the field dependent person. For example, Frank and Noble (1984) found that field independents solved both easy and difficult anagrams more quickly than did field dependents. This could not be explained by differences in verbal intelligence since the groups did not differ significantly on this factor

## Career Choices

Witkin (1977) proposed that because they rely on their own internal cues field independent people are logical and analytical. They tend to be found in occupations such as engineering, science and experimental psychology. They are often regarded by others as ambitious, distant and inconsiderate. Field dependent people, however, are more attentive to the environment and tend to be very good with people. They are usually thought of as friendly, warm and sensitive. They tend to gravitate towards occupations which involve dealing with people, such as social work, primary school teaching and clinical psychology. A study by Quinlan and Blatt (1973) showed that a group of very successful surgical nursing students were significantly more field independent than equally successful psychiatric nursing students, who tended to be field dependent.

## Social Differences

Research in the social domain has tested the hypothesis that the extremely field dependent person would tend to be more responsive to social cues and would rely more heavily on the attitudes and judgements of others than the field independent person. Linton (1955) tested this hypothesis by investigating the relationship between field dependence and conformity. She found a significant ($+0.60$) correlation between these two factors.

A study by Ruble and Nakamura (1972) examined the relationship between FD-I and attention given to social stimuli, which in this case was represented by the amount of time spent looking at others. In a problem-solving task, field dependent children were found to look at the experimenter's face more than did field independent children. However, this did not improve their performance in a follow-up trial. It could be assumed that it would have been more helpful to watch how the experimenter solved the problem rather than looking at her face. In a second task, where children were asked to choose from three possible correct solutions, looking at the experimenter's face was more useful. In this case, the experimenter provided social cues by looking at and leaning towards the correct example. This resulted in field dependent children performing better than field independent children.

## *Evaluation of FD-I*

Witkin's theory has received a great deal of supporting evidence from a wide range of sources, For example, Wapner (1976) believes that the study of FD-I provides a creative and novel approach to some central problems of education. Chickering (1976) believes that Witkin's studies of FD-I are important to higher education in particular in that they offer valuable insights on how institutions may adapt educational environments and practices to suit students with varying cognitive styles. However, a number of criticisms of Witkin's theory have been made:

1. FD-I AND INTELLIGENCE   Witkin has argued that FD-I cannot be equated with intelligence. Unlike the scores on IQ tests, he argues, measures of FD-I provide a value-free picture of an individual's functioning in that it is neither better nor worse to be either field dependent or field independent, since each has both strengths and weaknesses. Some investigators, for example Vernon (1972), have argued that tests of FD-I do not measure anything which is not revealed by IQ tests and therefore, FD-I is not

distinguishable from intelligence. It is known that between the ages of 8 and 17 years, people become more field independent. Since IQ also increases with age, the view that FD-I is merely an aspect of intelligence is supported.

However, research into sex differences in FD-I reveal that from the age of 12 up males, tend to be more field independent than females (Maccoby and Jacklin, 1974). Since there are no known sex differences in general intelligence it does not seem likely that FD-I and intelligence are equivalent.

2. LINKS WITH PERSONALITY  As already noted, Witkin (1976) argues that FD-I is a perceptual manifestation of personality and social behaviour. Gruen (1957) has challenged Witkin's claims of a direct link between perception and personality. He claimed that Witkin's procedures focus too much on people's perceptions of a task without taking account of processes within the person which may be involved in their perceptions, for example their attitudes towards or feelings about particular testing situations. Gruen suggests that the same score in an FD-I task might reflect quite different processes in different individuals.

*Self-assessment Questions*

1. What do you understand by single-trait theories? Give some examples.
2. What is the relationship between perception and the cognitive style field dependence–independence?
3. How might an extremely field dependent person be identified through the use of the Embedded Figures Test?
4. Give some examples of likely personality differences between field dependent and field independent people.
5. Critically evaluate the usefulness of the concept of field dependence-independence.

**FURTHER READING**

P. Fonagy and A. Higgitt, *Personality Theory and Clinical Practice* (London/New York: Routledge, 1984).

S. E. Hampson, *The Construction of Personality: an introduction*, 2nd edn (London: Routledge, 1988).

P. Kline, *Personality: Measurement and Theory* (London: Hutchinson, 1983).

I. Roth (ed.), *Introduction to Psychology*, Vol. 1 (Laurence Erlbaum Associates/Open University, 1990).

NOW'S OUR CHANCE TO GET A GLIMPSE OF
HIS UNCONSCIOUS MIND.

# Psychoanalytic Theories of Personality

# 3

At the end of this chapter you should:

1. Be able to critically evaluate Freud's psychoanalytic theory of personality;
2. Have an appreciation of the theories of post-Freudians, Jung and Erikson, and some ways in which they differ from classical psychoanalysis;
3. Have considered the nature of projective tests and the case for and against their use in assessing personality.


## INTRODUCTION

Psychoanalytic theories of personality propose an account of human behaviour which relies heavily on the notion of an **unconscious mind** and which emphasises the dynamic inner forces which regulate and control behaviour. All psychoanalytic theories are based to varying degrees on the theory of **Sigmund Freud**. His theory is the first to be examined below.


## SECTION I SIGMUND FREUD (1856–1939)

Trained as a doctor in Vienna, Freud's interest in neurology led him to specialise in the treatment of nervous disorders. He noted that many neurotic symptoms exhibited by his patients appeared to stem from earlier traumatic experiences rather than from physical complaints. Freud gradually developed his now famous psycho-analytic treatment of emotional and personality disorders. A major technique used was that of **free association**, where patients were encouraged to relax and express the free flow of thoughts entering

87

their minds. (See Chapter 6 for an examination of psychoanalysis as a therapeutic treatment.) The aim of free association was to penetrate the **unconscious mind** of the patient and reveal thoughts, feelings and motivations of which the patient had not hitherto been aware. It was from this early work in a clinical setting that Freud developed his famous theory of the human mind and personality, a theory which continued to grow and develop throughout his life.

Central to Freud's theory was his belief in:

1. The existence of the unconscious mind harbouring repressed memories which motivate and influence conscious thoughts and behaviour. Freud's view of the unconscious mind was largely negative in that he believed the contents were repressed because they were painful or threatening; burying unacceptable memories in the unconscious, therefore, is likely to make our conscious existence less painful. For most people this is a healthy defensive process but for some it may lead to psychological disorder. (See the later discussion of defence mechanisms.)

2. The existence of **instincts** which motivate and regulate human behaviour even in childhood, for example:

   **Eros** (a general life instinct made up of life-preserving and sexual drives) and
   **Thanatos** (a death instinct which involves aggressive and destructive drives)

   The source of these instincts is psychic energy and the most dominant, the **libido**, is sexual in nature. Freud regarded the libido as a force which compels humans to behave in ways which are likely to reproduce the species. He proposed that the amount of psychic energy for a particular individual is fixed and that energy could be linked to objects, people, thoughts and actions. He called this process **cathexis**.

**The Structure of the Personality**

Freud held that the personality encompassed three major parts, the **id**, the **ego** and the **superego**. Each part has its own function and in the healthy, mature personality the three parts produce well-balanced, integrated behaviour. Note that these parts of the personality should in no way be thought of as tangible biological entities.

**ID**  The id is biologically determined and is the most primitive part of the personality. It represents all the instinctual drives: sexual, aggressive and those concerned with the satisfaction of bodily needs. It operates on the '**pleasure principle**', that is to say, it seeks to obtain pleasure and avoid pain. Unsatisfied desires create tension, so release must be sought either through real solutions or through fantasy. The id is irrational and impulsive and is unaffected by social restrictions. In the newborn baby, all mental processes are id processes.

**EGO**  As the infant develops and attempts to adapt to the demands of the outside world, the ego emerges. It operates on the '**reality principle**', that is to say gratification of needs are postponed until the appropriate time and place. For example, the young child learns that hunger will only be satisfied when someone is available to prepare food. This does not imply that the ego is concerned with what is 'right' or 'good' only that it takes account of the constraints and restrictions of the outside world. The ego is often said to be the 'executive' or 'manager' of the personality, in that it attempts to strike a balance between the realities of the outside world and the irrational, self-seeking drives of the id.

**SUPEREGO**  Around the age of four to six the third part of the personality, the superego, emerges. The superego represents the individual's own internal framework of what is 'right' and 'wrong' as represented by the moral sanctions and inhibitions which exist in the surrounding culture. Largely unconscious, it has two components: the **ego-ideal** and the **conscience**. The ego-ideal is concerned with what is right and proper. It represents the individual's view of the sort of virtuous behaviour that would be rewarded by others, initially the parents. The conscience, on the other hand, watches over what is bad. It intercepts and censors immoral impulses from the id and prevents them from entering the consciousness of the ego. Psychoanalytic theory predicts that the individual with a strong superego is likely to experience greater feelings of guilt in a situation involving a moral dilemma than is a person with a weaker superego and is therefore less likely to transgress the rules.

Freud believed that the three parts of the personality are in continual conflict with the id trying to attain gratification of impulses and the superego setting often unreasonably high moral standards. The ego is obliged to maintain an appropriate balance between these two opposing forces and the external demands of social reality.

Unresolved conflict results in anxiety which may show itself in

1. dreams, which Freud believed are the disguised fulfilment of suppressed wishes. Dream interpretation became a major strategy used by Freud when treating his patients
2. neurotic symptoms such as extreme anxiety attacks, irrational fears or in some cases physical symptoms, such as paralysis or blindness.

## Defence Mechanisms

During the development of his theory, Freud identified a number of **defence mechanisms** and these were later refined and elaborated by his daughter Anna Freud (1936).

Defences are unconscious strategies used by individuals to protect themselves from painful anxiety or guilt. Such feelings may occur in one of three ways:

1. through moral conflict (ego versus superego, e.g. temptation to commit a crime)
2. through conflict over impulses (ego versus id, e.g. a desire to inflict harm on an opponent)
3. through external threat (ego versus reality, e.g. severe family conflict)

The short-term use of defence mechanisms is thought to be a 'normal' and healthy device for coping with life's pressures; where they are excessively used on a long-term basis they are considered to be dangerous and unhealthy.

Defence mechanisms are probably the most widely accepted aspects of Freud's theory, partly because they are described in relatively precise terms and partly because they receive intuitive credibility from the personal experiences of many people. Numerous defence mechanisms have been proposed by psychoanalysts; a number of them are briefly explained below.

**Repression**. Forcing painful or frightening memories, feelings, wishes, etc. out of conscious awareness and into the unconscious ('motivated forgetting'). For example, repressing the memory of a harmful experience or an unacceptable truth or feeling. According to Freud this is the most basic and important defence mechanism which is often supported by other defences.

**Denial**. Refusing to accept reality, for example that you are seriously ill or that a partner is unfaithful. This is considered to be the most primitive defence.

**Regression**. Reverting to behaviour characteristic of an earlier stage of life when no conflict or threat was present; for example, a 2-year-old child faced with a newborn brother or sister may wish to be a baby again and insist on wearing nappies or being bottle fed once more.

**Displacement**. Re-directing feelings or behaviour onto a substitute object or person because you cannot express them towards their real target, for example shouting at your partner after a disagreement with the boss. (See also the reference to phobias in Chapters 5 and 6.)

**Sublimation**. A variant of displacement where unacceptable impulses are channelled into a substitute activity, for example re-channelling the desire to handle faeces into artistic activities or redirecting aggressive impulses into sporting activities. Psychoanalysts believe this to be a positive and beneficial defence mechanism.

**Projection**. Assigning your own unacceptable feelings or characteristics to someone else, for example saying 'She hates me' when your true feeling is 'I hate her'. (See also the discussion of the paranoid personality in Chapter 5.)

### Three Levels of the Mind

Freud distinguished three modes of thinking, each of which would operate at one of three levels. These he termed conscious, preconscious and unconscious. The term 'levels' is meant to convey how far particular thoughts are available to us, rather than the existence of different regions of the mind.

**Conscious**. The conscious part of the mind represents all the thoughts and feelings we are aware of at a given time. It manifests itself in the ego and is organised in terms of logic and reason. Its main function is responding to external reality, avoiding danger and maintaining socially acceptable behaviour. Anxiety is thought to occur if the conscious part of the mind is dominated by impulses which seek to satisfy unconscious desires.

**Preconscious**. The pre-conscious contains thoughts which may not be conscious at a given time but which are accessible to us. It acts as a kind of filter, censoring unacceptable wishes and only allowing them through to consciousness if they are sufficiently disguised to avoid recognition of their unconscious roots.

**Unconscious**. The unconscious operates at the deepest level and is largely inaccessible except through psychoanalytic techniques such as free association or dream analysis. It is thought to be made up of all repressed material including desires and impulses which are largely sexual and sometimes aggressive.

Figure 3.1 illustrates the relationship between the three levels of consciousness and the id, ego and superego.

---

**FIGURE 3.1**

**The Relationship between Freud's Structure of Personality and Three Levels of Consciousness**

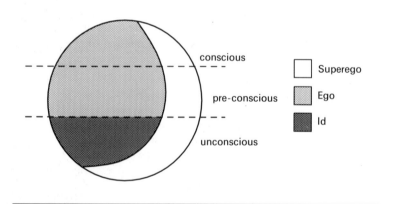

---

From A. Malim, A. Birch and A. Wadeley, *Perspectives in Psychology* (Basingstoke: Macmillan, 1992).

## Development of the Personality

Freud proposed that in the course of development children pass through a series of stages. During each stage satisfaction is gained as the libido (or sexual energy) is directed towards a different part of the body. He referred to 'sexual instincts', though in attributing this term to children, he used the term 'sexual' in a rather special way to mean something like 'physically pleasurable'. Each stage entails a set of problems to be overcome in relation to later development. Failure to negotiate satisfactorily a particular stage results in **fixation**, or halting of development at that stage. Fixation causes the individual to retain some of the characteristics of that stage in later life and in severe cases results in neuroses in adult life.

Below is a brief description of Freud's psychosexual stages:

### Oral Stage (Birth to 1 year)

The id is dominant. Libidinal energy is centred on the mouth and the child gains satisfaction from sucking and biting. Freud proposed that:

1. The oral stage can be subdivided into the passive, receptive, sucking subphase of the earlier months and the later active, aggressive, biting subphase
2. Fixation may be caused either by the over-indulgence or by the frustration of a child's oral needs. A child whose oral needs are not satisfied or are over-indulged will exhibit the characteristics of this stage in later life. Fixation may express itself in addictions such as smoking, gluttony or alcoholism; nailbiting; the excessive use of sarcasm.

### Anal Stage (Second Year of Life)

This stage focuses on pleasurable sensations experienced in the mucous membrames of the rectum. The child gains satisfaction from expelling and withholding faeces and is now in a position to exercise some control over these bodily functions. S/he can either please the parents by being 'clean' or can thwart them by making a mess. Thus the pleasurable sensations associated with 'letting go' or 'holding on' become associated with behaviour that has social implications. A significant event in the child's life is the parents' efforts to impose toilet training. Fixation at the anal stage, perhaps resulting from parent/child conflict over toilet training, may give rise to a personality who is exceedingly preoccupied with cleanliness and orderliness (expelling) or who is mean, obstinate and obsessive in adulthood (withholding).

### Phallic Stage (3 to 6)

Now libidinal energy centres on the genitals and feelings become overtly sexual. Describing first the sequence of events for the male child, Freud defined important issues arising from the **Oedipus complex**. The boy's fantasies include wishes for sexual intimacy with his mother. He envies his father's intimate relationship with his mother and fears punishment in the form of castration for his forbidden wishes. The Oedipus complex is resolved when the child **identifies** with his father in order to appease him and to become like him in as many ways as possible.

Freud's account of the progress of female children through the Phallic stage is less clear cut and he proposed various explanations for the girl's eventual identification with her mother. Possibly the most widely reported, the **Electra complex**, is that the girl, believing herself to be already castrated, since she does not possess a penis, suffers **penis envy**. This leads her to seek a strong love attachment to her father, the possessor of a penis, and finally to identify with her mother in order to become like her.

The satisfactory resolution of the Oedipus/Electra complex results in the child identifying with the same-sexed parent. Two important consequences stem from this identification:

1.  The child adopts the gender-role which will be assumed through life
2.  The child adopts the parents' moral standards, attitudes and prohibitions, together with the moral norms of the society they reflect. Thus, the superego is born and the values and beliefs of a culture are passed on from one generation to the next.

If, through insensitive handling by adults, the child does not satisfactorily overcome the Oedipus/Electra complex, problems lie ahead. Psychoanalysts believe that fixation at the phallic stage lies behind most adult neuroses.

## *Latency Period (6 to Puberty)*

This is a period of relative calm following the turmoil of the phallic stage. During this time, the libido is submerged and does not centre upon any bodily area. It is a time of ego-development, particularly in relation to social and intellectual skills.

## *Genital Stage (Puberty)*

Hormonal changes now stimulate the re-emergence of the libido. There is renewed interest in sexual pleasure and all previous sexual drives associated with particular regions of the body come together in an integrated set of adult sexual attitudes and feelings.

## **Studies of Freud's Theories**

Freud's work has generated an immense amount of research both into aspects of the theory of psychoanalysis and into the effectiveness of psychoanalysis as a therapy (Studies of the latter will be discussed in Chapter 6.) Detailed reviews of experimental investigations have been carried out by Kline (1981a) and Fisher and Greenberg (1977). Below is a selection of empirical studies which have attempted to test aspects of the theory.

## *The Oral Personality*

As noted earlier, fixation may be caused either by the over-indulgence or by the frustration of a child's oral needs.

Fisher and Greenberg (1977) see the oral personality as being preoccupied with issues of giving and taking, concerns about independence and dependence, extremes of optimism and pessimism, unusual ambivalence, impatience and the continued use of the oral channel for gratification.

A number of studies have examined whether these traits do tend to exist together in a single cluster or whether two clusters exist reflecting the oral passive (sucking) and oral aggressive (biting) subphases. Kline and Storey (1977) reviewed these investigations and found the strongest support for the oral personality in Goldman-Eisler's (1948) studies where traits such as pessimism, passivity, aloofness, oral verbal aggression and autonomy were found to cluster together as were their opposites. However, Goldman-Eisler provided evidence only of face validity for the scales used. Lazare *et al.* (1966) provided similar results using Goldman-Eisler's items in a questionnaire. In their own study, Kline and Storey (1977) found that characteristics associated with the first 'optimistic' subphase of the oral stage (including dependency, fluency, sociability and relaxation) tended to cluster together as did characteristics (including independence, verbal aggression, envy, coldness and hostility, malice, ambition and impatience) of the second 'pessimistic' subphase.

A second series of investigations examined the relationship between feeding practices and later behaviour. For example, Yarrow (1973) found a significant correlation between the time spent feeding and later thumb-sucking, those children with the shortest feeding times being the most persistent thumb-suckers. Though some support is claimed for the effects of fixation in the oral stage, an alternative explanation might be that children whose greater need for sucking, for whatever reason, led them to feed more quickly and later to satisfy the need through thumb-sucking.

*The Anal Personality*

As we have seen, Freud proposed that anal fixation is linked to the child's conflicts with the parents during potty training. The struggle which results either from over-harsh potty training or from exceptionally intense pleasure associated with the anal period can later reveal itself in the character traits of orderliness, rigidity, obstinacy and a dislike of waste. The kind of personality in which these traits are combined is known as the anal or obsessive-compulsive personality. Three major reviews of research evidence (Kline, 1972; Fisher and Greenberg, 1977; Pollak, 1979) concluded that these traits do tend to cluster together in the anally-oriented personality. However, Hill (1976) identified major methodological weaknesses in six of the studies considered by Kline to be sound ones. Howarth (1982) recognised that there does appear to be a personality type characterised by the orderly, pedantic, self-controlled and controlling individual who runs the bureaucracy of most nations who might be described as an anally-oriented personality. Fonagy (1981; 1984) points out that no evidence exists which suggests that this type of personality received toilet training that was different from that of less obsessive-compulsive types.

## Defence Mechanisms

Many researchers have attempted to demonstrate the effects of repression ('motivated forgetting') in the laboratory, often by causing an individual to experience anxiety in relation to a particular kind of material or activity and then looking to see if the rate of forgetting increased. Holmes (1974) in a review of such studies found no conclusive evidence of repression. However, Wilkinson and Carghill (1955) claimed that stories with an Oedipal theme were remembered less well than those that were neutral. Levinger and Clark (1961) showed that when asked to remember association words they had produced in response to a number of emotional and neutral stimulus words, participants recalled significantly less of the emotional associations. Kline (1972) claimed that these findings provide clear evidence of repression operating in memory. However, using Levinger and Clark's stimulus words, Parkin *et al.* (1982) found that if participants delayed recall for one week, emotional associations were *better* recalled than were neutral ones. They concluded that these findings support the known relationship between arousal levels and memory and offer no support for Freud's theory of repression. However, an objection to this study and others like it is that the stimuli used may be too trivial and artificial to activate the deep emotional responses described by Freud.

## Evaluation of Freudian Theory

1. Eysenck and Wilson (1973) have raised objections to psychoanalytic theory on a number of counts:

   (a) Freud's use of a limited sample composed mainly of adults who were suffering some psychological disturbance prevents generalisation of his theory to all human beings.

   (b) His use of the clinical case study method was criticised. Accounts of his sessions with patients were not written up until some time later and may have been inaccurate and selective.

(c)  Freud used no quantitative data or statistical analysis in support of his theories.

(d)  Most of the processes described by Freud, for example instinctual drives and defence mechanisms, cannot be directly observed and inferences drawn about human behaviour are often open to alternative explanations. This makes the generation of precise and testable hypotheses difficult. Not only can the theory not be supported, it cannot be refuted – a serious violation of the scientific method according to Popper (1959).

(e)  Freudian theory is unable to predict an individual's development. It can be used only to explain something after an event.

2.  Criticisms have been made of Freud's over-emphasis on the role of biological factors in personality development. His insistence that the goal of all behaviour is to satisfy biological needs was not shared by other psychodynamic theorists such as Jung, Adler and Erikson. Whilst recognising the importance of biological factors, these theorists subscribed also to the *social* nature of human beings.

3.  Kline (1984) whilst agreeing that some aspects of the theory, for example instinctual drives, cannot easily be tested and should be abandoned, other aspects can generate testable hypotheses which conform to the demands of the scientific method. Those hypotheses which can be tested should be restated in a refutable form and then subjected to an objective, empirical examination. Kline believes that psychoanalytic theory offers a coherent account of human behaviour in all its complexity and he pleads for bold and original thinking in future attempts to investigate Freudian concepts.

4.  The final comment should perhaps draw attention to the profound effect that Freud's theory has had on psychological thinking and on disciplines such as history, art and English literature.

'. . . it seems madness to jettison a set of ideas as stimulating as Freud's because they do not conform to a conventionalised methodology at present in favour in psychology. What is required is a scientific psychology that combines theoretical rigour with the rich comprehensiveness of psychoanalysis' (Kline, 1984, p. 157).

## Self-assessment Questions

1. Briefly explain the nature and function of the three major parts of the personality proposed by Freud: id, ego and superego.
2. What did Freud mean by 'defence mechanisms'? Briefly describe two of them.
3. Explain the concept of 'fixation' in relation to the development of the personality.
4. Comment on the findings of some studies which have investigated:

   (a) the oral personality
   (b) defence mechanisms.

5. Critically evaluate Freud's psychoanalytic theory.

## SECTION II  POST-FREUDIANS

### Carl Jung (1875–1961)

Jung, a onetime associate of Freud, found himself increasingly at odds with some of the ideas of classical psychoanalysis and consequently left his colleague to develop his own psychoanalytic theory and his own method of psychotherapy. His approach to psychoanalysis became known as Analytical Psychology. Jung's theory differs from Freud's in a number of important ways:

1. **Psychic Energy.**   Where Freud regarded the libido as primarily sexual in nature, Jung saw it as a more general life force.
2. **The Structure of the Personality.**   In Jung's view, the personality, or psyche, included three interacting systems: consciousness, the personal unconscious and the collective unconscious:

   **Consciousness.** This refers to that aspect of the mind that the individual is directly aware of. Jung proposed four different ways of experiencing the world: sensing; intuition; feeling; thinking, as summarised below:

SENSING    Experiencing the world through stimulation of the sense organs

INTUITION  Guessing about what is known through the sense organs

FEELING    Concentrating on the emotional aspects of experience and evaluating them as pleasant or unpleasant, beautiful or ugly

THINKING   Reasoning and abstract thought

Jung proposed that people differ consistently in the extent to which they emphasise each way of experiencing. One individual might tend to experience the world through the senses using little intuition or reasoning, another might typically favour intuitive thought. In addition to the four ways of experiencing, Jung also posited two attitudes, namely introversion and extraversion, one of which is dominant in the conscious side of the personality while the other influences the unconscious. (The concepts of introversion and extraversion were discussed in Chapter 2, Section II.)

**The Personal Unconscious**. This is similar to Freud's conception of this aspect of the personality in that it represents the whole of the individual's experience and contains much that has been forgotten or repressed. Jung viewed the unconscious not just as the source of instincts but as a rich and vital part of the individual's life containing symbols expressed through dreams. The methods of Jungian psychology encouraged people to be receptive to their own dreams and to allow their unconscious to act as an indication of how to live.

**The Collective Unconscious**. This represents a fundamental departure from Freud's account of the structure of personality. Jung proposed that the contents of the collective unconscious, which are common to all individuals, have never been conscious and owe their existence to heredity. They are made up of ancestral and racial memories which form the psychic residue of human development and which have become embedded in the human mind. These memories are known as **archetypes**. Examples of archetypes include God, the wise old man, the Fairy Godmother, rebirth, the hero and others found to occur in the fables and legends of many different cultures.

3. **Repression**. Jung's theory focused far less than did Freud's on the role of repression in the development of neurosis. Jung

believed that humans should be understood not only in relation to their past experiences but also in the light of their present purposes and future goals.

**Status in Psychology**. Though Jung is generally admired and considered to be a great intellect, many aspects of his theory have proved difficult to validate. As noted in Chapter 2, the influence of his concepts of introversion and extraversion can be seen in the work of Hans Eysenck and his more optimistic view of the nature of human beings can be detected in the ideas of later personality theorists such as Carl Rogers and Abraham Maslow.

In terms of practical applications, a Jungian version of psycho-analytic psychotherapy is still practised by some clinicians. Also, Jung's theory of introversion/extraversion and the four ways of experiencing the world form the basis of one of the most commercially used personality tests, the Myers–Briggs Type Indicator (Briggs and Myers, 1962), used in business, commerce and industry for career counselling, team building and assessments for promotion and management potential.

## Erik Erikson (born 1902)

Erikson's (1963) view of personality is an extension and elaboration of Freud's theory. Although he accepted many Freudian concepts, there are a number of important differences between the two theories.

### Comparison between Freud and Erikson

1. Where Freud regarded the adult personality as fixed by events reaching back into childhood, Erikson saw the individual as subject to change throughout the lifespan. Thus, Erikson is less deterministic than Freud.
2. Erikson generally accepted the validity of Freud's psychosexual stages but considered that Freud overemphasised the importance of sexual drives to the exclusion of broad social and cultural influences such as family relationships and the standards of behaviour expected in a particular culture.
3. Erikson described a series of eight stages which extend from birth to old age and which he termed **psychosocial** (rather than psycho*sexual*) stages.

4.  Erikson placed more emphasis than did Freud on 'ego development'. He saw the ego as being capable of reacting independently of instinctual drives and internal conflicts with the id and superego. Given an adequate environment, the ego could achieve a satisfactory balance between inner forces and social influences.

### Erikson's Stages of Psychosocial Development

*Figure 3.2* gives a brief summary of Erikson's psychosocial stages, including an indication of the possible favourable and unfavourable outcomes associated with each. Points to note are as follows:

1.  Erikson sees each stage as marked by a crisis or struggle, which the individual must confront and attempt to resolve. At any given point in development, personality is the product of the way these crises have been resolved. (Note that the stages are named in relation to the opposite extremes of the crisis; for example during the first stage the crisis is termed 'Trust versus Mistrust' indicating the individual's need to develop a sense of trust in the environment).

2.  The level of success with which each crisis is managed will determine that individual's psychological well-being at a particular time. The person who is unable to deal satisfactorily with a crisis will continue to experience problems in later stages and thus development will be impaired. However, Erikson believed that it is possible to compensate later for unsatisfactory experiences at a particular stage. Similarly, satisfactory negotiation of a crisis at an early stage could be diminished if the individual suffers deficiencies later in development.

3.  The first three stages are similar to the Freudian oral, anal and phallic stages. Like Freud, Erikson believed that the major determining factor to govern satisfactory progress through the early stages was the kind of care given by parents. According to Erikson, the crisis 'identity versus role confusion', which occurs during adolescence, marks a key stage in development and is seen by many psychologists as the central crisis of all development.

Erikson believed that the psychosocial stages are pan-cultural; that is, applicable universally to individuals in different cultures; the conflicts are the same though each culture will have its own way of dealing with them.

## Some Studies of Erikson's Theory

1. Central to Erikson's theory is the notion that personality change arises in relation to the different crises that characterise each developmental stage. A study by Ryff and Heinke (1983) asked the question 'Do people perceive their own personality changes in this way?' Perceptions of personality change were studied in three adult groups: young, middle aged and old-aged. Participants completed a number of personality scales including two which related to the Eriksonian concepts of integrity (related to old age) and generativity (related to middle age). Concurrent, retrospective and prospective self-reports were obtained. Support for Erikson's theory was found in that all age groups perceived themselves as being most generativity-oriented at middle age and having higher integrity at old age

2. A series of studies by Block (1971, 1981) have offered support for Erikson's belief that personality changes occur during the adult years and that adolescence is a critically important time in personality development.

3. A longitudinal study by Kahn *et al.* (1985) found support for Erikson's proposition that establishing an identity in adolescent is crucial for later successful intimate relationships. Students' identity scores taken in 1963 were related with their marital status some twenty years later. Interesting sex differences emerged: women with low identity scores were more likely to be divorced or separated; men with low identity scores were found more often to remain single.

## Evaluation of Erikson's Theory

Erikson is a practising psychoanalyst who has treated large numbers of individuals both normal and disturbed over a wide age range and in several different cultures. In general, his theory is highly regarded not only in psychology but in the fields of education and psychiatry, However, there have been some criti-

**FIGURE 3.2**

**Erikson's Stages of Psychosocial Development**

| Life Crisis | Favourable Outcome | Unfavourable Outcome |
| --- | --- | --- |
| **First Year** | | |
| **Trust-v-mistrust** The child needs consistent and stable care in order to develop feelings of security | Trust in the environment and hopes for the future | Suspicion, insecurity, fear of the future |
| **Second and third years** | | |
| **Autonomy-v-shame and doubt** The child seeks a sense of in-dependence from parents. Parental treatment should not be too rigid or harsh | A sense of autonomy and self-esteem | Feeling of shame and doubt about one's own capacity for self-control |
| **Fourth and fifth years** | | |
| **Initiative-v-guilt** The child explores her environment and plans new activities. Sexual curiosity should be sympathetically handled by parents | The ability to initiate activities and enjoy following them through | Fear of punishment and guilt about one's own feelings |
| **Six to 11 years** | | |
| **Industry-v-inferiority** The child acquires important knowledge and skills relating to her culture | A sense of competence and achievement. Confidence in one's own ability to make and do things | Unfavourable reactions from others may cause feelings of inadequacy and inferiority |

## Adolescence (12–18 yrs)

**Identity-v-role confusion**

| | | |
|---|---|---|
| The young person searches for a coherent personal and vocational identity | Ability to see oneself as a consistent and integrated person with a strong, personal identity | Confusion over who and what one is |

## Young adulthood (20s and 30s)

**Intimacy-v-isolation**

| | | |
|---|---|---|
| The adult seeks deep and lasting personal relationships, particularly with a partner of the opposite sex | The ability to experience love and commitment to others | Isolation: superficial relationships with others |

## Middle adulthood (40–64)

**Generativity-v-stagnation**

| | | |
|---|---|---|
| The individual seeks to be productive and creative and to make a contribution to society as a whole | The ability to be concerned and caring about others in the wider sense | Lack of growth: boredom and over concern with oneself |

## Late adulthood (65+)

**Integrity-v-despair**

| | | |
|---|---|---|
| The individual reviews and evaluates what has been accomplished in life | A sense of satisfaction with one's life and its accomplishments: acceptance of death | Regret over omissions and missed opportunities; fear of death |

From A. Birch and A. Malim, *Developmental Psychology: from Infancy to Adulthood* (Basingstoke: Macmillan, 1988).

cisms. For example, Booth (1975) questions whether the eight psychosocial stages are applicable to individuals in different societies and cultures. The validity of the crises described at each stage and agreement about what constitutes a desirable outcome may depend heavily upon the norms and values of a particular culture. For example, stage 4, industry versus inferiority, may only apply in cultures such as ours which heavily emphasise competitiveness and which frown upon children who do not succeed in particular skills at a particular time.

Though researchers have not found Erikson's ideas easy to test, as has already been noted, findings from studies that have been carried out have lent encouraging support to his theory.

Erikson's extension of his theory to cover young, middle and late adulthood, is generally regarded as a major stimulus to the study of development over the whole lifespan, in contrast to earlier theories which tended to focus primarily on child development.

### Self-assessment Questions

1. Discuss three ways in which Jung's Analytical Psychology differs from Classical Psychoanalysis.
2. What is the present status of Jung's theory in psychology?
3. Briefly outline four ways in which Erikson's theory differed from that of Freud.
4. Discuss one study which has investigated an aspect of Erikson's theory,
5. Make an evaluation of Erikson's theory.

### SECTION III   ASSESSMENT OF PERSONALITY RELATED TO PSYCHOANALYTIC CONCEPTS: PROJECTIVE TECHNIQUES

Freud did not develop an assessment technique to coincide with his theory in the way that, for example, Cattell developed the 16PF (see Chapter 2). However, during the time that psychoanalysis was developing, some complex, subjective methods of assessment known as **projective tests** were popularised. Projective tests have been loosely defined as ambiguous stimuli to which participants are required to respond. It is assumed that the individual 'will project much of his own personality, his conflicts and his motivations into his response' (Marx, 1976) to a test stimulus. Participants are not aware of the purposes of the test, so may disclose things about themselves that they would normally be unwilling to reveal. In psychoanalytic terms, this happens by avoiding normal defence mechanisms and gaining access to preconscious or unconscious matter. The tester's task is to interpret these signs.

Although Freudian ideas have inspired the development of projective techniques, other devices have been used to explore psychoanalytic concepts, for example standard personality inventories. As noted in Section II of this chapter, the **Myers–Briggs Type Indicator** is a widely used personality test which is based on Jung's theory. Conversely, whilst projective techniques are most likely to be used by psychodynamically-oriented psychologists in a clinical setting, other psychologists have used them from a non-psychodynamic perspective, for example McClelland *et al.* (1953) in their work on achievement-motivation.

Three widely known projective tests are described below.

## The Rorschach Test (Rorschach, 1921)

1. **Description**. The test consists of ten symmetrical shapes which resemble ink blots and which participants are required to describe. The tester notes down what the participant says, how long before the response is made, whether the whole shape is used or just parts of it, any recurring themes emerging and the participant's general reaction to the test.
2. **Responses**. Characteristic responses are 'a flower' or 'a bearskin rug' which do not suggest any significant anxiety or conflict. Responses which reveal themes relating to sexual matters or death are often seen as indicating serious underlying conflicts.
3. **Scoring**. Interpretation and scoring are highly complex tasks which require substantial training (Kline, 1983). There is a large body of research evidence which relates Rorschach scores to largely clinical phenomenon though Eysenck (1959) argues that much of this work lacks scientific rigour. A number of elaborate scoring systems have been devised (Beck, 1952;

Klopfer *et al.*, 1956) Critics hold that scoring is a highly subjective and unreliable process.

### Thematic Apperception Test (TAT) (Murray, 1938)

1. **Description**. The TAT consists of a series of pictures mainly depicting human beings in a range of situations, for example a boy holding a violin and gazing into the distance or a woman standing in the doorway of a room. The participant is asked to describe the pictures in turn and tell a story about what is portrayed in each.
2. **Responses**. Participants' responses are timed and the content recorded in detail for later analysis. The tester is looking for basic themes which may reveal the participant's motives and needs or characteristic ways of dealing with problems.
3. **Scoring**. Many scoring schemes have been empirically devised on the basis of the ability of the scores to discriminate between different groups. Kline (1983) contends that the scientific rigour of the studies, as with the Rorschach test, is not impressive. However, he draws attention to some special reliable scoring schemes for the TAT which have been developed by Zubin *et al.* (1966).

### The Blacky Pictures (Blum, 1949)

1. **Description**. This test, which is one of few projective techniques specifically designed to tap psychoanalytic psychosexual stages, consists of a series of cartoons in which Blacky, a puppy, is depicted in a number of family situations. The participant is asked to explain what is happening in the pictures The test is used mainly with young children.
2. **Responses**. Responses, which are noted in detail, are thought to reveal whether the individual is fixated at a particular psycho-sexual level. The analyst aims to detect clues relating to Oedipal castration fears, anal fixation, parental rejection, sibling rivalry and other stressful events related to early childhood,
3. **Scoring**. Part of this test is objectively scored, and according to Kline (1983), there is some evidence that the test has certain valid indices.

**Criticisms of Projective Test**

The main objections to projective tests have been summarised by Vernon (1964) as follows:

1. There is no adequate theory or evidence to support claims that the tests tap the participant's deeper layers of personality.
2. Reliability of projective test scoring on different occasions by the same scorer is not high.
3. Studies of the validity of projective tests are poor; the more rigorous the validity studies, the lower are the validity coefficients that emerge.
4. Test results have been shown to be affected by such factors as the mood of the participant or the tester, the attitude of the participant or the tester and the race of the tester.

Fonagy and Higgitt (1984) point out that though the tests are still quite widely used in the United States (Wade and Baker, 1977), they no longer form part of the training of British clinical psychologists who seem to have been influenced by critical assessments of the technique (Eysenck, 1959)

**The Case for Projective Tests**

Many psychologists propose that, despite their shortcomings, the use of projective tests provide valuable 'clinical hunches' which can be followed up using more reliable and valid devices. Kline (1983) argues that there are two points that should be raised in defence of projective tests, the second of which clearly supports their continued use:

1. The usual method of assessing the validity of projective tests is for the responses of the participants to be rated blind, that is with the rater having no knowledge of the participant. Kline suggests that this is nonsense. The interpretation of projective tests must be undertaken in the context of the participant's life in the same way as the psychoanalyst interprets dreams. In the light of this it might be assumed that demonstrations of invalidity are not so severe as they first appear.

2.  The basic objection to projective tests relates to the unreliability of scoring and interpretation. This could be overcome if a method were developed for reliable scoring and analysis. Kline argues that such an objective method has been developed for the Rorschach and used successfully by Holley (1973) – G analysis. G analysis has been used with tests other than the Rorschach also by Vegelius (1976) and Hampson and Kline (1977). In Kline's view, G analysis does allow projective tests to be used in the quantitative study of personality.

Semeonoff (1981) argues that if projective techniques are abandoned, psychology will be the poorer and a source of insight will have been lost.

### Self-assessment Questions

1.  What are projective tests and in what ways are they thought to useful in exploring psychoanalytic concepts?
2.  Briefly describe one projective test and explain what the tester may be looking for in the testees' responses.
3.  Make a judgement about the value of projective techniques in assessing aspects of personality.

### FURTHER READING

M. N. Eagle, *Recent Developments in Psychoanalysis: a Critical Evaluation* (New York: McGraw-Hill, 1984).

P. S. Holzman, *Psychoanalysis and Psychopathology* (New York: McGraw-Hill, 1970).

P. Kline, *Psychology and Freudian Theory: an Introduction* (London/New York: Methuen, 1984).

A. Storr (ed.), *Jung: Selected Writings* (London: Fontana, 1983).

AS I ALWAYS SAY, ALL THE WORLD'S ODD
EXCEPT YOU AND ME — AND EVEN YOU ARE A
BIT PECULIAR.

# Psychopathology: The Normality/ Abnormality Continuum 4

At the end of this chapter you should be able to:

1. Discuss the concepts of normality and abnormality.
2. Consider whether abnormality should be viewed as mental illness and evaluate alternative views;
3. Understand the structure and outline of the two main diagnostic systems in use in Western societies, the ICD 10 and DSM III R;
4. Consider evidence regarding problems of diagnosis, such as those relating to validity, reliability and labelling.

## SECTION I  NORMALITY AND ABNORMALITY

### Introduction

This chapter examines whether normality and abnormality should be regarded along a continuum, merging imperceptibly at some undefined point. If this is the case, where does behaviour become 'abnormal' and be deemed to need changing? Each individual tends to regard him or herself as the norm, so what ruling is acceptable? There is no dividing line separating 'normal' people from 'abnormal' people; the most normal occasionally exhibit abnormal behaviours, just as the most abnormal patients exhibit recognisably normal behaviours and reactions. In addition, normal behaviour in one set of circumstances would not be regarded as normal in other circumstances; behaviour suitable at a party would be regarded as unsuitable at a funeral.

Psychopathology can be defined as the scientific study of mental disorders. The immediate problem this poses is what constitutes a mental disorder and whether this should be regarded as a 'mental illness'. This point is discussed more fully in Section II of this chapter, but it needs to be noted here that the term covers a wide range, from brief transient episodes to lifelong incapacitation.

Approximately one in ten men and one in seven women will be treated for mental disorder during their lifetime; for the majority these are brief periods, possibly of depression or a delusional state.

Overt behaviours which are unacceptable may be the external symptoms of abnormality which are brought to the notice of **psychiatrists**; these are doctors who specialise in mental illnesses and attempt to unravel and 'cure' the aberrant thought processes which lead to these behaviours. **Clinical psychologists** are psychologists trained in the administration and analysis of tests of mental functions: personality tests, cognitive tests, projective tests and other diagnostic tools.

They also design programmes using a wide range of therapies, to assist both in-patients and out-patients who have mental problems and are seeking to change their thought processes and behaviours. Diagnosis and classification of these problems is examined in Chapter 5 and treatments and therapies in Chapter 6.

### Defining Abnormality

There is no general agreement on how abnormal behaviour may be distinguished from normal behaviour, but one or more of the following criteria are usually applied.

### *Statistical Abnormality*

Behaviour which occurs frequently is viewed as normal, therefore by definition, behaviour which occurs infrequently must be abnormal. (Readers may wish to refer back to the description of the normal distribution in Chapter 1, Section I.) By implication, extremely intelligent people are as likely to be defined as abnormal as extremely unintelligent people; likewise the statistical frequency of a Einstein or a Hitler would be the same although society may not regard them as being equally preferable. Clearly the desirability of a behaviour is not allowed for in this definition and it is insufficient on its own (Mackay, 1975).

## Social Abnormality

The criteria for social norms varies from society to society. What is considered acceptable or desirable behaviour in one society may be considered undesirable or abnormal in a different culture. For example, some African tribes revere their members who claim to hear voices; in Western society this may well be viewed as a symptom of schizophrenia or other mental abnormality. Also behaviour within any one society is temporally based, it can only be judged by reference to any one period of time. For example, in Great Britain seventy years ago, bathing machines were used, yet nowadays no one is surprised at 'topless' beaches. On the other hand, fifth-century temples in mid-Asian countries are decorated with partially clad figures, whereas nowadays it is considered an insult to go to a temple scantily clad – even some of the statues have been draped to preserve propriety! In order to be universally acceptable, a definition of abnormality must include more than social compliance.

## Maladaptiveness of Behaviour

Another suggested definition investigates how an individual's behaviour affects people's lives, or their social group. Some deviant behaviours interfere with the individual's lifestyle, for example, a man so fearful of crowds he cannot ride to work on a bus or a woman so afraid of contamination she cannot hug and kiss her own children. The quality of life for such people is severely impaired, whereas some behaviours are harmful to society. The paranoid who guns down innocent people in the street, or the assassin who believes his action will right wrongs, or even the person who has uncontrollable verbal outbursts and intimidates all around him, are exhibiting abnormal behaviours detrimental to other members of society.

## Personal Distress

Symptoms of mental disorders often include feeling miserable, anxious or depressed, insomnia, lack of appetite, many aches and pains, feelings of panic or agitation. These all cause the individual some distress, although in many cases other people are unaware of their suffering. Occasionally an individual's depression is deep enough for attempted suicide, while family or friends had no idea of these depths of despair. However, personal distress is not an infallible indicator of mental abnormality; the psychopath who continually offends against society may do so without any feelings of personal distress, but such behaviour can only be viewed as abnormal. Some psychopaths and schizophrenics feel no personal distress, except when society imposes treatment upon them (Cleckley, 1976) (Descriptions of what is meant by the terms 'psychopath' and 'schizophrenic' can be found in Chapter 5.)

*Legal Definition of Abnormality*

Let us say immediately, this does not have direct influence on the psychological concept, but as abnormal people also live in the real world, the legal definition is obviously relevant. The term 'insane' is used in law, but not by psychiatrists or psychologists for diagnostic purposes; the word implies a clear dividing line. In Great Britain the law is governed by the case of McNaghten, 1843: 'to establish a defence of insanity, it must be clearly proved that, at the time of committing the act, the party accused was labouring under such a defect of reason, from disease of mind, as not to know the nature and quality of the act he was doing; or if he did know it, that he did not know he was doing what was wrong.' This relates to criminal proceedings.

Lack of responsibility for one's actions is also invoked to protect individuals with diminished responsibility, so that others may not take advantage of them by, for example, convincing them to sign away money or property.

**Models or Paradigms of Abnormality**

Different investigators use different models (or paradigms) for conceptualising abnormal behaviours, how they develop and how best to treat them. The major paradigms reflect the five major approaches to psychology; these are: the physiological (or medical) model, the psychoanalytic model, the learning-theory (behaviourist) model, the cognitive model and the humanistic model. The theoretical basis of each is outlined here, the treatments and therapies based on each approach can be found in Chapter 6. (A fuller description of the major approaches to psychology can be found in the book in this series entitled *Perspectives in Psychology* (1992) by Malim, Birch and Wadeley.)

1. **The Psychoanalytic Model** .Based on the work of Sigmund Freud, psychoanalytic theorists believe that many of our motivations are unconscious. Conflicts between the three facets of the personality, id, ego and superego, produce defence mechanisms and anxieties which may be maladaptive (see Chapter 3 for a full description of Freud's theory). Post-Freudian theorists may have different perspectives, but all hold that abnormality is rooted in conflicts which need to be brought to the surface, examined and rectified or reconciled.

2. **The Physiological or Medical Model** .This model views abnormality as an illness which can be treated by physical methods, such as chemotherapy, to effect control or cure. Diagnosis is carried out in a prescribed, routine manner and the most suitable treatment is prescribed, often in conjunction with non-physical therapies. Whether abnormality should be viewed as 'mental illness' is a current discussion point, which is explored at greater depth in Sections II and III of this chapter.

3. **The Learning Theory Model** .Classical conditioning, discovered by Pavlov (1849–1936), and Operant Conditioning, the work of B. F. Skinner, form the basis of this theoretical model.

   **Classical conditioning** looks at the **involuntary responses** made by individuals, which can be related to previous learning. For example, Pavlov's dogs learned to salivate when a buzzer was sounded because it was sounded at the same time as food was presented. They later salivated at the sound of the buzzer only – the food was absent. However, the paired association had been made and the involuntary response had been 'programmed in'. Classical theorists would suggest that people's inappropriate responses to stimuli may arise because in the learning situation the responses were appropriate, but subsequently one of the stimuli was absent. This may account for the formation of the irrational fears of phobics.

   **Operant conditioning** looks at **voluntary responses**, which are repeated because they are rewarded or reinforced. Skinner's original experiments examined the situations whereby a rat would press a bar in order to obtain food pellets, or a pigeon would peck at coloured lights for food; neither is the 'natural' action of the animal to obtain food, but both soon learned what action brought the desired end-result. In the real-life human situation, reward or reinforcement is usually appropriate to the action made to obtain it; if a child looks to a parent for love, he or she expects love, not food or punishment. If the parental response is not as expected, the child learns a faulty response pattern; that pattern may be the one produced by the child later on, which is then considered an abnormal behaviour, because it is inappropriate.

4.  **The Cognitive Model** .The cognitive theorist looks beyond the stimulus–response associations of the learning theorist and recognises that learning does not occur in a vaccuum. New information will be perceived, assimilated, judged and rationalised by the individual in the context of existing knowledge and ideas. Faults in rationalisation and conception, or irrational beliefs already held, may produce subsequent abnormal behaviours. In order to change these behaviours, cognitive restructuring (or reorganising thought patterns) may be necessary.

5.  **The Humanistic Model** (also discussed in Chapter 2, Section IV).   This is really a loose group of theories whose connecting point is that they all study individuals in the context of each one's unique experiences of the world. (Chapter 2 looks at the work of some of these theorists.) The individual is seen as striving for self-actualisation, seeking to achieve one's full potential as an individual, once one's basic needs have been satisfied. Rogers suggests that everyone has a need for positive self-regard, which is prompted by the positive unconditional regard of others. Personality problems arise when individuals concern themselves too much with other people's evaluations of them; central to the humanistic model is the idea that there may be a mismatch between the perceived self and the ideal-self.

All the above paradigms or models view abnormality from their particular theoretical position. In order to assess any one problem, it may be necessary to view it from more than one standpoint. No one model offers a sufficient answer for all the problems of abnormality which may arise.

## Normality

Having realised the difficulties inherent in defining abnormality, it is obviously no less difficult to define normality; both are relative concepts, rather than hard and fast rulings. However certain characteristics, which are present in the majority of people who are regarded as normal, have been suggested (Jahoda, 1958; Mackay, 1975; Maslow, 1968).

### Efficient Self-perception

Most individuals have a realistic awareness of their own capabilities and limitations, feelings, motivations and emotions. As a rule, a normal person does not make false attributions or blame extra-terrestrial forces, for 'making me behave like this'.

### Realistic Self-esteem and Acceptance

It is normal for a person to realise one's own value as an individual and in relation to family, friends and workmates, rather than feeling 'useless', 'worthless' – or, conversely, exhibiting megalomania: 'I am better than everyone at everything'. Knowledge of oneself as an individual can be put into the perspective of one's environment, together with the realisation that one is fulfilling one's role in society. However, this is often undermined by periods of unemployment, where work is seen as an intrinsic part of the person's role, and thereby 'self'.

### Voluntary Control over Behaviour

It is accepted that everyone acts impulsively on occasions – life would be dull and predictable without impulse – but when the occasion demands, normal people can exert self-control. Sometimes, for example during natural disasters, it is amazing to see how controlled some individuals' actions are, in extremely adverse circumstances. On the other hand, people who feel that they have no control over their actions, or think that they are being controlled by forces outside themselves, are regarded as being in need of help. A frequent observation made by those suffering from depression is that they feel 'powerless' to assist themselves, or indeed to do anything.

## *A True Perception of the World*

Usually people know what is going on in the world around them, they are aware of other people's actions and intentions, and are interested in happenings outside themselves. To someone with abnormal perceptions, the only area of interest may be their internalised world; the external world seems to have no relevance to them or, conversely, seems only to wish to punish them.

## *Sustaining Relationships and Giving Affection*

Sensitivity and the ability to recognise the feelings of others is a necessary prerequisite to sustaining relationships. The ability to give affection is normal, not just constantly seeking love, affection and reassurance, but being able to reciprocate with a real depth of feeling.

## *Self-direction and Productivity*

The majority of people try to organise their lives to some sort of design, in order that they experience a fulfilling lifestyle: a career, family, possessions, hobbies. However, even minor depressions can create feelings of aimlessness, tiredness and lethargy. If one assumes that mental disorder restricts an individual's activity, it is then surprising to regard the productivity and energy of Van Gogh, Munch, Dali, Dylan Thomas and many others who were recognised as suffering from mental disorders as well as being in possession of genius. The courses of mental disorders are not always the same, in some, periods of normality interweave with periods of abnormality, giving rise to pockets of energy and productivity.

## Evaluation of Views of Normality/Abnormality

No single definition of abnormality given here is sufficient alone: statistical frequency, social norms, maladaptiveness of behaviour and personal distress must all be taken into consideration when defining and describing abnormal behaviour. Different approaches to psychology attribute different reasons for the development of abnormality. In addition, it should be recognised that there is the potential for abnormal behaviour within everyone and most people will manifest abnormal behaviours at some time in their lives, whether prompted by external circumstances such as a highly stressful environment, or by internal changes. Even less satisfactory is the legal definition of abnormality, where a person is declared insane largely on the basis of a perceived inability to judge between right and wrong or exert control over his or her behaviour. Remember, the term 'insane' is a legal one and is not used in psychiatry.

With regard to the characteristics suggested as belonging to 'normal' people, it is likely that the vast majority of people would admit to falling short of at least one of these, at some time in their lives. Perhaps the easiest route to adopt is to suggest that, as humans, we like to be able to predict the behaviour of others with reasonable accuracy. If we cannot, if it does not seem commensurate with the circumstances as we perceive them, we are concerned and worried at what we perceive as abnormal behaviour. This still leaves open the question of whether it is the actor or the observer who has an abnormal perception. If a person's behaviour seems to be what the majority of people would expect in that particular set of circumstances, it is accepted as normal behaviour.

### Self-assessment Questions

1. What major criteria are applied when attempting to define abnormality, and what are the limitations of each?
2. What current models or paradigms are used in examining abnormality?
3. Briefly describe and contrast two models of abnormality.
4. How would you describe a normal person? Are there problems with your description?

### SECTION II   THE CONCEPT OF MENTAL ILLNESS AND THE MEDICAL MODEL

#### Introduction

A number of psychiatrists, among them Thomas Szasz and R. D. Laing, maintain that abnormality should not be called 'mental illness'. This misnomer, they suggest, implies an illness such as measles or cancer, which is totally out of the control of the individual, thereby removing any responsibility of self-control from him or her. If there is a demonstrable physical reason for the abnormality, it should be called an illness, not a mental illness.

### *Evidence from Signs and Symptoms*

Physical illnesses are diagnosed from patients' **symptoms** (pains or problems reported by the patient or others who have connection with him) and these can be confirmed by **signs** such as the outcome of X-rays, blood tests, scans, etc. Psychiatrists diagnosing mental illness rely a great deal on symptoms, reports from the patient or relatives; these may not necessarily be reliable. Signs such as psychological tests may be open to more than one interpretation and therefore are not conclusive. Supporting observations from trained staff are not wholly reliable, as evinced by Rosenhan's two experiments (see Section IV). The lack of agreement on diagnosis by psychiatrists is well known, as demonstrated by Fransella (1975) and Shapiro (1982) (see Problems of Diagnosis: Section IV).

### *Responsibility*

It has been argued that society is absolving abnormal behaviour by referring to abnormality as mental illness, thereby removing the responsibility for those actions from the individual; it also removes the responsibility for the cure from the individual ('I am ill, Doctor, please cure me.') On the other hand, it could be argued that some physical illnesses attach blame to the individual: AIDS or venereal diseases have – rightly or wrongly – moral implications, but some stigma also attaches to leprosy or cancer sufferers, for example, who report that they are treated with aversion.

   **Deviant or Ill?**   Society today has an ambivalent attitude towards abnormality: Whilst recognising that individuals may be 'victims' of their internal or external environment, they are also expected to take a degree of responsibility for their behaviour in certain circumstances. These are not always well-defined. Is it more humane to label someone mentally ill, rather than deviant or morally defective, as Blaney (1975) suggests? Is it better to be 'mad' than 'bad'? This question has a bearing on the way the person is treated.

**Prison or Hospital?**   Certainly treatment has progressed since the days of torturing the patient to exorcise the devils within; the question now posed is whether, in the last resort, abnormal behaviour should be treated by imprisonment or confinement in a mental hospital? Szasz suggests that when criminals are imprisoned, they believe it is because society will not tolerate their behaviour; they are still responsible. This may not be strictly true; a number of them regard their circumstances as being responsible for promoting their behaviour (for example, 'poverty made me steal') therefore their attitudes may not be very different from the attitudes of those in mental hospitals labelled 'mentally ill'.

**Free to Leave**.   It must be remembered that very few patients in Great Britain are locked up or detained under any Section of the Mental Health Act. Most are free to leave whenever they want provided they understand they are free to go. Many do understand this, and may not want to leave because they feel their behaviour is in some way abnormal; they want to be 'cured'. Undoubtedly there are others who do not understand that they are free to leave, or feel that they are pressured into remaining as voluntary patients, for fear that, if they leave, they will be brought back with a detention order. Szasz argues that there are no 'voluntary' patients; he suggests they are coerced into psychiatric hospitals on threat of being certified if they do not co-operate voluntarily.

## Moral not Medical Context

Heather (1976) suggests that abnormality should be viewed in a moral rather than a medical context. Neurosis and personality disorders he instances particularly as lacking evidence of organic causes. Therefore, he argues, these should be treated as moral or behavioural disorders, or alternatively, not disorders of the individual at all, but disorders of a sick society. This emulates Laing's (1965) view of schizophrenia, as a 'sane response to an insane world'. Heather also points out the cultural and temporal differences in defining abnormality, both within a society and between different societies; for example, the diagnosis of schizophrenia is ten times more frequently made in the United States of America than in Great Britain.

## The Anti-psychiatry Movement

*Against the Medical Model*

The anti-psychiatry movement was started in the 1950s by psychiatrists such as Laing, Cooper and Esterson. they rejected the 'disease' model of mental illness. Laing, while initially recognising schizophrenia as a cluster of symptoms and behaviours (1964), later suggested that the people labelled as schizophrenic simply needed time to voyage within their 'inner space' and work out their problems for themselves. Offering the patient treatment interferes with this natural healing process (1967). Laing put forward the view in the 1960s that society is far more disturbed by the behaviour of schizophrenics, than are the individuals themselves. They perceive their own behaviour to be rational, under what they believe are their circumstances.

**A Safe Environment**. Laing proposed and inaugurated 'safe houses' for schizophrenics, where they could live without pressures, thereby, he said, removing the need for abnormal behaviours. It must also be remembered that, at that time, the currently fashionable theory of schizophrenia was the 'family theory': this theory suggested that the family, usually led by the mother (denoted the schizophrenogenic mother), picked on one member of the family, and by constant carping and bullying, turned them into a schizophrenic. Family therapy is offered today, where problems are not seen as located solely within one individual; this rarely applies where the diagnosis is that of schizophrenia. In the same way, Laing's 'safe houses' may have been the forerunner of the Community Homes and hostels being set up today (see Chapter 6, Section 5).

**Organic not Mental Illness**. Thomas Szasz, in his book *The Myth of Mental Illness* (1967), puts forward the seemingly irrefutable argument that if the 'mind' does not exist, how can it be ill? This book was written during a period when overt behaviour was seen as of paramount importance, and any mental conflict preceding the behaviour could be discounted. Possibly Szasz may have been unwittingly instrumental in the resurgence of the concept of 'mind'. Psychologists today are readier to admit to 'mind' being of importance. As Clare (1980) argues, the idea of a mind without a body is untenable in science, therefore so must be the concept of a body without a mind, the two are inextricably linked.

Szasz argues forcibly that if a so-called 'mental illness' has a demonstrable physical cause, such as deterioration of the brain or nervous system, hormonal or chemical imbalance, then the patient has an illness not a mental illness, which should be treated medically not mentally. If the 'illness' has no physical origin, then it is not an illness, but a 'problem of living' and should be called such. The patient should be helped, if he or she so chooses, to adapt problematic behaviour to reach a compromise with society. People should be made to realise that they are responsible for their own behaviour.

**Tolerance of Unusual Behaviour.** Szasz lays blame at society's door for being too rigid in its expectations of people's behaviour. We are not all identical, he argues, therefore it is unreasonable to expect everyone to behave identically in any given situation. Society should be more tolerant of unusual behaviours: people are being treated as mentally ill when they are just different from others. (Those who try to live with someone diagnosed as schizophrenic or manic depressive may disagree, but Szasz would say they are only serving their own ends.) Szasz says that society desperately needs to predict behaviour; if it cannot, if people do strange, unpredictable things, then they are labelled 'mad' or 'mentally ill'. This labelling process is a kind of symbolic capture, which precedes the physical capture of hospitalisation, drugs or other treatment. Before the advent of asylums in the nineteenth century, Szasz points out, there was no segregation of the 'mentally ill': society was more tolerant and these people mixed with everyone else. Except, one might argue in return, for 'witches' who were burned at the stake, or those who simply could not cope and died of starvation or exposure. The parallel might be drawn that more physical illnesses are identified and treated today, whereas in the past their sufferers would have died without diagnosis or treatment.

**Points of View.** One major difference between Laing and Szasz is that while Laing denied the existence of a disease called schizophrenia, he still offered suggestions for its management; whereas Szasz denies that schizophrenia exists, and argues that it is simply a label set up by society to describe behaviours with which society itself cannot cope.

Bailey (1979) agrees with Szasz on two major points:

1. Organically-based mental illnesses are not mental but physical illnesses, which manifest mental symptoms.
2. Functional mental illnesses (those without physical or organic causes) are not illnesses, but disorders of psychosocial or interpersonal functioning; the mental symptoms which are manifest should help to decide the type of therapy the patient needs. Bailey sees the need for patients to adapt their behaviour to the more recognisable norm, rather than for society to become more tolerant.

### Evaluation of the Medical Model and the Anti-psychiatry Movement

It has been questioned whether mental problems can be assessed and verified in the same way as physical diseases, also whether the acceptance that these problems are an 'illness' absolves the individual from any responsibility for those problems.

The ideas of Szasz and Laing may seem both forward-looking and retrograde at the same time. To expect society today to simply tolerate what are regarded as abnormal behaviours is idealistic; large cities such as London or New York are currently trying to prevent displays of abnormal behaviour such as 'living on the streets'. Populations have now become too overcrowded and too sophisticated to accept aberrant behaviours. Families of those with mental disorders would be put under intolerable pressures trying to continue their lives in the ordinary manner, whilst one of their members was perceived as suffering.

The value of Laing's and Szasz's contributions must not be underestimated; they have made society – and psychiatrists – question anew whether each patient needs to be confined, and for how long. As mentioned previously, the development of community homes, family therapy, moral therapy and facets of other treatments, may well have been influenced by their ideas.

In addition the separation of illnesses with an organic cause, from those with no apparent organic causes, may help to determine treatments. Whether their sufferers are regarded as ill or mentally ill would probably be immaterial to those sufferers, were it not for the stigma of 'labelling' (see Section V of this chapter).

**Self-assessment Questions**

1. Describe how a parallel is drawn between the diagnosis of physical illnesses and mental illnesses.
2. Discuss whether the concept of mental illness should relate to morality and responsibility for one's own actions.
3. What is Szasz's view of the medical model of abnormality seen as a mental illness?
4. Discuss how tenable these views are in society today.

## SECTION III  DIAGNOSIS AND CLASSIFICATION OF MENTAL DISORDERS

Stressful or traumatic events in a person's life sometimes result in abnormal behaviours which are acute and transitory; other forms of abnormality may be chronic, life-long or degenerative. Each individual is unique and no two people necessarily follow the same identical pattern, just as no two people share identical environments, life experiences and genetic inheritance.

However, cognitive psychology has demonstrated that human beings find it advantageous to use classification as a method of grouping things, a useful reduction to lengthy descriptions (Bruner, 1966); if a person is described as 'an African' or 'European' a mental image is immediately formed, which may be wrong in some respects but gives us a broad outline. In the same way, classification of the many areas of abnormal behaviour attempts to give a broad picture.

Diagnosis of abnormality was, historically, a judgemental affair, which is outside the scope of this book to examine. Kraepelin (1913) made the earliest formal attempts at classification. The necessity for standardisation of description and classification of illnesses worldwide was recognised and extended to include abnormal behaviours, the purpose being that a diagnostic label would communicate information quickly and concisely about an individual. For example, the diagnosis of 'schizophrenic' conveys a great deal of immediate information to an informed observer.

Accordingly, the World Health Organisation's publication, the *International Classification of Diseases*, incorporated mental illnesses. The tenth edition of this (ICD 10) is currently in use. In the United States a more extensive diagnostic document has been developed, by the American Psychiatric Association: *The Diagnostic and Statistical Manual of Mental Disorder*, the third edition of which has recently been revised: DSM III R.

Historically, mental illness fell into two major categories, psychosis and neurosis.

**Psychosis** was described as involving the whole of the personality; an individual's whole life and behaviours are bound up with his or her problem. There is loss of touch with reality; everyday behaviours such as maintaining social relationships, or cleanliness may be totally discarded. Usually the term psychosis was used for long-standing problems, of some severity, such as schizophrenia.

**Neurosis** was thought not to affect the whole personality, as the individual was said not to entirely lose touch with reality. Frequently the individual realised that he or she was not functioning normally and could recognise and discuss the threads of their pre-illness behaviours as being the desirable state to which they wish to return.

Currently, both ICD 10 and DSM III R have both discontinued the usage of these major divisions; the band was so broad that sweeping generalisations such as 'loss of insight' became meaningless. Categories are now narrower-banded and more specific. One might also suggest that the use of modern psychoactive drugs (see Chapter 6) have changed the outlook on the psychoses. A brief discussion of these two diagnostic documents follows. Readers may also wish to refer to the Table of Classifications of Disorders, in Chapter 5 (Figure 5.1), in conjunction with the following discussion.

## ICD 10

One major difference between the organisation of the ICD 9 and the ICD 10, is that the latter does not use psychosis and neurosis as major classifications, although the terms 'neurotic' and 'psychotic' are both still used in conjunction with specific categories: for example, 'Neurotic, stress related and somatoform disorders' and 'Acute and transient psychotic disorders' (see Figure 5.1).

Diagnosticians using the ICD 10, identify symptoms which indicate one of the ten major group categories (called Two-factor Categories),then further investigations are made to refine the diagnosis to a specific category (called Three-factor Categories), for which diagnostic guidelines are provided by ICD 10; these are necessarily flexible.

Problems of terminology are addressed by ICD 10, including the question of using the term 'mental illness'. In order to avoid implications inherent in that term, the word 'disorder' rather than 'illness' is used throughout. Although this is not an exact term, it implies the existence of a set of symptoms which cause distress and interfere with the functioning of the individual.

The terms 'psychogenic' and 'psychosomatic' are not used in ICD 10, due to their differential meanings and interpretations in different psychiatric conditions and different countries.

## DSM III R

Only one level of categories is given in the DSM III R: these are, in the main, similar to the ICD 10 Two-factor Categories, plus a few of the Three-factor Categories, although Mental Retardation is not given a separate category, but is included as a sub-category of Developmental Disorders of Childhood. The disorders described and listed are similar in both diagnostic manuals, but DSM III R prescribes how the diagnosis should proceed.

Investigations using DSM III R are organised along five axes. Axes I to III have to be explored by the psychiatrist for each patient, while Axes IV and V are optional and can be used if the psychiatrist judges them to be relevant.

This multi-axial system requires the diagnostician to utilise a broad range of information:

**Axis 1**. What type of problem is the individual currently presenting? For example, do they have symptoms of schizophrenia or substance use disorder, etc.

**Axis 2**. Has the patient any known previous problems, such as a long-standing history of Personality Disorder?

**Axis 3**. enquires whether there are any physical disorders or enduring conditions, for example diabetes or a recent heart attack, which may or may not be relevant to the current problem, but should be noted.

**Axis 4**. examines the severity of psychosocial stressors experienced by the individual, and rates them on a 1 to 6 scale, for example whether there have been any deaths in the family, or marital break-up.

**Axis 5**. makes a Global Assessment of the individual's psychological, social and occupational functioning, both currently and the highest level attained during the past year for comparison. Scores range from 90 (a wide range of interests, general satisfaction with life, no more than everyday problems or concerns) down to 1, where the individual is seen to be in danger of hurting the self or others, or has a persistent inability to maintain personal hygiene, or has shown a serious suicidal attempt. See Figure 4.1 for an example of the way in which DSM III R can be used.

In addition to using one of these classification systems, the psychiatrist may well use a structured interview technique where standardised questions are asked of the patient, in order to arrive at an informed, objective decision as regards classification. There will be consultation with the clinical psychologist, who has given the patient standardised psychological tests in order to decide diagnosis and optimum treatment. It may be necessary to run a neurological investigation to establish whether there is an organic basis to the problem.

---

**FIGURE 4.1**

**Fictitious Example of DSM III R Multi-Axial Diagnosis**

| | |
|---|---|
| Client: | A. N. Other |
| Axis 1: | Psychoactive substance use disorder (heroin addiction) |
| Axis 2: | Antisocial personality |
| Axis 3: | HIV positive |
| Axis 4: | Psychosocial stressors: death of several close friends recently |
| Axis 5: | Current level of functioning, 25; highest level in past year, 41 |

## Two Broad Categories of Mental Disorder

Although the term 'mental illness' is not used in ICD 10, there still remains inherent the division between 'mental handicap' and 'mental illness', largely because, in Great Britain at least, care specialisations fall into one of these two categories. For example, common usage recognises 'psychiatric hospitals' for the mentally ill and 'sub-normality hospitals' for the mentally handicapped. Changes of terminology take a long time to filter through to the real-life situation.

Mental illness is not the same as mental handicap (or retardation), although both can be alleviated or exacerbated by social and environmental conditions.

**Mental handicap** is a condition usually present from birth, representing a failure of pre- or post-natal development of intellectual capacity, due to a variety of causes, either genetic, or unfavourable inter-uterine circumstances, birth trauma or subsequent early damage. Mental handicap ranges from slight learning difficulties to failure of development of the fetal brain. (Mental handicap is discussed at greater length in Chapter 5, Section III.)

However, there are 'grey' areas between determining whether some individuals are mentally handicapped or mentally ill; there is still some dispute as to whether autism, for example, should be regarded as a form of mental handicap or a developmental disorder. In addition, there is nothing precluding a mental illness being superimposed on the mentally-handicapped.

**Mental illness**, which will also be discussed at much greater length in Chapter 5, presents the idea that individuals can become imbalanced at some time in their lives, and that this illness is diagnosable, treatable and possibly curable. There are others, Laing, for example, who argue that abnormal behaviours may be due to abnormal social circumstances, and changes in these will produce a change in the individual, thereby proving how inaccurate is the term 'mental illness' (as discussed in Section II of this chapter).

## Self-assessment Questions

1. What are the two major classificatory systems used by western society? What professional bodies have drawn up these documents?

2. How does diagnosis proceed, using each of these two classificatory systems?
3. Apart from these classificatory systems, what are the two main functional categories in Great Britain, as regards treatment and hospitalisation?

## SECTION IV   DIAGNOSTIC TOOLS

This term is used for the various techniques used by the diagnostician, psychiatrist or psychologist, in trying to determine the cause and thereby the classification for abnormalities.

### Clinical Interview

This is not just a 'cosy chat' with the clinician, but rapport is established with the client, in order to draw out problem areas. Clinicians of humanistic or psychodynamic orientation may work from the premise that clients do not know what is troubling them, and they have to endeavour to find out. Not only answers to questions are recorded, but the client's emotional accompaniment to those answers. In fact, if emotion overcomes, they may not reply in words. In this way the clinician's notes would vary qualitatively from a survey interviewer's, who would simply tick 'No reply'.

The need for empathy in the clinical setting is of great importance; situational factors, such as age, sex and appearance of the interviewer may exert strong influence on the client's replies to probing personal questions.

Structured interviews respond to the need to collect standardised information: an example is **SADS**, the Schedule for Affective Disorders and Schizophrenia. Reliability of diagnosis using SADS is impressive, according to Endicott and Spitzer (1978).

### Psychological Tests

These fall into three major categories: projective tests, self-report personality inventories and intelligence tests (described and discussed in Chapters 1, 2 and 3).

**Physiological Tests**

An X-ray will show a fracture of the skull, a depressed fracture may indicate reasons for loss of function, but X-rays will pass straight through soft brain tissue, and not show problems within the brain itself. Harmless dyes injected into the blood circulating the brain, will show up on X-ray plates, and can indicate sites of blocking or haemorrhage.

Also available for use nowadays are sophisticated techniques such as **PET** scans (Positron Emission Tomography), **CAT** scans (Computerised Axial Tomography) and **MRI** scans (Magnetic Response Imaging) which give computerised pictures of the brain. Non-functioning, and therefore probably damaged, areas can be identified, and explored as the possible sites of abnormality (see Figure 4.2 for descriptions of these scanning techniques). However, many psychological disturbances have no demonstrable physiological abnormalities, and as scans are expensive tools to use, these are not implemented without good reason. They are rarely used in routine diagnosis.

Abnormalities of the brain's electrical activity can be identified with **EEG** (electroencephalogram): electrodes are attached to the patient's scalp with a sticky substance and the electrical activity of specific areas can be recorded on a record sheet. Normal patterns have been identified for various functions, such as sleeping, restful waking and cognitive activities; however, there is no specific pattern relating to particular mental illnesses.

Many brain abnormalities and injuries are so slight, that these may not be recognised by physical examination.

Clinicians may also take measures of heart rate, galvanic skin response (the conductivity of the skin, related to sweating) and blood flow, to compare the patterning of these with overt behaviours.

**Behavioural Observation**

It is difficult to observe most behaviour as it actually takes place. The family situation or setting preceding the actual abnormal behaviour may be as important as a description of the isolated behaviour. Many therapists contrive situations in their consulting rooms in order to observe behaviours; this of course invokes the

---

**FIGURE 4.2**

**Scanning Techniques Used in Diagnosis**

---

1. **CAT Scan**   In Computerised Axial Tomography, a moving beam of X-rays is passed across the patient's brain, in horizontal cross-section. The moving X-ray detector on the other side measures the amount of radioactivity that gets through, thereby detecting any difference in tissue density. The computer takes up this information and constructs a two-dimensional black and white image of the cross-section. Cross-sectional images of all areas of the patient's brain can be produced. This is a non-invasive technique, since it does not require surgery or the introduction of foreign substances into the patient's body.

2. **PET Scan**   In Positron Emission Tomography, a substance used by the brain, for example glucose or oxygen, is tagged with a short-lived radioactive isotope and injected into the bloodstream. The radioactive molecules emit positrons which can be detected by the scanner. The computer analyses millions of these detections and converts them ino a moving picture of the functioning brain, in horizontal cross-sections. These can be projected onto a colour screen; the metabolic rates of specific areas (where the tagged substance is being used more quickly) is indicated by a variety of specified colours on the screen. Moving pictures can not only indicate the sites of injury, tumours, non-activity but also the distribution in the brain of psychoactive drugs, and may indicate possible abnormal physiological processes in the brain. This is an invasive technique.

3. **MRI Scan** (sometimes called NMR Scan)   Magnetic Response Imaging (or Nuclear Magnetic Response Imaging) is superior to CAT scans because it produces higher quality pictures and therefore more information, yet does not require the invasive techniques of the PET scan. In MRI the patient is placed inside a large circular magnet that causes the hydrogen atoms in the body to move. When the magnet is turned off, these revert to their original positions, producing an electromagnetic signal which is translated by the computer into pictures of brain tissue.

---

phenomenon of **reactivity** of behaviour – behaviour which changes simply because it is observed.

The **reliability** of behavioural assessment depends heavily on the diagnostician's categorisations. Inter-observer reliability may be improved through training (Paul, 1966), but this does not necessarily relate to observations made in another institution, let alone across the Atlantic.

Bernstein and Nietzel (1980) found that the random observing of observers increased their reliability.

The **validity** of whether the observed behaviours relate to the client's problem, should be established; if a clinician assumes that frequent lateness for clinic appointments is an indication of hostility, is he or she justified in making such an assertion? Also, is the observed behaviour typical of that individual's behaviour when not being observed?

Zeigob *et al.* (1975) found that mothers acted more positively towards their children when they knew they were being observed, than when they were observed surreptitiously.

The situation may influence the observed behaviour; Mischel (1968) argued that situation is more important in determining behaviour than internal factors. (See Chapter 2, Section III.)

**Observer expectations** can also influence observations (as demonstrated by Rosenthal, 1966, where outcomes were found to be as the observer had been led to believe they would be; see Chapter 1, Section II for a description of this experiment).

### Self-monitoring

The self-monitoring of behaviour can be undertaken by clients, although this is not always reliable (Nelson, 1977) as clients are not always motivated to be honest – they may not wish to attribute faults to themselves. Careful questioning about reported behaviour may indicate the point at which intervention should be made, in order to change behaviour. For example, if attention is paid promptly by a client's family to a reasonable request, unreasonable or confrontational behaviour may be averted.

### Self-assessment Questions

1. Evaluate the 'face-to-face' techniques used by diagnosticians to aid diagnosis of mental problems.
2. Describe the physiological tools which may be used by clinicians.
3. Discuss the usefulness of behavioural observation and self-monitoring techniques.

## SECTION V   PROBLEMS OF DIAGNOSIS

**Introduction**

The main problems associated with diagnoses are:

1. **Reliability**. Would the diagnosis always remain the same, even if conducted by another diagnostician?
2. **Validity**. Does this cluster of symptoms really represent a named diagnosis? Does this classification category have real-life representation?
3. **Labelling**. What is going to be the outcome of assigning an individual to a category – is that person effectively 'labelled' for life?

Let us look at these problems in more detail.

**Reliability**

Does the diagnosis remain the same throughout the patient's illness? If the patient is seen by more than one psychiatrist, are their diagnoses the same?

**Ullman and Krasner (1975)** found reliability to be better for the major categories of disorders, but disturbingly low for other categories.

**Rosenhan (1973)** carried out what is now regarded as a classic experiment. Eight 'normal' people requested appointments, at various psychiatric hospitals in USA; the only symptoms they presented were that they claimed to hear voices saying single words, such as 'hollow' or 'thud'. They were all admitted as patients, subsequently exhibiting no false or aberrant behaviours, although their normal behaviours were sometimes misinterpreted by the staff; for example, one who took notes of his treatment in hospital, was identified as having a compulsion to write. None of the psychiatric staff reported any suspicions that these were anything other than genuine patients. Eventually all were discharged, with the diagnosis of 'schizophrenia in remission'; confinement varied from nine to fifty-two days.

In a second experiment, a teaching hospital was told of the previous experiment and warned that some pseudo-patients might apply for admission, over a three week period. During that time, 193 patients were admitted; the staff were confident that 41 of these were not genuine patients, and various others were suspected. In fact, they were all genuine patients.

**Cooper (1972)** suggests that ten times as many people are diagnosed as schizophrenic by American psychiatrists as British ones, out of a proportional number presenting.

**Fransella (1975)** advises that diagnostic categories are not mutually exclusive and may therefore show overlap; on the other hand, different schizophrenics, for example, may exhibit no symptoms in common.

**Beck *et al.* (1962)** reports that he and three other psychiatrists diagnosed 153 patients; each patient was seen by two psychiatrists. All four diagnosticians had agreed the current diagnostic manual, but not on the techniques to be used for gathering information. Overall agreement on diagnosis was only 54 per cent. When these cases were re-examined, **Ward *et al.* (1962)** suggested reasons for the low rate of agreement.

1. Inadequacies of the diagnostic system, with unclear criteria, or major categories which were not specific enough, accounted for 62.5 per cent of disagreements.
2. Inconsistencies in information presented by the patient.
3. Inconsistencies in techniques used by the diagnostician, for example, differences in interviewer techniques.

(Points (2) and (3) accounted for most of the balance of the disagreement.)

**Shapiro (1982)** claims that a severely anxious patient with delusions, may be classified as either neurotic or psychotic, depending on the view taken of the intensity of the problem.

**Validity**

Validity, as discussed in Chapter 1, looks at whether a test, a diagnosis, or a situation really is what it says it is. In the context of diagnosis for example, does the descriptive term 'broken leg' adequately and truly describe what the patient is suffering from? In the field of mental disorders, the answer may not always be so self-evident. If reliability is a prerequisite of validity, there have already been shown some doubts. In addition, **Heather (1976)** states that very few 'causes' of mental illness are known, and there is only a 50 per cent chance of predicting treatment once diagnosis has been made.

**Bannister** *et al.* **(1964)** suggest that factors other than diagnosis seem to dictate what treatments are used.

**Mackay (1975)** asserts that because the notion of 'mental illness' is such a vague one, the diagnostic process cannot be a valid one; the choice of treatments is likely to be haphazard.

**Clare (1980)** suggests that the diagnosis of physical illnesses is not as clear-cut or reliable as generally believed: criticism should be directed at those diagnosing, not the diagnostic process.

This supports the view of **Falek and Moser (1975)**, where doctors' diagnoses of illnesses such as tonsillitis, or angina, without the support of a definitive laboratory test, showed no greater agreement than psychiatrists' diagnoses of schizophrenia.

## Labelling

Once a diagnosis has been made, it is entered in the patient's records and that diagnosis may become synonymous with that individual – they are effectively 'labelled'.

The person's family and friends may come to regard him or her differently because of the label and the label may replace the individual.

Even when the person is finally discharged, they are not rid of their label; others still remember them by it and it is still on their medical records, which are allegedly confidential, but confidential to how many? In these days of computerisation, who knows?

**Laing (1967)** suggested that the patient is labelled by a diagnosis in order that he or she may be institutionalised and dehumanised; the label is the 'symbolic capture' of the individual.

**Scheff (1966)** suggested that the disorder is a learned social role; the labelled individual acts according to the stereotype. This became known as Labelling Theory. However, there is little evidence to support this theory. Given that the behaviours shown by schizophrenics, for example, are so disparate and wide-ranging, there is no one stereotype to follow.

**Gove's (1970)** study showed that there is little conclusive evidence of the social stigma allegedly attached to mental illness, although others have challenged this.

The differing views of normality and abnormality held by different cultures, was investigated by **Murphy (1976)**, who found that both Eskimos and the Yoruba tribe differentiate between their 'shamans' (those who have visions) and their 'crazy people', who exhibit behaviours such as talking to oneself, refusing to speak, delusional beliefs and strange behaviours. Both cultures have different words in their languages for 'shaman' and 'crazy person'.

There are arguments for and against labelling. On the one hand there is the diagnostic convenience of a category, recognisable to other professionals who may encounter the individual. On the other hand there is the suggestion that the person may choose to 'act the part' of the label, or be stigmatised by its attachment, by family, loss of job or friends, or decline in social status.

### Evaluation of Diagnosis and Classification

The fact that many surveys have shown medical diagnosis to be unreliable is not a valid argument for ceasing to diagnose; the same applies to psychiatric diagnosis.

**Spitzer (1976)** gave a spirited rebutal of Rosenhan's studies: the diagnosis 'schizophrenia in remission' is rarely used with genuine patients, therefore the diagnoses were a function of the pseudo-patients behaviours, and therefore should not reflect badly on the psychiatric hospital. He defended the hospital procedures and suggested that any problems with diagnosis lay with individual psychiatrists. He also criticised Rosenhan for his use of the terms 'sane' and insane', which as he said, are legal terms and not used by psychiatrists in hospitals. However, many other psychiatrists and psychologists assert that 'schizophrenia in remission' remains a common diagnosis.

**Fonagy and Higgitt (1984)** suggested that instead of using diagnostic categories to describe specific 'diseases', terms such as 'anxiety' and 'schizophrenia' should be used descriptively, to make testable hypotheses about mental disorders. If this suggestion were adopted, it might obviate the problem of labelling.

### Self-assessment Questions

1. What studies have suggested that the diagnosis of mental illnesses is not wholly reliable?

2. Discuss whether these studies suggest that diagnosis should be discontinued?
3. What assumptions have been made as to the validity of diagnosis?
4. What are the problems associated with categorisation or 'labelling' of mental illnesses?

## FURTHER READING

A. Clare, *Psychiatry in Dissent* (London: Routledge, 1992).

T. W. Costello and J. T. Costello, *Abnormal Psychology* (New York: Harper Collins College Outline, 1992).

R. D. Laing, *The Divided Self* (Harmondsworth: Penguin, 1965).

T. Szasz, *The Myth of Mental Illness* (London: Paladin, 1972).

INSANITY **IS** HEREDITARY — YOU GET IT
FROM YOUR CHILDREN.

# Causes, Categories and Descriptions of Medical Disorders

# 5

At the end of this chapter you should be able to:

1. Understand the categorisation systems used by both ICD 10 and DSM III R;
2. Be familiar with descriptions of a variety of mental disorders, including their aetiology and prognosis;
3. Discuss the genetic, environmental and neurochemical contributions to causes of both childhood and adult mental disorders.

## SECTION I  CATEGORIES OF MENTAL DISORDERS

### Introduction

As discussed in the previous chapter, major diagnostic categories of mental disorders are delineated in **ICD 10** and **DSM III R**. Although they are not identical in the two diagnostic systems, they are very similar, and for the purposes of this book are treated in conjunction with each other. In both, specific mental disorders are grouped with others that have similar symptoms or origins, to form major categories which are then given a comprehensive title.

Figure 5.1 lists ten major categories; under each of these are listed a number of specific disorders assigned to each. These are not exhaustive lists but examples, some of which may already sound familiar to the interested reader. (A description of some of these disorders is given in Section II of this chapter.)

### Self-Assessment Questions

1. Give the major category under which the following specific disorders fall:

**FIGURE 5.1**

**Specific Mental Disorders in Major Categories**

| | 1. Organic Mental Disorder | 2. Psychoactive Substance-use Disorders | 3. Schizophrenia and Delusional Disorders | 4. Mood (affective) Disorders | 5. Neurotic and Stress-related Disorders |
|---|---|---|---|---|---|
| **SPECIFIC DISORDERS** | Various dementias, e.g. HIV, vascular | Intoxication, dependence, abuse and withdrawal of substances, e.g. alcohol, opioides, stimulants, cannabis, sedatives cocaine, tobacco, solvents, hallucinogens | Schizophrenia, e.g. simple, hebephrenic, paranoid, catatonic | Mania | Phobias |
| | Alzheimer's disease | | Persistent delusional disorder | Bipolar affective disorder | Anxiety disorders e.g. panic attacks |
| | Disorders due to brain damage or disease | | Acute and transient psychotic disorders | Single depressive episode | Obsessive-compulsive disorder |
| | Organic amnesias | With or without complications (e.g. coma, convulsions) | Schizophrenia affective disorders | Recurrent depressive | Severe stress e.g. post-traumatic stress syndrome |
| | | | | Other mood (affective) disorders | Dissociative disorders, e.g. fugue, amnesia multiple personality |
| | | | | | Somatoform disorders, e.g. hypochondria |

FIGURE 5.1 continued

| 6. Behavioural Disorders Associated with Physical Disturbances | 7. Adult Personality Disorders | 8. Mental Retardation | 9. Disorders of Psychological Development | 10. Childhood and Adolescence Disorders |
|---|---|---|---|---|
| Eating disorders e.g. anorexia, bulimia | Specific personality disorders, e.g. paranoid, schizoid, dissocial | Mild, moderate, severe or profound categories | Specific language and speech disorders | Hyperkinetic disorder |
| Non-organic sleep disorders e.g. insomnia, sleepwalking, nightmares | Personality changes after catastrophe | | Specific scholastic disorders, e.g. dyslexia | Conduct disorder |
| Sexual dysfunction (non-organic) | Habit and impulse disorders, e.g. gambling pyromania | | Pervasive disorders, e.g. autism | Emotional disorders, e.g. phobic anxiety, separation-anxiety |
| Puerperal disorders, e.g. puerperal psychosis, post-natal depression | Psychosexual disorders | | | Social functioning disorders, e.g. elective mutism |
| Abuse of non-dependence substances e.g. laxatives, vitamins, steroids | | | | Tic disorders e.g. Tourette's syndrome |
| | | | | Other, e.g. stuttering, enuresis, feeding disorder |

SPECIFIC DISORDERS

(a)  Alzheimer's disease
(b)  Catatonic schizophrenic
(c)  Bipolar affective disorder
(d)  Phobias
(e)  Anorexia
(f)  Autism
(g)  Hyperkinetic disorder


## SECTION II    DESCRIPTIONS OF MENTAL DISORDERS

### Introduction

This section describes various mental disorders. Included are examples of disorders from each of the main categories named in the previous section. Their aetiology (causes), symptoms and prognosis (prediction of the course of the disorder) is outlined wherever possible, unless previously dealt with elsewhere in this book.


### Category 1    Organic Mental Disorders

These are due to physical deterioration of the brain or degeneration of the nervous system. Specific disorders in this category include:

(a)  **Parkinson's Disease**. Dopamine-producing cells in the brain no longer function effectively. Tremor and a shuffling gait are typical symptoms. In many patients, this can be treated effectively with a drug called L-dopa, but careful monitoring is necessary to prevent overdose. The L-dopa is a synthetic form of dopamine which replaces this necessary neurotransmitter and restores activity to the dopamine circuit. An overdose of L-dopa may produce hallucinations or other symptoms reminiscent of schizophrenia (see The Dopamine Theory, Section III of this chapter).

(b)  **Alzheimer's Disease** was first identified in 1860 by the German neurologist Alois Alzheimer. It has been identified in people in their forties and fifties, as well as the elderly, and is classified as a pre-senile dementia. It usually commences with difficulties of concentration, absent-mindedness and irritability, and mental faculties deteriorate as described in Dementia (above). In Alzheimer's, **primary degeneration of neurons** (brain cells) occurs. (Information on neurons and nervous transmission is contained in Figure 5.3.) Cells in the cortex atrophy to such a degree that **ventricles** in the brain may become larger and **sulci** (the folds in the cortex) may widen. In place of the atrophied cells are senile or **neuritic plaques**: these contain the remnants of the cells plus amyloid, a substance deposited when protein metabolism is disrupted. Bundles of abnormal protein filaments (neurofibrillary tangles) accumulate within the cell bodies of neurons.

**Hyman *et al.* (1984)** found that cell-degeneration particularly affects the **hippocampus** (a structure in the brain important for laying-down memories).

Many potential causes of Alzheimer's disease have been indicated, but none actually proven as yet. It is difficult to establish which of the observed changes is cause, and which effect. The prognosis is poor, with deterioration occurring over 10–12 years.

Treatment of Alzheimer's is primarily to reassure the person and provide care and comfort. In the early stages, individuals are better in their own homes, with family and familiar surroundings. Reminder 'notes' (e.g. turn off the cooker, lock the front door) can provide the necessary prompts. Later symptoms may include paranoid delusions, aggression and other behaviours with which the family cannot cope. Institutionalisation is not a decision to be taken lightly and counselling is an excellent form of support for the individual and his or her relatives (**Zarit, 1980**). Practical and moral support for families caring for an Alzheimer's sufferer at home is currently recognised as being of importance, although funds are not always available to provide all the help needed.

Current research into the cause of Alzheimer's disease is looking into a possible genetic component.

(c) **Dementia in HIV. Human Immunodeficiency Disease** is a virus infection which destroys the body's immune responses. It also produces mental disorders, initially presenting with complaints of slowness, forgetfulness, poor concentration and difficulties with problem solving and reading. Apathy and social withdrawal are common; less frequent are seizures or psychoses. It is possible that a degree at least of the apathy and social withdrawal are due to the individual's perception of his state of health, as well as physiological deterioration; counselling is always offered to AIDS sufferers, to try to combat despondency, as well as help with day-to-day problems.

Nurnberg *et al.* (1984) found that patients exhibited problems with concentration and memory months before AIDS-related illnesses appeared.

(d) **Disorders Due to Brain Damage or Disease**

(i) **Brain damage** can be caused by tumours, infections (such as meningitis), accident or trauma and physical damage can be located and related to loss of function in the individual. Infections which are cured and tumours which are benign or removed, rarely leave residual psychological problems. Clinical studies in this area have provided much evidence for localisation of functions in the brain. Unlike other parts of the body, the brain does not regenerate, and as a rule, if functions are lost, they will not be regained. Notable exceptions to this rule are young children, under five or six years of age, where the brain is still plastic and substitute connections can still be forged. Patients who are comatose after an accident, sometimes for months, may show a complete recovery of functions, even if this is gradual; the younger the patient, the more complete the recovery. A **concussion** (a brief loss of consciousness), or a **contusion** (bruising of neural tissue, when the brain shifts and compresses against the skullbone, through forceful impact, possibly resulting in coma) are unlikely to cause a change in personality, whereas a laceration (where brain tissue is pierced or torn) is likely to result in personality change. The best-known case was that of Phineas Gage (late nineteenth century) who was working on excavation for the railroad, when a three-and-a-half-foot tamping iron was blasted right through his left cheek and out of the top of his skull. He recovered, with no resultant sensory or motor deficits, but his personality had changed so radically his employers would not give him his job back. One wonders if he wanted it back!

(ii) **Alcohol** causes brain damage: sufferers of **Wernicke's Disease** have damage to the pons, cerebellum and mamillary bodies, and exhibit drowsiness, confusion and unsteady gait.

Those suffering from **Korsakoff's Psychosis** have a similar pattern of damage and behaviour, but in addition exhibit lesions in the thalamus and anterograde amnesia (loss of memory for events following an illness or trauma), often **confabulating** ('inventing' memories) in order to fill gaps in their memories.

### Category 2    Psychoactive Substance-use Disorder

Dependence syndrome is a cluster of physiological, behavioural and cognitive phenomena in which the use of a substance takes on a much higher priority than any other behaviours previously enjoyed by the individual. Tolerance occurs, thereby necessitating more frequent or higher doses of the substance. Persistence with the substance may have physiological consequences (for example, alcohol causing liver damage) or social consequences (for example, loss of a job through drug-related impaired performance or depressive mood-states). Deprivation of the substance produces a physiological withdrawal state, which may range from anxiety, through convulsions, to delirium, such as delirium tremens experienced by alcoholics, where vivid hallucinations combine with confusion and tremor.

The **opioids** such as heroin have a similar chemical 'shape' to some of the brain's own chemicals, the **endorphins**. These appear to have a calming, pain-reducing effect on the individual in the normal situation. When opioids are used the endorphins are underproduced. During withdrawal from heroin the painful effect is enhanced through the under-production of the natural calming chemicals. Withdrawal from substance use is best undertaken under medical supervision.

### Category 3    Schizophrenia and Delusional Disorders

(a) **Schizophrenia.** Whether this is one disorder or many, is still a point for discussion, as is the possibility that the origins of schizophrenia may be organic. If so, it should therefore be regarded as an organic disorder.

Kraepelin first presented his description of **dementia praecox** in 1898, as follows: an early onset, progressive intellectual deterioration, hallucinations, delusions, negativisim (doing the opposite of what is required), attentional difficulties, emo-

tional dysfunction and stereotyped behaviour. Not all schizophrenic patents will show all of these symptoms; in fact no two
cases are identical (for examples of symptoms, see Figure 5.2).
DSM III R determines for the diagnostician how many areas of
disturbance should be present, from thought, perception,
attention, motor functions, affect or emotion, and life function; however, there is no essential symptom which determines
classification. ICD 10 does not prescribe what exactly should
be included in the diagnosis; this may partially account for the
difference in frequency of diagnosing schizophrenia, between
the United States and Great Britain.

Duration of the disorder must be taken into account, in order to
distinguish true schizophrenia from brief psychotic episodes
(reactive psychoses) or other schizophrenic disorders. **Cooper** *et
al.* **(1972)** showed that many patients with a DSM II diagnosis of
schizophrenia were actually suffering from brief psychotic episodes,
as duration of the problem was not a factor for consideration at
that time. These are now diagnosed as personality disorders.

**Endicott** *et al.* **(1982)** found that diagnoses of schizophrenia
varied according to the diagnostic system used.

**Schneider (1959)** identified what he called 'first rank symptoms'
which he said are central to defining schizophrenia; these include
particular forms of hallucinations and delusions. The layman's idea
of a 'split personality' is incorrect, this is more descriptive of
multiple personality (see Category 5) than schizophrenia.

Four subtypes of schizophrenia are identified in ICD 10, (three in
DSM III R). At one time it was thought that these were sequential
and the disease would progress from one 'stage' to another. This is
not now thought to be true. There is less tendency nowadays to
regard it necessary to classify people into one of these sub-
categories.

(i)  **Simple schizophrenia** appears during late adolescence. Symptoms include increasing apathy, decline in academic or work
performance, gradual social withdrawal, may be regarded by
others as idle, or a drifter. (This sub-category is not included in
DSM III R.) Diagnosis depends on establishing the gradual progression and worsening of these symptoms. Hallucinations and
delusions are not usually manifest.

**FIGURE 5.2**

**Examples of Symptoms of Schizophrenia**

*Perception and Thought Disorders in Schizophrenia*

1. **Schizophrenic slip**: an apparently lucid flow of conversation from the person, but 'slipping' from topic to topic, concept to concept, with no apparent logical relationship.
2. **Clang associations**: the use of words, without regard for their meanings, because they sound similar 'He's a pig like a swig in the dig'.
3. **Literal interpretations**: of proverbs for example: the schizophrenic may literally go looking for 'the light at the end of the tunnel', or commence a discussion about how quick is 'a flash'.
4. **Lack of insight**: schizophrenics rarely have an idea why their behaviours are unacceptable and frequently cannot understand why they should be hospitalised.
5. **Delusions** means holding beliefs that the rest of society would disagree with. Common delusions are **delusions of grandeur**: 'I am God/ Napoleon/the Queen' or of **persecution** (paranoia), where individuals believe others are planning to kill or harm them in some way.
6. **Hallucinations**, most often auditory, are experienced by many schizophrenics. The 'voices' they hear are often saying derogatory or threatening things.
7. **Thought control**: individuals feel that thoughts are no longer their own. They are controlled by others, they may believe that thoughts are transmitted to them by radio waves. The delusion may be so strong that sufferers are convinced there are wires attached to their heads, or radio antennae. They may blame radio or television for this control, and avoid it. Sometimes the insertion is of feelings or sensations rather than words or thoughts.

*Other Typical Symptoms*

**Affective symptoms**: the mood of the individual may either be said to be 'flat' – stimuli fail to elicit an appropriate emotional response, or they may exhibit **inappropriate affect**, for example laughing at sad news, or becoming extremely angry at a simple, uncontroversial question.

    **Motor symptoms**: bizarre motor movements, e.g. waving the hands without cause, or complete immobility or purposeless rushing up and down.

(ii) **Hebephrenic schizophrenia** (called 'Disorganised' in DSM III R) is characterised by hallucinations and delusions which are profuse and less directed than those of the paranoid schizophrenic. Behaviour is changeable, even violent at times, mannerisms are adopted and discarded, as are behavioural rituals. Appearance and personal hygiene may be forgotten. Disorders of thought, perception and attention are prevalent (see Figure 5.2). Onset is usually during the early twenties.

(iii) **Catatonic schizophrenia** is typically represented by motor disturbances which tend to fall into extremes. At one extreme, the sufferer is completely immobile for long periods of time, often 'posed' in odd positions, seeming oblivious to all around, yet may later relate details of what has happened during that time. At the other extreme, in the excited state, the individual may run or walk up and down, shouting or talking with great agitation. Between these two extreme states are other distinctive motor disturbances: hand or finger-waving or strange, jerky movements.

(iv) **Paranoid schizophrenia is characterised by delusions. These may be grandiose**, where individuals are full of their own self-importance or power, sometimes convinced that they are a well-known historical figure such as Napoleon or Jesus Christ, and everyone else is conspiring to keep them prisoner. Alternatively they may be delusions of **persecution**: everyone is talking about them, snippets of conversation in the street are about them, radio and TV programmes refer to them, there are plots to kill them. Sufferers of paranoid schizophrenia are frequently argumentative, agitated and sometimes violent, but they are more alert and verbal than other sub-categories and their thought processes although deluded, are not as fragmented.

A discussion of the views of Szasz and Laing, who take differing views on the existence or treatment of schizophrenia, was included in Chapter 4, Section II.

### Category 4   Mood (Affective) Disorders

(a) **Mania** The manic person exhibits high activity, elation, is full of grandiose plans, buys things he or she cannot really afford, talks volubly, taking the whole population into his or her confidence.

(b) **Single depressive episodes** (called Reactive depression in DSM III R) The sufferer feels in a sad, depressed mood, no longer enjoys usual activities, has disturbed sleep patterns or sleeps a great deal, poor appetite and loss of energy and drive. This type of depression differs from Recurrent depressive disorder in that this form is usually triggered by an external event but the sadness or mood disturbance exceeds the bounds of a normal reaction, to a death, for example. Many people become depressed for short periods of time (one might almost say it would be abnormal not to do so!) and recover with no treatment at all. Times of hormonal changes, such as adolescence and menopause, sometimes produce emotional changes which may include depressive episodes.

(c) **Recurrent depressive disorder** (Endogenous depression in DSM III R) has no immediately recognisable cause. The patient has recurring bouts of depression; some may be triggered by seemingly minor external events, others not. The result is deeply sad, depressed mood, poor appetite, disturbed sleep patterns, loss of energy, loss of pleasure in any activities, difficulties in concentration or decision making, recurrent thoughts of suicide or death.

(d) **Manic-depression** is where the two extreme states, mania and depression, alternate in the same individual. It is very difficult to treat; if the depressive state is lifted too high for example, by chemotherapy, then the person may swing into the manic phase; if the manic state is 'damped down' too much, then the person may slip into depression. These are known as bipolar swings.

**Category 5   Neurotic and Stress-related Disorders**

(a) **Phobia** is an irrational fear of an object or situation. By far the most common is **arachnaphobia (fear of spiders). Other common phobias include agoraphobia** (fear of public spaces or fear of leaving one's own safe haven) and **social phobia** (where an individual cannot cope with meeting new people: this is often confused with agoraphobia, as in both cases the affected individual may refuse to go out). Fear of snakes is another common phobia, also claustrophobia (fear of confined spaces), tophepophobia (fear of being buried alive) and acrophobia (fear of heights).

Phobias are common but most people can keep them under control and simply practise avoidance. If you are afraid of snakes, and live in the city you have no real problem; if you are afraid of heights, don't become a steeplejack!

Agras *et al.* (1969) found that fewer than 1 per cent of phobics required treatment for their phobias; treatment may be necessary when the individuals have to organise their own lives around their phobias. Phobics realise their fears are irrational.

Phobias are thought by learning theorists to originate through faulty learning; either through classical conditioning, by contiguous association, the fear object being present at the same time as a real fear or punishment, or through operant conditioning, by reinforcement of the individual's fear of the object, usually in childhood (as discussed in the learning theory model in Chapter 4). Freud and other psychodynamic theorists suggest that phobias are a defence against the anxiety that is produced by repressed id impulses (discussed in Chapter 3).

(b) **Obsessive-Compulsive Disorder**. Obsessions are recurring thoughts and ideas which dominate a person's consciousness, without his or her active volition. A compulsion is a need to perform a stereotyped action or movement, to ward off the feared situation. Anxiety and tension are produced if the individual tries to resist the compulsion.

(c) **Somatoform Disorder** (conversion type of hysterical neurosis in DSM III R). This is where the individual's actual problem is changed into an acceptable problem. The classical case, described by Freud, is that of Anna O, the lady who could not admit to her resentment at having to look after her invalid father, and therefore developed a 'paralysed' arm, although there was no physical problem present.

(d) **Multiple Personality**. In ICD 10 this is classified as a dissociative type of hysterical neurosis and in DSM III R, a Dissociative Disorder. The person with multiple personality disorder has two or more distinct personalities at the same time, either of which may take over without bidding. Sometimes these personalities are unaware of each other; at other times there is a central personality who is aware of some or all of the others. One of the most interesting was that of Sybil, who had

16 different personalities (Rheta Schrieber, 1973). Cases are few and far between. Autonomic responses, such as heart-rate, blood pressure and galvanic skin response, have been taken and found to differ for each personality.

Psychoanalytic theory views multiple personality as repression of infantile sexual wishes; Bliss (1980) believes it becomes established in childhood through self-hypnosis. Learning theorists regard it as avoidance responses, to avoid punishment or protect the individual from highly stressful events. Selective memory loss could be accounted for by state-dependent learning (if you learn something when you are happy you are more likely to remember it when you are happy). Because of the rarity of dissociative disorders, they are among the least understood and researched clinical syndromes, relying for data only on clinical case studies.

(e) **Post-Traumatic Stress Disorder**. A delayed and/or protracted response to a stressful event or situation, either man-made or natural disaster. This may involve the individual either as a witness or a participant in, for example, earthquake, serious accident, war, witnessing violent death of others, being a victim of rape, torture or other crime. Symptoms include repeated reliving of the trauma ('flashbacks'), emotional blunting, detachment from other people, fear and avoidance of cues associated with the original trauma. Anxiety and depression are commonly associated with post-traumatic stress disorder.

**Paton (1990)** looked for these symptoms in two classes of people who helped after the earthquake in Armenia: trained firefighters and volunteers with little or no experience of disasters. The volunteers displayed a lower level of post-traumatic stress on all symptoms. Paton suggests this may be due to higher expectations in the professionals to be able to give help and save lives, and their disappointment at being unable to do so.

Recently these same symptoms have been identified in some individuals who have not been involved in a major catastrophe. Severe reprimands at work, for example, have triggered the same level of anxiety, flashbacks and avoidance responses usually associated with catastrophes (**Stradling and Scott, 1992**, unpublished).

**Category 6    Behavioural Disorders Associated with Physical Disturbances**

(a) **Anorexia Nervosa**. Three principal symptoms are: serious weight loss, an intense fear of becoming obese, and refusal to eat sufficiently to gain or maintain body weight. The problem is usually first manifest during adolescence and is twenty times more common in girls than boys. The girl fails to menstruate regularly; this and the loss of weight has prompted theorists to suggest that the girl is showing an unwillingness to grow up. Family conflict has also been suggested as a cause; the conflict is deflected on to the sufferer's 'disease'. Learning theorists suggest the young woman is trying to emulate the slim models so valued by society. Psychoanalytic theorists who equate food with sexuality, suggest that refusal of food is really a rejection of sexuality. The anorexic is usually of above average IQ, a perfectionist, well-behaved and conscientious, and frequently comes from a family of high-achievers.

Some anorexics have to be hospitalised and fed intravenously; a percentage die. Behaviour therapies include regimes of isolation followed by company at mealtimes. If the patient eats a meal, rewards follow, such as company of nurses, access to TV, radio or music. Family therapy includes 'the family lunch', where mother and father are asked to unite to persuade the sufferer to eat (Minuchin *et al.*, 1975), the idea being that, if conflict has promoted anorexia, perceived unity will solve the problem.

(b) **Bulimia** has now been recognised as a separate disease from anorexia nervosa. The bulimic seldom reduces weight, never to life-threatening dimensions, as does the anorexic, but does have an equal fear of obesity. Life is a series of 'binges' followed by vomiting; they often feel disgust and helplessness while binging, they are aware their eating patterns are abnormal and go to great lengths to hide them. The continual vomiting has physiological consequences such as intestinal damage and nutritional deficiencies. Various therapies and anti-depressant drugs have been tried with bulimics, with varying claimed successes. No really effective treatment has been found.

(c) **Puerperal Disorders**. Post-natal depression is an abnormal reaction to what is usually considered a happy event: the birth of a baby. The mother feels unable to cope, and in very severe cases may commit suicide or infanticide. Causes are likely to be biochemical or social. Puerperal disorders are recognised at two levels, mild (**post-natal depression**) and severe (**puerperal psychosis**). Commencing within six weeks of the birth of the baby, the mother is depressed and cannot relate to her new infant. In severe cases she ignores the infant or threatens to harm it or herself. Because of the danger of suicide or infanticide, prompt treatment is necessary. If anti-depressant drug treatment is ineffective, electro-convulsive therapy may be used (see Chapter 6). Mother and baby are kept together as much as possible, in special 'mother and baby' units, while treatment is undertaken.

**Category 7    Personality Disorders**

Explanations based on the trait approach to personality, described in Chapter 2, suggest that these disorders have long-term, inflexible and maladaptive patterns of behaviour. DSM III R lists eleven specific disorders, ICD 10 lists five. The individual does not lose contact with reality and behaviours are integrated into the person's life-style, making treatment difficult. A number of personality disorders are described below.

(a) **Dissocial Personality** (called psychopathic or sociopathic personality in DSM III R). This has usually revealed itself by the age of 15, through truancy, vandalism or delinquency. In adulthood, the individual may be indifferent to holding a job, keeping within the law, acting in a caring or responsible manner to partners or relatives. Many psychopaths do hold down ordinary jobs, but extend their immorality to the work situation. Frequently they are clever enough to avoid being caught.

 **Cleckley (1976)** suggests that characteristics of the psycho-path may include: considerable charm, absence of anxiety, irrational thoughts or other 'neurotic' symptoms, lack of remorse or guilt, while exhibiting unreliability, untruthfulness and insincerity, pathological egocentrism, leading to incapacity for real love and attachment, inability to see oneself as others do (therefore lack of insight).

**Hare (1980)** lists lack of empathy and lack of concern for others, as characteristics typical of psychopaths. Robins (1966) suggests that some psychopaths come from families where discipline is inconsistent or absent and are usually referred to guidance clinics during childhood, for a range of antisocial behaviours. **Retrospective studies** (studies which look back at a person's past after they have been identified as belonging to a group or category) unfortunately lack comparable control groups, either of peers who also were referred to clinics and did not become psychopaths or psychopaths who have not been identified by the law during adulthood, and are therefore not included in research data.

(b) **The Schizoid personality** is aloof, with few friends, and is indifferent to praise and criticism. They may have recurrent illusions and 'magical thinking' (that they are telepathic for example). Spitzer *et al.* (1979) suggest that the disorder may be a mild form of schizophrenia. It may be related by virtue of a genetic predisposition to schizophrenia.

(c) **The Narcisstic personality** has an extreme sense of self-importance, requires constant attention from others, fantasises about great successes and exaggerates modest ones, and is likely to exploit others.

(d) **The Paranoid personality** is suspicious of people, expects to be mistreated and assumes others are discussing him or her. They are argumentative, overly sensitive and tend to blame others even when at fault themselves. Their extreme jealousy, especially of sexual partners, makes it difficult to maintain close relationships.

## Category 8    Learning Difficulties or Retardation

*Introduction*

It was extremely difficult to find a title for this section without causing offence to someone. Terminology for mental handicap tends to change periodically as stigma becomes attached to current terms. Historically, those who were judged to be below normal were classified as either 'idiots' or 'imbeciles', often with scant attention to testing for real potential. When these terms became unacceptable to society, the terms 'subnormal' and 'severely subnormal' were substituted. These, too, became unacceptable, and the term 'mentally handicapped' was used, which did not seem to imply the same stigma; recently there has been a move to use the term 'people with learning difficulties' or sometimes 'challenging behaviour'. How accurate these descriptive terms are of all forms of mental handicap, is debatable. What is needed is more acceptance, by the population at large, that humans are not all the same in their intellectual and functional capacities, otherwise the stigma will re-attach itself in time to whatever term is used.

Perhaps some parallels could be drawn here, from the field of physical handicaps. Is the term 'cerebral palsied' preferable to 'spastic'? You may think so, sufferers may not. The cerebral palsied Christopher Nolan (in 'Under the Eye of the Clock') refers to himself simply as a 'cripple'. An American professor once commented 'We have done terrible things to the American Indians, the least terrible of which is to call them American Indians!' He was commenting on the move to stop the usage of this terminology. The same seems to apply to the mentally handicapped. As they are all individuals, they may not wish to use the terminology chosen for them.

Mental handicap does not describe a total syndrome, it includes many types of problem. Some are genetically related, some biochemical, all can be made worse by poor social conditions or alleviated by good management. Some examples are given here, but there is not space to cover every category.

**Four levels of mental retardation** are categorised by both ICD 10 and DSM III R: **mild** mental retardation (IQ of 50 to 70), **moderate** mental retardation(IQ of 35 to 49), **severe** mental retardation (IQ of 20 to 34) and profound mental retardation (IQ below 20). The latter group often exhibit physiological malfunctions as well: childhood mortality rate is high in this category. (Readers are reminded of the discussion on controversies surrounding the use of IQ tests in Chapter 1.) The American Association on Mental Deficiency suggests that the criterion of IQ scores should only be applied after adaptive functioning is assessed. In other words, the way in which the individual adapts and functions in the real world is of greater importance than a scored IQ test.

In Great Britain all children have a right to education, whether retarded or not, until the age of 18. After that, there is no guarantee of training, employment or any further education, yet development is lifelong for all individuals, and necessarily protracted for retarded individuals. They may well be among those who would benefit from having no ceiling to educational age. It is not unknown for mentally handicapped adults to start to learn to read at the age of 30-plus. The following descriptions are subcategorised into what is currently believed to be the three main causes of mental retardation: genetic conditions, infectious diseases, and environmental hazards.

**Genetic Conditions**

(a)  **Down's Syndrome**. Probably the most easily recognisable and best known form of mental handicap, the syndrome covers a wide range of ability levels. Physically, individuals are recognisable by being short, usually stout, with a round face and heavy-lidded, usually slanting, eyes (this is why Down's syndrome people were called 'mongols' at one time – nothing to do with the inhabitants of Mongolia!). Some have a large tongue which may protrude, this also relates to an increased flow of saliva. Finger joints may well be shorter than most people's. Internally many Down's syndrome sufferers have respiratory and heart complaints, especially as they get older. Longevity is not expected; forty is about the maximum age.

Sufferers have a chromosome abnormality; most people have 46 chromosomes, 23 from each parent. Down's sufferers have 47, three of Chromosome 21 instead of two, hence the term **Trisomy 21**. In some, all the body cells are affected, in others, only some of the cells. It is difficult to ascertain whether this corresponds directly to the degree of impaired mental functioning, as Down's sufferers are extremely susceptible to influences in their social environment, and may also be limited by their own level of physical health. Nearly all have a good comprehension of speech, but production of speech varies, and is not assisted by a large tongue.

The cause of Down's Syndrome is still not fully established; statistically it seems to most commonly affect babies of older mothers (over 35 years of age). It was at one time suggested that the origins could be a virus infection of the maternal grandmother during her pregnancy; a woman's eggs remain in a suspended state of division from the fetal stage, until they begin to mature after puberty. Alternatively, an explanation could be that the longer the eggs are stored, the greater the chance of damage; this would explain why more Down's Syndrome babies are born to mothers over 35. In 1973 women over 35 had only 13 per cent of all pregnancies, but bore more than 50 per cent of the infants with trisomy 21. Men after puberty form new sperm cells daily yet research (**Magenis *et al.*, 1977**) indicated that in as many as 25 per cent of Down's Syndrome cases, the fathers' sperm carried the extra chromosome. And again, advanced parental age is implicated. Trisomy 21 can be detected in the early stages of pregnancy by sampling the cells of the amniotic fluid which surrounds the fetus. A new blood test has recently been devised, which will be much simpler and cheaper (and can therefore be offered to all pregnant women, not just those over 35). It obviates the slight risk of unintentional abortion, which is present with the amniocentesis test. If a Down's Syndrome baby is detected, in Great Britain the mother has the right to choose an abortion or not.

(b) **Phenylketonuria (PKU)**. PKU is a relatively rare disease (about one in 14,000 live births) although it is estimated that one person in seventy carries the recessive gene responsible. When a pair of defective recessive genes misdirect the formation of an enzyme, metabolic processes are disrupted. The infant, who is born with normal intellectual capabilities, suffers from a deficiency of the enzyme phenylalanine, and its derivative, phenylpyruvic acid, builds up in the body. Myelination of the axons in the nervous system is prevented and the brain is affected especially the neurons of the frontal lobes. Mental retardation is profound, while outward physical signs are not obvious. Fortunately this biochemical abnormality is detectable easily in the blood test given routinely to the baby a few days old. If the test is positive, the child can be given a special diet, until six or seven years of age, when brain formation is relatively complete. In this way, damage to the central nervous system is minimised.

*Infectious Diseases*

An infectious disease of the expectant mother can affect the fetus *in utero*; the first three months of fetal development is especially important to development of a healthy brain and nervous system. Diseases such as rubella (German measles), syphilis (a venereal disease, contracted through sexual intercourse with an infected person) and herpes simplex (the same virus which causes cold sores, but can cause more serious problems in other parts of the body), can all cause mental as well as physical abnormalities.

After birth, some infectious diseases in the young child can affect the child's developing brain, causing mental retardation; for example, meningitis (inflammation of the meninges, one of the layers of membranes covering and protecting the brain,) can cause mild or severe retardation or even death. This is likely to be less serious in the child over six years old, as the brain is largely developed by this age.

## Environmental Hazards

(A) IN THE UTERUS   In the pre-natal environment, the greatest hazard comes from substances ingested by the mother. For example:

(i)     **Alcohol,** particularly if ingested during the first three months of pregnancy, has been related to fetal alcohol syndrome (FAS). This is characterised by a small head, flat nose and deep upper lip, small stature and a degree of mental retardation, usually related to the amount of alcohol consumed.

(ii)    It has also been recently suggested that **smoking** affects the mental development of the fetus; presumably this has implications for passive smoking, and expectant fathers as well as expectant mothers are now urged to give up smoking.

(iii)   **Drugs** taken during pregnancy (prescribed or otherwise) are necessarily transmitted to the fetus; everyone knows of the horrendous physical after-effects of the drug thalidomide, administered to pregnant women for morning sickness. Not all drugs taken by women are recorded and related to mental abnormalities, but undoubtedly many could cause major or minor problems. Heroin, of course, produces babies who are already addicted.

(B) DURING EARLY CHILDHOOD   Damage to the developing brain and nervous system can have permanent effects. Causes may be due to:

(i) **Pollutants** in the environment, such as mercury, which can be transmitted through affected fish. Lead poisoning, through chewing or sucking items painted with a lead-based paint, or in the past, lead soldiers, can cause kidney and brain damage. Lead-based paint production is now prohibited, but the paint may still be in existence in old houses or on old furniture. Lead soldiers are now mainly collectors' items. Lead piping for water supplies is not used nowadays, but may still exist in old buildings.

(ii) **Accidents** involving head injuries to young children can cause permanent brain damage. Attempts to minimise this have been made by legislation for the wearing of seat belts, or use of child seats in cars. Falls or blows to the head can also produce brain damage.

(iii) **Birth injury**, either physical damage or anoxia (lack of oxygen) during the birth process can result in a degree of mental retardation. Prolonged labour can cause anoxia, as can the placenta or umbilical cord becoming damaged during or before the birth process. Vitamin K injections are routinely given to neonates, in order to minimise bleeding from tiny blood vessels in the brain (haemoraghic disease of the newborn), as this causes mental retardation. However, it has been suggested that these injections may be related to a rise in childhood cancers, and possibly Vitamin K by mouth would be an acceptable compromise.

**Category 9   Disorders of Psychological Development**

*Autism*

Many mentally handicapped children are readily identifiable on sight (e.g. Down's Syndrome) but most autistic children have no identifiably physical abnormalities. This led people to believe that autistic children were all of normal or even superior intelligence, especially as a few show exceptional abilities in a specific direction such as music, for example. These anomalies inaugurated the discussion over whether autism should be regarded as a form of mental retardation or mental illness. Recent research, however, suggest that 80 per cent of diagnosed autistic children score below

70 on IQ tests. However, the scoring pattern for these children is not uniformly low; some score average or above average on tests such as visual spatial tests and most score below average on items associated with language (DeMyer, 1975; Rutter and Lockyer, 1967). The validity of using IQ tests on autistic children has been questioned, as it is difficult to hold their attention long enough to indicate what is required of them. They are also unlikely to have had the same cultural or social experiences as other children.

Autism was originally described as a syndrome by **Kanner** in 1943, Where he described an 'extreme autistic aloneness', an inability to relate to other people, severe limitations of language and an obsessive desire that everything around them remain the same. In addition **Rutter** in 1966 noted ritualistic and compulsive activities. Autism begins before the age of two-and-a-half-years, affects four times more boys than girls (about 5 children in 10,000 are affected), and is distributed throughout all socio-economic, racial and ethnic groups. Those autistic children who learn to speak, seldom use speech effectively; the most common form used is **echolalic speech** – repeating back to someone what they have just said. Words are produced but without, apparently, much comprehension, and without the effect of communication, which to other children is the whole point of speech.

The **prognosis** for adult autistics is not encouraging; some can work in undemanding environments but most shut themselves in their own self-imposed prisons, living out a solitary life within their families or institutions.

Autism was not accepted into official categorisation until the publication of DSM III in 1980. Until then, autistic children had frequently been diagnosed as 'childhood schizophrenics', as their symptoms fitted with those of adult schizophrenics. However it is not that they have withdrawn from the world, like the schizophrenics, but have simply never entered it.

**Useful treatments** often include operant conditioning techniques and modelling (a description of these can be found in Chapter 6). The drug fenfluramine has been used to reduce serotonin levels, which may lessen some of the aloofness and stereotyped ritualised behaviours.

**Category 10   Childhood and Adolescent Disorders**

*Introduction*

This category comprises a seemingly unrelated group of disorders, mostly with unidentified causes. Their common factor is that they are all first observed during childhood.

(a)   **Tourette's Syndrome**. Named after the French physician who first described it, this syndrome involves not only a tic (an involuntary movement) but is often accompanied by spitting or shouting brief phrases or words, frequently rude or swear-words. The cause has not been positively identified, but tics may be exacerbated by stress and disappear during sleep. As the reader can imagine, it was some time before this syndrome was clinically recognised; very few cases are presented. A case study is described by Sacks (1985).

(b)   **Feeding Disorder**. Extremely common in childhood in its mildest form; the child exhibits faddiness and refuses food, mainly from the primary care-giver. Diagnosis of feeding disorder is only made if food refusal is beyond the normal range of behaviour or if the child loses or fails to gain weight over a trial period. There may be repeated regurgitation without nausea. This syndrome was identified and treated in a child as young as nine months (Lang and Melamed, 1969). (See Chapter 6, Section II and Figure 6.2.)

**Self-assessment Questions**

1.   (a) Describe some of the typical behaviours associated with schizophrenia.
     (b) Explain why these would not all be exhibited by all sufferers from schizophrenia.
2.   Describe one form of mental handicap.
3.   What are current views on mental handicap and how are these changing?
4.   What is the difference between Single Depressive Episodes and Recurrent Depressive Disorder?

## SECTION III    POSSIBLE CAUSES OF MENTAL DISORDERS

If a skier falls and breaks a leg, the doctor can identify the cause of the break: a fall while skiing. Prevention could be suggested, such as make sure you do not fall, or alternatively do not ski at all. Not all physical illnesses have such a direct, uncomplicated cause-and-effect pattern; causes of mental disorders are usually even less easily identifiable.

Discussed in three sub-sections below are three major areas of research relating to causes of mental disorder: genetic, environmental and neurochemical/neurological. These areas are not mutually exclusive, they interact and overlap. The possible causes of mental handicap or retardation were examined in Section II, Category 8, on Mental Handicap.

### Genetic

There may well be a **genetic predisposition** for some mental illnesses, as there is for some physical illnesses such as diabetes, but the disease may not be manifest until prompted by some precipitating event, such as a virus infection.

Likewise with mental disorders, for example a woman may have a genetic predisposition to depression, but a precipitating event such as the birth of a baby happens before the recognisable clinical syndrome of post-natal depression is manifest.

There may be links between genes and mental illnesses which have not yet been identified. It has been suggested that Alzheimer's Disease (a degenerative brain disease which was thought only to affect the elderly, but has now been identified in people in their forties) may well begin with a chromosomal abnormality.

**Twin studies** and **family studies** have shown that there seem to be strong genetic links in some types of mental disorder. A brief description of some of this research follows.

**Allen (1976)** looked at the incidence of depression among twins. In monozygotic twins (from one egg-cell) when one twin was diagnosed with depression, 40 per cent of their partners also suffered from depression, in other words there was a 40 per cent **concordance**. In dizygotic twins (from two egg-cells) the concordance dropped to 11 per cent, which is a considerable drop, indicating that where twins share identical genes (**monozygotic**) the concordance is much higher than where twins only share 50 per cent of their genes (**dizygotic**).

No exact chromosomal defect has as yet been identified as responsible for depression. Research was carried out among the Amish community in USA, who only marry within their own community and therefore present a restricted gene-pool. There **Egeland** *et al.* **(1987)** identified a genetic marker on chromosome 11 as being implicated in manic-depression.

However, other studies have identified various different chromosomes as being implicated in depression, so the true situation may not be 'a defective chromosome'. In fact there may be many types of depression, all of which may have different genetic origins, or some may have no genetic links.

In the same way it may be wrong to regard schizophrenia, for example, as one homogeneous disorder; it may be a group of disorders with separate origins.

**Gottesman and Shields (1982)** studied twins, where schizophrenia had been presented and found a 45 per cent concordance rate among monozygotic twins and 14 per cent concordance among dizygotic twins.

**Kety** *et al.* **(1968, 1975)** points out that the incidence of schizophrenia in the general population is 1 per cent (or 1 in 100), but if one or both parents are schizophrenic, 40 per cent of the offspring are also diagnosed as schizophrenic if living with one or more of the parents. However, this concordance rate drops dramatically to 3 per cent, according to Kety, if the offspring have been adopted. This would indicate a strong environmental influence mediating the genetic component.


### Environmental

As shown above, even when there seems to be a genetic predisposition to mental disorders, such as depression or schizophrenia, environmental influences appear to play a part. As a simple example, if genetics alone were involved in the transmission and exhibition of mental disorder; the monozygotic twin studies should show 100 per cent concordance. As this is not so, environmental or other influences must be intervening. Various environmental theories have been put forward to account for mental disorders; some are discussed below.

**Family Theory** was one of the earlier theories of the cause of schizophrenia. The family is said to treat one of its members in such a bizarre manner that he or she is forced into irrational thought processes and strange behaviours and becomes schizophrenic. At one time the mother was thought to play a major role and the term **'schizophrenogenic mother'** was coined to describe the mother who promoted this situation. However, although there may be disordered communications and double bind situations arising in some families with a schizophrenic member, research does not offer support for Family Theory. (An example of a double bind situation is where a mother may not show affection or want her child to hug her, yet accuses the child of not loving her if s/he does not show affection.)

The importance of the family's attitudes to a schizophrenic member are highlighted by **Brown's (1966)** study, which showed that family attitudes towards expressing support and emotion have a profound effect on whether a schizophrenic relapses and returns to hospital.

**Sociogenic Hypothesis** suggests that schizophrenia is prevalent in lower socio-economic groups. Hollingshead and Redlich (1958) carried out a ten-year study in Connecticut, USA, and found that schizophrenia rates were twice as high in the lowest socio-economic group as in the next group. Kohn (1968) reports that this is supported by studies in Denmark, Norway and England. Interpreted in causal terms, being in the lowest social class may in itself cause schizophrenia, due to simply being a member of this social class. One would urge caution in using this interpretation, there may be other factors, such as infections, eating and drinking habits, and even diagnostic problems as discussed in the last chapter, which may be clouding the issue. There is also the possibility that they may not have started in the lowest socio-economic group, but have drifted downwards as a result of their schizophrenia.

**Social Drift Theory** suggests that individuals who are schizophrenic are unable to sustain social status and drift downwards to the lowest socio-economic group. This theory can be examined by comparing the parents' occupations and socio-economic status with that of the schizophrenic. Goldberg and Morrison (1963) did this and found evidence of social drift, but Hollingshead and Redlich (1958) did not, and supported the Sociogenic Theory, as did Kohn and other researchers.

**Socio-Cultural Factors.** The influence of cultural factors may be indicated in societies where there is more than one sub-culture and where diagnostic processes and classification are the same for both. Crocetti, in a study in Yugoslavia, found that the incidence of schizophrenia in the Istrian peninsula was twice that of Croatia; each region is occupied by a separate sub-culture.

**Reactive Depression.** Some types of reactive depression may be thought to have a solely environmental cause, in that they are a reaction to an event in the individual's environment, for example, a death in the family. However, not everyone who loses a close family member suffers from clinical depression which goes beyond the bounds of the normal grief suffered by others. There must be extra factors involved in reactive depression, either genetic, biological or further environmental factors.

### Neurochemical and Neurological

Neurochemicals are biochemicals which are located in the brain (see Figure 5.3 for a brief description of Nervous Transmission). Neurotransmitters are chemicals held in the synapse which are released in order to make the next neuron in that circuit fire. This is the way information is passed on through the nervous system. If too much of a neurotransmitter is present (or too little of the enzyme which deactivates it) then the neuron will fire too frequently and misinformation will be passed on.

**The Dopamine Theory.** In some schizophrenics too much of the neurotransmitter dopamine is present; this may account for hallucinations and strange motor movements produced, for the dopamine circuit is involved in perception and motor control. Of course, excess dopamine production could be the result of schizophrenia, rather than the cause; research is not entirely conclusive as yet.

---

**FIGURE 5.3**

**The Brain and Nervous Transmission**

---

Q.  **How are messages passed around the body?**
A.  Messages are passed around the body via a series of **axons** (or nerves) which are linked to **neurons** (or nerve-cell bodies). Transmission of messages along axons both within the brain and the body is an **electrochemical process**; different molecules along the axons are positively and negatively charged. These 'change places' during stimulation and cause a ripple effect of electrical activity along the axon.

Q.  **What goes on in the brain?**
A.  The **brain** decodes the incoming messages, sent along incoming axons, decides what action is to be taken, and sends out messages along other axons, to **effectors** such as muscles. Some areas of the brain have been found to have specific functions, but the exact mode of functioning of the brain as a whole is still a mystery to us. This is essentially a simplified explanation; the interested reader is referred to a specialised text for further information (see end of chapter for further reading).

Q.  **Are neurons joined together by axons?**
A.  Not directly. There is a minute gap between the axon of one neuron and the **dendrites** (tentacle-like outgrowths of the neuron) of the next cell body. This gap is called the **synaptic cleft** and messages are passed across this by the chemical action of **neurotransmitters**.

Q.  **What is a neurotransmitter?**
A.  A chemical contained in a **synapse** (a bulb or button at the end of an axon) which is released on excitation, to take up its position on the receptor sites in the dendrites of the next neuron in the chain.
    The action of neurotransmitters can be either **excitatory** (stimulating) or **inhibitory** (damping). When neurotransmitters have transmitted their chemical message and stimulated the neuron to fire, or inhibited it from firing, they are **deactivated**, usually broken down by an **enzyme**, or taken up again into the system. Absence of adequate neurotransmitter substance means that the neuron will not be stimulated enough for the message to be passed on. Too much neurotransmitter means that the neuron will be over-stimulated. Absence of the enzyme means that the neurotransmitter will not be broken down and will continually stimulate the neuron. Some neurotransmitters you will encounter in this book are:

| | | |
|---|---|---|
| **Dopamine** | **Acetylcholine** | **Serotonin** |
| **Norepinephrine** | **GABA (gamma-amino butyric acid)** | |

---

Phenothiazine drugs block the action of dopamine, thereby lessening schizophrenic symptoms. However, Haracz (1982) found that this only applies to one sub-group of schizophrenics, suggesting that not all produce excess dopamine. This would serve to reinforce the view that schizophrenics are not all suffering from the same disorder.

**Mood Disorders**. Investigations have shown low levels of the neurotransmitters serotonin and norepinephrine seem to be implicated in depression. Drugs which have been found to alleviate depression are those which are known to raise the levels of serotonin and norepinephrine in the brains of animals. (See Chapter 6, Section I.)

**Neurological Findings**. Neurological investigations of the brains of schizophrenics, using CAT or PET scans, show that the ventricles are enlarged, suggesting deterioration or atrophy of brain tissue. Rieder *et al.* (1983) also found enlarged ventricles in the brains of other psychotic patients, besides schizophrenics.

### Summary

Genetic, social and neurological factors have all been indicated as possible causes of mental disorders. It appears from research so far that more than one factor, probably from more than one of these areas, may be responsible for any specific disorder. Even when events are found to correlate (for example, high dopamine levels and the occurrence of schizophrenia), it is still not possible to state with certainty which of these events is cause and which effect. More research will be necessary before scientists can say they have pinpointed the exact causes of most mental disorders.

### Self-assessment Questions

1. What evidence is offered from genetic studies as to the causes of mental disorders?
2. What part might a person's environment play in the course of mental disorder?
3. What are the findings of neurological and neurochemical research into mental disorders?

## FURTHER READING

C. Blakemore, *The Mind Machine* (London: BBC Books, 1988).

N. R. Carlson, *Foundations of Physiological Psychology* (Boston, Mass.: Allyn & Bacon, 1992).

G. Davison and J. Neale, *Abnormal Psychology* (New York: Wiley, 1990).

*Diagnostic and Statistical Manual*, 3rd edn, revised (The American Association of Psychiatrists, 1987).

*International Classification of Diseases*, 10th edn (The World Health Organisation, 1990).

I'M USING FLOODING THERAPY FOR HER
SPIDER PHOBIA.

# Treatments and Therapies

At the end of this chapter you should be able to:

1. Differentiate between various forms of treatment available for mental disorders;
2. Relate those treatments to the various models or approaches to psychology from which they are derived;
3. Discuss research that indicates which treatment may be beneficial for a specific form of mental disorder;
4. Discuss the concept of 'cure' in relation to mental disorders;
5. Evaluate different forms of accommodation available to patients and clients who are undergoing treatment for mental disorders.

## INTRODUCTION

There are five major areas into which treatments are divided; these relate to the theories or assumptions of the five main approaches to psychology, as briefly described in the models or paradigms discussed in Chapter 4. The **psychoanalytic model** utilises **insight therapies**, where clients are encouraged to examine their past in order to gain insight into their current problem (see Section III of this chapter). Many of the theorists who are referred to as **humanistic psychologists** may have started from a psychoanalytical perspective (for example, Rogers), but now believe that their therapies are best concentrated on the here-and-now situation, rather than looking to the client's past. **The medical model** suggests that **somatic** (physical) treatments are appropriate in order to put right physical maladjustment of the body. This would then automatically be followed by a commensurate adjustment by the mind; these treatments are described in Section I. The **learning theory model** forms the basis of treatments used by the behaviourists, who aim to right problem behaviours instilled through faulty learning, by learning appropriate behaviours. This is also the basic assumption from which treatments are derived which are applied by the **cognitive theorists**, who also aim to change the faulty thinking which they believe is the precursor of maladaptive behaviours. Methods of doing so vary according to their theoretical persuasion. These treatments also involve the client's active use of cognitive processes, such as reasoning, in order to change resultant behaviour. A few of these are discussed in Section III.

The latter part of this chapter looks at some studies of treatment effectiveness, and also the suitability of different forms of accommodation currently offered to people suffering from mental disorders.

## SECTION I   SOMATIC TREATMENTS

Somatic treatments are physical treatments designed to redress a balance in the individual's physical body (soma), in order that psychological functioning will be affected and normalised. This is based on the premise that there is a mind/body relationship (Clare, 1980) and that an imbalance or malfunction of the body, especially the brain, may be the cause or the result of mental disorder. This has already been discussed in Chapter 5 with regard to schizophrenia, for example; this section looks at somatic treatments for mental illnesses.

### Chemotherapy (Administration of Drugs)

There are five main groups of drugs used in psychiatry (see Figure 6.1). As with all drugs, care must be taken in their administration. Clinicians must be sure of the capabilities of a patient before sending them home with a bottle of tablets saying, 'Take one three times a day for two weeks, them come back and see me'. Many drugs are addictive, promoting psychological or physiological dependence and therefore must be used under close supervision for short periods of time only.

(a) **Minor Tranquillisers**. As the name suggests, these are used to reduce anxiety in patients who are not deeply disturbed. They are also used for patients who suffer depression where anxiety

**FIGURE 6.1**
Some Psychoactive Drugs

| Effect Group | Chemical Group and Examples | Neurochemical Affected | Effect on Mood or Behaviour |
|---|---|---|---|
| Minor tranquillisers | Benzodiazepines (e.g. Librium, Valium) | Enhance release of GABA (inhibitory) | Calming effect, reduces anxiety |
| Neuroleptics (antipsychotics) | Phenothiazines (e.g. chlorpromazine) butyrophenones (haloperidol) | Dopamine – drug occupies receptors | Reduces psychotic experiences and strange motor movements |
| Stimulants | Amphetamines (Dexadrine) | Blocks reuptake of dopamine and norepinephrine | Increase alertness and feelings of confidence |
| Antidepressants | (1) Tricyclics | (1) Blocks breakdown of norepinephrine and serotonin | Produces lifted mood, feelings of euphoria, blocks REM sleep |
|  | (2) Monoamine oxidase inhibitors | (2) Blocks action of enzyme MAO, thus enhancing action of norepinephrine and serotonin |  |
| Antibipolar disorder | Inorganic salts (lithium carbonate) |  | Sedative effect, maintains emotional balance |

is also a feature (mainly reactive or exogenous depression, those classified as suffering from Single Depressive Episode syndrome, as described in Chapter 5). These drugs are usually prescribed by general practitioners, and began to be widely used in the 1950s to replace barbiturates, which had been found to be addictive. However it was later discovered that the minor tranquillisers also produced psychological and physiological dependence; therefore they are now prescribed less frequently and monitored more carefully than in the 1960s. Many people who take **benzodiazepines** complain of drowsiness and lethargy; for this reason and also because of the problem of addiction, long-term usage is not recommended. Noyes *et al.* (1984), found that these drugs produce greater improvement in patients with panic disorders or anxious depression, than patients given a **placebo**. (A placebo is a form of treatment which, unknown to the patient, is not expected to have any effect upon the problem. This is a truer method of comparison than non-treatment of the control group, who would not be expecting to get any better without treatment – as previously shown, expectation is a powerful force in humans. In chemotherapy the placebo would be a pill or capsule with no active chemical constituents. Of course, one should question the ethics of treatment by placebo; all patients should expect to receive the optimum available treatment for their problem.)

(b) **Major Tranquillisers** (also called neuroleptics, or antipsychotic drugs) are used mainly to reduce extreme anxiety in acute psychotic episodes. These drugs are also used for schizophrenics as in addition they appear to reduce the level of delusions and hallucinations as well as anxiety. This was discovered initially by accident; a French surgeon, Laborit, in the 1950s, noted that the drug he gave his patients to reduce surgical shock also made them less anxious about their impending operations. The drug was refined to enhance its anxiety-reducing properties and shortly afterwards Charpentier produced a new **phenothiazine** derivative, called **chlorpromazine**, which proved very effective in calming schizophenics. It appears to block impulse transmission in the dopaminergic pathways to the brain (see Figure 6.1).

A study of various treatments available to schizophrenics, carried out by **May (1968)** found (a) phenothiazines or (b) phenothiazines plus psychotherapy, to be the two equally most effective therapies available, rather than (c) ECT (discussed later), (d) psychotherapy alone or (e) Milieu therapy (a therapy based on the idea of a therapeutic community where patients are kept busy for 85 per cent of their waking hours, given responsibilities and expected to participate in community decisions). The same pattern of results was found in a five-year follow-up (May, 1976).

Phenothiazines cannot be regarded as a cure for schizophrenia; patients need to be kept on a maintenance dose in order to prevent relapses. **Vaughn and Leff (1976)** showed that schizophrenics discharged without drugs were much more likely to relapse and needed to return to hospitalisation. Side-effects of phenothiazines can be unpleasant, ranging from dryness of the mouth and blurred vision, to tremors closely resembling Parkinson's disease (an organic disease linked with inadequate dopamine in the brain). These motor effects stem from dysfunction of the nerve tracts descending from the brain to spinal motor neurons.

(c) **Stimulants. Amphetamine** and **Piperidyl** derivatives are currently prescribed for hyperactive children; this may sound strange, giving stimulants to children who are already hyperactive! However, the drug seems to give direction to the activity by increasing concentration. Optimum performance seems to occur when combined with behaviour therapy (Gittleman-Klein *et al.*, 1976).

Side-effects include changes in appearance (for example sunken cheeks, dark circles under the eyes (Mattes and Gittleman, 1983) and in large doses may even interfere with learning and performance on cognitive tasks (Sprague and Sleator, 1977.) The drugs may be prescribed in the short term to conteract lethargy, increase alertness and confidence; they are of course open to abuse.

(d) **Antidepressants.** The **tricyclics** and **MAO** (monoamine oxidase) **inhibitors** are sub-categories of antidepressants which produce therapeutic effects by facilitating neural transmission. The tricyclic drugs were found to be more effective in relieving endogenous depression (Stern *et al.*, 1980). Klerman (1975) found MAO inhibitors to be less effective than tricyclics in relieving depression, but they are still prescribed for patients who do not respond to tricyclics. Care needs to be taken as side-effects of MAO inhibitors can be severe; toxicity can cause damage to liver, brain and cardiovascular system; they also interact with other drugs and foods high in tyramine (for example broad beans, cheese, chicken liver, yeast extracts) and can cause death.

Both MAO inhibitors and tricyclics have been used success-fully to treat obsessive-compulsive disorder (Insell *et al.*, 1983), bulimia (Walsh *et al.*, 1984) and panic attacks (Zitrin *et al.*, 1983).

(e) **Anti-Bipolar Disorder.**   As discussed previously, the difficulty in treating manic depressive patients arises because over-treatment of either phase can 'tip' the patient's balance into the other phase, or pole. Treatment with **lithium carbonate**, (inorganic salts) seems to iron out the problem of these bipolar swings, although Shopsin *et al.* (1975) found no difference in effectiveness between neuroleptics and lithium carbonate. However, lithium carbonate also acts as a proplylactic – it forestalls subsequent episodes of mania or depression (Prien *et al.*, 1984).

The drug requires the careful monitoring of blood levels, as an overdose can prove fatal.

**Psychosurgery**

Pioneered by Moniz, in the late 1930s, early psychosurgery was a crude affair. Incisions were made either through the side of the skull or through the orbital region (eye socket) into the **frontal lobes**, where rotation of surgical instruments destroyed a considerable amount of brain tissue. The rationale was that the frontal lobes controlled the thought processes and emotional expression, there-fore if the tracts connecting these to the thalamus and hypothala-mus (sub-cortical brain structures) were severed, irrational, emotional thoughts and behaviours would be lessened.

Exaggerated claims of success for the treatment of schizophrenia, depression, personality and anxiety disorders were made, which were not borne out by later studies of outcome. **Robbin (1958, 1959)** found that lobotomy produced a slightly higher discharge rate, but these patients were later re-admitted. **Barahal (1958)** did five to ten-year follow-up studies on lobotomy patients and found that most suffered undesirable side-effects: listlessness, stupor, seizures and even death.

Adverse publicity and the advent of use of phenothiazines in the 1950s lowered the rate of lobotomies performed. Currently, surgical techniques are precise and refined, so that very small areas of brain tissue are destroyed. Patients are selected carefully, when other treatments have been ineffective for their severe, long-lasting problems. Higher rates of success have been shown with obsessive compulsive disorder, severe depression and anxiety; the technique is rarely if ever used for schizophrenia.

### Electroconvulsive Therapy (ECT)

The introduction of ECT replaced insulin therapy – a treatment whereby non-diabetics were injected with insulin to produce coma, and then 'brought round' with intravenous dextrose – Sakel (1938) reported that patients thus treated were less confused and the treatment reduced psychotic symptoms. About the same time, it was observed (mistakenly) that schizophrenia patients did not suffer from epilepsy, therefore if they could be given epileptic seizures, it might 'cure' their schizophrenia. **Cerletti** first used the technique in 1938, in Rome, of administering an electric current to the skull to induce a grand mal seizure to a schizophrenic patient. Nowadays patients are given a sedative and muscle relaxant, which lessens the possibility of broken bones during seizures.

A course of six to ten treatments is spread over 3 to 4 weeks. Often patients show an improvement after only one or two treatments. Currently, **unilateral ECT** is used, inducing seizure in only one brain hemisphere; this has the effect of causing less confusion and memory loss to the patient, than previously experienced in bilateral ECT, but has been shown to be equally therapeutic (Inglis, 1969; Abrams, 1975).

ECT is now used primarily for profoundly depressed patients, who have failed to respond to drug treatment, especially if there is any threat or risk of suicide. It appears to be extremely successful in a number of cases, although the way in which it works is not understood; it does not prevent future episodes of depression. It is not used for schizophrenia as chemotherapy is usually more effective.

**Evaluation**

Somatic treatments aim to alter abnormal functioning by intervening directly in the body's processes. Drugs act at the biochemical level, usually by action at the synapse, either reducing or enhancing the action of the neurotransmitter. Psychosurgery changes behaviour by severing brain tissue and physically lessening transmission routes, although whether these changes are for the better or worse, is a point for discussion. The action of ECT, causing brain seizures to reduce depression is not understood, but may possibly cause a temporary change in neurochemical levels.

Chemotherapy is by far the most popular treatment and that which is always tried first. ECT is used selectively and only after drug treatment has been shown to be ineffective; criticisms of this treatment include the problems of side-effects, such as confusion and memory-loss, and the argument that we do not know how ECT works, or even (some might argue) if it does work at all; perhaps patients' abnormal behaviours are simply 'damped down' by the trauma of the treatment. Ethical questions have been raised as to whether it is permissible to give patients electric shocks, given that it is not known for certain how or even if the treatment provides a 'cure'. Objections have been raised on these grounds by MIND (the National Association for Mental Health) and PROMPT (Protect the Rights of Mental Patients) and similar organisations in the United States. Protagonists (e.g. Klerman, 1972, 1988) maintain that it is the most effective treatment for depression and should therefore be continued. The alternative of chemotherapy may provide after-effects which are just as unpleasant. Psychosurgery is practised rarely, because of the uncertainty of success or side-effects in individual cases and because of the irreversibility of the procedure. Patients are within their right to refuse any form of treatment with which they do not agree and ask that an alternative form of treatment be made available. Whether they always understand their rights, given that they are in a disturbed frame of mind, is another matter. The psychiatrist may regard alternative treatments requested to be inappropriate; if that treatment is refused, is the clinician then in the wrong for refusing treatment? The areas of *consent* and *ethics* need careful clarification if the best interests of the patient are to be served.

**Self-assessment Questions**

1. What are somatic treatments?
2. What are the major categories of drugs used in psychiatry?
3. What are the problems of using somatic treatments?

## SECTION II   BEHAVIOURAL THERAPIES

These are based largely on the theories of **operant** or **classical conditioning** described in Chapter 4. The premise is that all behaviour is learned; faulty learning is the cause of abnormal behaviour, therefore the individual has to learn the correct or acceptable behaviour. The first part of this section deals with therapies based on classical conditioning (where involuntary associations and responses are made by the individual); these are usually referred to as behaviour therapies. Those based on operant conditioning (described in the latter part of this section) are called behaviour modification or sometimes operant conditioning techniques, in order to distinguish them from techniques based on classical conditioning (Walker, 1984). Behaviour modification involves the use of voluntary responses.

### Behaviour Therapy, Based on Classical Conditioning

This theory suggests that a response is learned and repeated through contiguous association (a chance association in time or place). Pavlov's dogs salivated when a buzzer sounded, because initially the buzzer had sounded when their food was presented. Why do you like a particular name? Is it because the first time you heard it, it was paired with a person you liked? Classical conditioning suggests that a great deal of human learning occurs in this way, not all of it quite so innocuous as this example.

Treatments which aim to replace a disadvantageous response pattern with a more appropriate response include: systematic desensitisation, implosion, flooding, aversion therapy, covert sensitisation. These are described below.

(a) **Systematic Desensitisation**.   Patients are taught to relax and then shown pictures of their feared object or problem, to desensitise them, or reduce their unfavourable response patterns. These stimuli systematically commence with less-threatening and proceed to more-threatening representations of the real object. Phobias are often treated successfully in this way. Exposure to the feared object or situation (rather than avoidance, which is usually practised by phobics) shows the patient that there is no real reason for their anxiety. Between therapy sessions they are given 'homework' and asked to put themselves into what are to them progressively threatening situations. Paul (1966) found systematic desensitisation more effective for phobics than insight therapy or attention plus a placebo pill.

(b) **Aversion Therapy** is used mainly for addictions or unwanted behaviours. The aim is to attach negative feelings to stimuli which are considered inappropriately attractive. For example, if an emetic is paired with alcohol, the next alcoholic drink becomes less attractive. Electric shocks have been used as the 'pairing' but the ethical questions posed by these discourage their use (see Figure 6.2). The effects of aversion therapy may be short-lived and, when used, it is often accompanied by other positive techniques.

   **Covert sensitisation** is similar to aversion therapy but clients are asked to **imagine** their attractive stimuli and accompanying negative states, such as electric shocks or vomiting. This obviates the ethical question of unpleasant stimulus pairings.

(c) **Implosion Therapy and Flooding**.   Used mainly for the treatment of phobias, the essence of both these therapies is to expose the client at the outset to a most fearful situation. The premise is 'fighting fear with fear'. Once the client has been exposed to the most horrific situation they can possibly imagine, the object or situation is feared no longer. The therapist encourages the high arousal levels of the situation for up to an hour at a time.

   In **implosion therapy** the therapist also elaborates the situation by constructing stories and outrageous scenarios, as, when linked to psychodynamic theory, it is seen to represent repressed sexual or aggressive id impulses. For example, the spider phobic may be asked to imagine a giant spider who devours their eyes, crawls into the eye sockets and eats its way into the brain! Implosion therapy takes place in the client's imagination, whereas **flooding** takes place *in vivo* (a real-life situation). For example, Wolpe (1958) took a patient with a fear of cars for a four-hour car journey. The girl became hysterical as her anxiety levels rose, but eventually became calm and by the end of the journey her fears had disappeared. Extinction of the client's fear responses occur because the usual route of escape or avoidance is blocked by the therapist.

Other therapists (e.g. Emmelkamp and Wessels, 1975) found flooding to be more effective than implosion.

### Evaluation

Systematic desensitisation seems a relatively benign techique; it is difficult to realise that flooding, implosion and aversion therapy stem from the same theoretical position. There are serious questions about the ethics of using these strenuous methods, especially if they are no more effective than less traumatic methods. Supporters of flooding and implosion therapy claim its effectiveness (Marks, 1981; Barratt, 1969). It is quick and therefore less costly for the client than other protracted therapies. However, the cost to the client may not only be in monetary terms, and some therapists suggest these should be used only when other means fail.

---

### FIGURE 6.2

**Aversion Therapy to Save a Life**

---

Lang and Melamed (1969) reported the case of a nine-month-old baby, who exhibited **vomiting** and **chronic rumination** (regurgitating food and rechewing it). Tests had been run and no physiological problem was revealed. The child was suffering from malnutrition and was being fed by tube directly into the stomach.

Aversion therapy treatment consisted of one-second shocks delivered to the baby's calf, each time he showed signs of vomiting. The baby quickly learned that the way to avoid shocks was by not vomiting. After just two sessions shock was rarely required.

Throughout three weeks of observation and treatment the child steadily gained weight and was able to be discharged from hospital. Five months later he was regarded as completely normal, both physically and psychologically. Aversion therapy had undoubtedly saved his life, although the ethical question of cure through pain remains.

---

Aversion therapy is not often used nowadays for alcohol-related problems, as pairings have to be repeated in order to be effective, and other methods are more successful. There are ethical controversies about whether therapists should hurt people with electric shocks, even when those people have requested that treatment; they may be requesting punishment rather than treatment. At one time this treatment was used for homosexuals, pairing electric shocks with photographs of attractive men. The effectiveness of this treatment was never satisfactorily proven and the practice has now ceased for ethical reasons. Some investigations have failed to show any superiority of aversion therapy over placebo treatment (Diament and Wilson, 1975).

### Behavioural Therapies, Based on Operant Conditioning

(a) **Behaviour modification** is based the premise that actions which are rewarded (or reinforced) are more likely to be repeated. Actions or behaviours involved are **voluntary** behaviours, because the **reinforcement** is recognised by the individual as relating to that action over which they have control. Behaviour modification aims to instil appropriate behaviour through the reinforcement of desired or more acceptable actions. This is best achieved in situations where the therapist is in control, as reinforcement must be consistent and unwavering (**Wilson and O'Leary, 1980**).

A range of childhood problems are dealt with by operant techniques, for example bedwetting, thumb sucking, hyperactivity, poor school performance, extreme social withdrawal. Children are under the control of adults, and therefore susceptible to operant conditioning. It generally produces better rates of improvement than other therapies. (**Franks, 1984; Ross, 1981**). This technique has also been extended, with success, to autistic and mentally retarded children, to improve social skills (Williams *et al.*, 1975), and table manners (Plummer *et al.*, 1977). Lovaas (1973) found that gains achieved in therapy with autistic children were only maintained when their parents continued to reinforce the behaviour.

Reinforcers include praise, attention and some tangible rewards such as special food, sweets or toys. These are **primary reinforcers**, which the child has instant access to, and can use immediately. Non-reinforcers include ignoring the child when inappropriate behaviours are displayed. (Getting cross with the child, shouting or smacking involve giving the child attention and could therefore be construed as reinforcement of undesirable behaviours.)

A fictitious example of how the programme might be used is contained in Figure 6.3.

---

## FIGURE 6.3

**Behaviour Modification Programme (Based on Operant Conditioning)**

---

Jenny is a teenage hostel resident with learning difficulties. She is not yet able to feed herself at meal times and staff have devised a reinforcement programme to encourage Jenny to eat with a spoon. The reinforcement they decided upon was red currant jelly, as Jenny is very fond of this. Each time Jenny performs the correct steps in her programme, she is reinforced with a small teaspoonful of jelly. Tasks must be broken down into a sequence of steps.

**Task Breakdown**

1. Picks up spoon, right way up.
2. Scoops food from dish on to spoon.
3. Raises spoon to mouth.
4. Tips food into mouth.
5. Returns empty spoon to dish.
6. Retains grip on spoon.
7. Repeats above sequence till food is eaten.

NOW can you devise a task breakdown to teach Jenny to clean her teeth? Of course, red currant jelly would not be appropriate reinforcement in this situation, but Jenny does enjoy catching sight of herself in the mirror.

---

(b)   **Token Economy**.   A natural progression from operant conditioning, uses the idea of **secondary reinforcement**, where the rewards are not to be used instantly, but take the form of tokens which have to be saved and exchanged later for a reward of the individual's choice. One method used is to give the individual tokens as desirable behaviours occur. These can be saved and exchanged for whatever the person wants; in hospitals, they are exchangeable at the hospital shop for sweets, cigarettes, or other items; on the ward they may be exchanged for special privileges such as extra TV viewing time. This technique is generally used with adults, or older children, who can make the association between the immediate, non-usable reinforcer and the later reinforcement.

**Paul and Lentz (1977)** compared three hospital wards of long-term institutionalised patients. One ward used token economy; one used Milieu therapy (where residents are kept busy 85 per cent of their waking hours, and expected to contribute to the common good of their 'community'); the third ward used routine hospital management. Patients were checked monthly over four and a half years of hospitalisation and 18 months follow-up. Both token economy and Milieu therapy groups reduced symptomatic behaviour more than the routine group. More token economy patients were discharged to community placements, and were better at remaining in their placements than members of the other two groups. However, other social learning methods were used in conjunction with tokens, which were regarded as an excellent method of gaining the severely regressed patients' attention.

Problems of both token economy systems and behaviour modification are similar. Firstly, reinforcement must be kept the same by all people who have dealings with the individual, and secondly, the behaviours may not be generalised to the 'real world' situation. The latter of course is a criticism of most types of therapy. Behaviour modification seems to cope with this better than most, as indicated by the Paul and Lentz study quoted above. A third problem suggested by insight theorists, is that the problem underlying the abnormal behaviours has not been resolved, even when the overt behaviour has been changed; consequently other abnormal behaviours may arise in their place; this is called **symptom substitution**. Reinforcers must always be appropriate to each individual; these must be carefully chosen, as what is reinforcement to one person may be anathema to another.

(c) **Biofeedback**   This technique utilises the theoretical bases of both classical and operant conditioning.

Patients are trained to control bodily processes such as heart rate and blood pressure, which are normally under autonomic control rather than voluntary control. Patients are connected to a machine which gives a continuous reading of heart rate and blood pressure, and asked to consciously try to reduce one or both. When the readout falls to a given target level, a bell or tone sounds. The patient aims to maintain that level. The reinforcement for hypertensive patients, in doing this, is the knowledge that they are helping to improve their own health. Initial results were encouraging, but biofeedback has not been established as a standard treatment for raised blood pressure (Shapiro and Surwit, 1979). Blanchard *et al.* (1979) believes that relaxation training is more effective. Added to which, it might be necessary for individuals to change their life-styles, in order to effectively lower blood pressure in the 'real-world' situation, rather than use biofeedback and assume that a 'cure' has been effective.

Various forms of epilepsy have been treated by biofeedback: patients are trained to increase cortical activity in the sensori motor cortex. However, improvement was not sustained when training sessions lapsed (Sterman, 1973).

Neuromuscular disorders, such as cerebral palsy, paralysis following stroke or poliomyelitis, have been treated by biofeedback (Basmajian, 1977). Patients are informed by biofeedback of the firing of single muscle cells, and trained to reactivate these. Neural pathways which are disordered are normally under voluntary control and should therefore be ideal for retraining by biofeedback techniques. In damaged tissue, signs of muscle movement are faint and need amplification; this therefore acts both as a reinforcement and as a prompt for further effort.

**Modelling**

This is based on experimental work in social learning (see Chapter 2, Section III), such as that of **Bandura (1965)** and has been very effective in a clinical setting (Bandura *et al.*, 1969). The technique involves allowing phobics to watch both filmed and live models dealing with their phobic object. This results in a reduction in anxiety displayed by the phobics when they came face-to-face with their feared object. A new approach to health psychology, pioneered by Melamed *et al.* (1975), utilises modelling to reduce children's fears of dental work or surgery.

**Lazarus (1971)** used **therapist-demonstration** to enable clients to rehearse difficult interpersonal behaviours; the therapist demonstrates for the client how to handle a difficult situation, which the client then practises in the therapy session. This approach is now frequently used in many areas of counselling and the technique is used with success in assertiveness training.

## Evaluation

The focus of behaviour therapies is on the 'here and now'. Overt behaviours are taken to be indicative of the patient's problem and these are to be corrected by therapy. Behaviour therapies are criticised on the grounds that they only change overt behaviour and do not root out underlying causes. Therefore the patient's problem may still exist, and symptom substitution may occur (another maladaptive behaviour may be substituted). Biofeedback has its applications in behavioural medicine, but its usefulness and applications are more limited than were originally thought. Again, biofeedback could be 'curing' the overt behaviour but not the underlying cause.

In a hospital situation, it has been suggested that improved interaction with staff, due to the introduction of behavioural programmes, is the real reinforcer that has brought about improvement in behaviour patterns (Fonagy and Higgitt, 1984).

Behaviour therapies have been criticised on ethical grounds, in that they aim to remove unacceptable behaviours and substitute acceptable behaviours; decisions on acceptability rest with the therapist. Do therapists have the right to make decisions which have effect on other people's lives? In the real-world situation, the therapist should discuss with adult patients what their goals are and work towards those; in the case of a child, consultation would be with the child and the parent or guardian.

## Self-Assessment Questions

1. Describe the theoretical bases of behaviour therapies.
2. Describe a technique based on classical conditioning.
3. Describe a technique based on operant conditioning.
4. What criticisms have been levelled at behaviour therapies?

## SECTION III   COGNITIVE-BEHAVIOURAL THERAPIES

Martin Seligman (1974) put forward his theory of **learned helplessness** as an explanation for depression. If an animal is given electric shocks from which it cannot escape, no matter which area of its environment it runs to, then that animal will lie down and passively accept the shocks. Learned helplessness theory views the depressed adult as having learned the helplessness of their own situation; depressed people often express negative views of themselves, the world around them and the future. Cognitive restructuring theorists aim not only to change the behaviour of clients, but to change the negative outlook which the client has learned over time. They assist clients to change their perceptions, to use reasoning and through changed thought-processes to alter their resultant behaviours. Descriptions of some of the main types of therapies follow.

(a) **Beck's Cognitive-Behaviour Therapy**.   Beck holds that mental disorders, particularly depression, are caused by the client's negative thought patterns which have been learned over years, possible due initially to early failures or negative events in life, such as death of a close relative. Over-generalisation takes place, and everything is seen as a 'failure'. Beck's therapy aims to change both cognitive and behavioural levels. Tasks are broken down into small steps, so that the client can see they are achieving something positive. Therapist and client work together to uncover what Beck calls **'automatic thoughts'** – for example, a boy tells his father he failed his exam or did not make the football team; unbidden, the father thinks, 'What a lousy father I am'. The therapist helps to restructure the idea that the father is responsible for his son's failures – does it really make him a bad father? What other proof can he offer that he is a bad father? Rush *et al.* (1977) compared two groups of depressed patients, one group given psychoactive drugs used for depression, the other twenty sessions of Beck's therapy. After the 12 week period of treatment, 79 per cent of the cognitive therapy group were much improved compared to 20 per cent of the drug group. They were also less depressed at follow-up.

(b) **Rational Emotive Therapy**.   Albert Ellis believes that people cause themselves emotional turmoil by repeating internalised sentences to themselves; a depressed person may continually internalise 'How worthless I am!' Ellis suggests that the therapist should concentrate on uncovering and restructuring those sentences, rather than looking at historical causes or overt behaviour, as self-statements can mediate emotional arousal. Clients are persuaded to substitute an internal dialogue to ease their problems, thus viewing their relationship to the world in a more rational light. The views of Beck and Ellis may seem somewhat similar, but their techniques differ in several ways. Beck requires co-operative interaction between client and therapist, to uncover the problem; Ellis believes that forceful interventions may be necessary to disrupt well-learned maladaptive patterns, and will use confrontational methods early in therapy. Where Beck would enquire what made his client think he was a bad father, Ellis would say, 'So what if you are a bad father? Is it logical to be depressed about it? You do not have to be competent at everything. You have other areas of competence.' Ellis has no conpunction about calling his client's thoughts '**irrational**' and is more directive than Beck.

(c) **Personal Construct Therapy.**  Based on Kelly's Personal Construct Theory (1955) (described in Chapter 2), the therapy aims to uncover the client's way of construing (interpreting) the world, and to change any false notions, in order to asist the client in 'functioning' more effectively (Fransella, 1984). Again, there is an interactive relationship between client and therapist. Kelly's Repertory Grid (see Figure 2.6) is used to measure the client's construct system and to monitor the therapeutic process. Kelly's therapy differs in many respects from that of Beck or Ellis, but still aims to uncover the client's cognitive processes which give a personal construct on the world, and may serve to explain and change resultant behaviours.

**Evaluation**

The cognitive-behaviour therapies, while not exploring the client's past, examine covert behaviour and internalised thoughts and aims to change those to rational, self-accepting statements. In doing so, the resultant behaviours will change too, and the client's problems will be resolved.

While the techniques of cognitive-behavioural therapists are similar to those of the behaviourists, they pay attention to what their clients perceive the world to be; situations are not regarded as uniform for everyone, so in that way the cognitive-behaviourists are approaching the platform of the humanists. However as Wessler (1986) states, cognitive restructuring (attempts to change people's cognitions) is only a means to an end, that end being permanent changes in emotions and behaviour.

Cognitive therapies have been criticised on **ethical** grounds; the client's problem behaviours or thoughts are being changed to those which the therapist sees as acceptable; who is to say that they are correct?

**Self-assessment Questions**

1.  How do cognitive-behavioural therapies differ from behaviour therapies?
2.  Describe an example of a cognitive restructuring therapy.
3.  Discuss criticisms which might be levelled at cognitive-behavioural therapies.

## SECTION IV   PSYCHOANALYTIC THERAPIES

These are based on Freud's psychoanalytic theory (see Chapter 3). Conflicts between the id and ego result in **anxiety**, which the individual tries to resolve by using **defence mechanisms** such as repression (pushing unwanted thoughts or memories back into the unconscious mind), regression (going back to an earlier stage in one's life), projection (projecting inadmissible feeling on to others). The unconscious mind being the keeper of the individual's secret fears and wishes, the therapist aims to uncover these and bring them forward into the conscious mind. This must be done non-directively, or the therapist could be suggesting his or her own wishes, which would then be used by the client, instead of drawing on the contents of the unconscious. The aim is to provide the client with **insight** into problems, to gain self-knowledge and under-standing.

There are many variations and therapies based on Freud's theory; here we shall look at just a few.

**Psychoanalytic Therapy**

As discussed in Chapter 3, the purpose of psychoanalysis is to uncover problems, fears and motivations which have been forced into the **unconscious mind**. When these are consciously recognised they can be dealt with by the client. Freud believed that all psychological problems are rooted in the unconscious. In **classical psychoanalysis** the patient lies on a couch, with the therapist sitting out of sight so that the therapist remains anonymous and does not inhibit communication. In this way, the client will not be intimidated or influenced at all by the therapist, even by his or her body language, and relaxation (encouraged by lying on the couch) promotes a free flow of ideas, thoughts and feelings from the client. The client is free to talk about whatever comes to mind, no matter how disjointed or irrelevant it seems. This process is called **free association**. Gradually the client's associations will lead to uncovering of unconscious material. The client may occasionally encounter 'blocks', where he or she will stop talking, or change direction, or even get off the couch and walk over to the window. These 'blocks', Freud said, are important, they may indicate **resistances** – a point of repression.

**Dreams** are regarded as important to analysis, as Freud assumed that during sleep the ego defences are lowered, allowing repressed wants and desires to come forward. They may also represent **wish-fulfillment**, not directly expressing what the individual desires, but disguised in symbolic form within the dream. This is why analysis has to be undertaken by a trained professional.

At some time during therapy sessions, **transference** occurs, when the client transfers emotions on to the therapist which were held previously for important others in the client's life. This transference is used in **interpretation**, explaining to the client what he or she has revealed, but specific advice on what to do next is not given; the person is encouraged to find his or her own solution. Drake and Sederer (1986) suggest that intensive, intrusive therapies such as psychoanalysis can have a negative effect on schizophrenics, necessitating longer periods of hospitalisation. They suggest this may be due to emotional overstimulation, which would concur with the findings of studies of schizophrenics from highly emotional families, discussed in the Chapter 5.

**Ego Analysis**. Theorists such as Karen Horney, Anna Freud and Erik Erikson emphasise the strength of the ego in the individual (as well as the id) and suggest that ego strength is why people take such an active role in trying to control their environment. Therapists seek to assist their clients in recognising their ego functions (a set of conscious aims and capabilities, which can control both the id and the environment) and to select the optimum ways of changing themselves in order to interact with their environment to their best advantage.

**Play Therapy** is the application of psychoanalytic therapy to children, who cannot – or will not – verbalise their problems. The child acts out problems in a **safe environment**, the playroom, while the therapist observes, never criticising or stopping the child from any form of play, however bizzare it may seem. From these observations, the therapist deduces what is the root of the child's problems.

Apart from this analytical process, the child has the opportunity to work through problems, to wreak vengeance on a doll, rather than a sibling or parent, to explore, seek solace and resolve emotional difficulties for him or herself. Opportunities are given for the child to **regress** to earlier developmental stages and work through childhood experiences again, to a more satisfactory conclusion.

One version of play therapy is admirably described by Axline, in her book *Dibs: in Search of Self* (1964).

**Evaluation**

The basic assumption of all psychoanalytical therapies is that the clients are not aware of what motivates their actions; it is rooted in the unconscious. Childhood fears and repressions are explored so that they may be rationalised by the adult ego-state; an understanding of the root of the problem is the start of the cure. There are problems of validation associated with psychoanalytical theory, as discussed in Chapter 3. There are further problems associated with evaluating insight therapies. How can internal id–ego conflicts be measured accurately? Who measures improvement – the client, by self report, or the therapist, by other methods? (For a fuller discussion for this, see Section VI of this chapter.)

**Self-Assessment Questions**

1. What are the fundamental principles and beliefs in psycho-analytic therapy?
2. How does ego-analysis differ from classical psychoanalysis?
3. What are some criticisms of psychoanalytic therapies?

## SECTION V  HUMANISTIC AND EXISTENTIAL THERAPIES

These are a loosely-banded group of therapies with features in common; they are insight-oriented, like psychoanalytic therapies, believing that problems can best be dealt with by increasing the individual's awareness of needs and motivations. However, there is a far greater belief in the individual's freedom of choice; clients are assisted to find their own choice of action and the courage to use it. While the past may be acknowledged, therapies are rooted in the present. Humanists also believe in the uniqueness of the individual, that no two cases can ever be identical, because everyone has their own unique combination of circumstances, characteristics and experiences; this is called phenomenology.

(a) **Rogers's Client-centred Therapy** (see Chapter 2 for a description of Rogers's theory). Emphasis is placed on the free will of the individual; however, Rogers suggests that freedom of choice is a gift which requires courage to use. The therapist assists the client through **accurate empathic understanding**, seeing the world through the client's eyes and understanding feelings from the client's phenomenological viewpoint. The **genuineness** of the therapist is essential; Rogers suggests that if a therapist cannot wholly relate to a client, he should agree with the client to see a different therapist. The therapist, through honest self-disclosure, provides a model for the client.

Carl Rogers therapy is essentially non-directive, the client must be encouraged, supported in a 'safe' environment, to find solutions and choose actions for him or herself. The client must be· given **unconditional positive regard**, in order to facilitate getting to know the self and learning to deal more effectively with problems, as learning is inhibited if the client feels that the approval of others must be constantly sought.

The possible mismatch between the 'perceived self' and the 'ideal self' can be monitored during therapy by use of the Q-sorts technique, described in Chapter 2, Section IV.

Rogers assumes that **self-actualisation** is the principal human motivation, and that people by nature are innately good. Both of these precepts have been questioned.

(b) **Encounter Groups**. A spin-off of the T-groups started by Rogers, where **participants** (rather than clients) are encouraged by a **facilitator** to break down barriers and talk about and act out their emotions and problems. The free interaction and responses by others give new perspectives and promote self-actualisation. Some writers (for example Rogers, 1970) state that the groups are effective in facilitating positive change; others suggest that they can precipitate psychological disturbances (Lieberman *et al.*, 1973)

(c) **Gestalt Therapy**. Founded by Fritz Perls, who like Rogers, believed that people have an innate goodness which is seeking to express itself. The therapy assumes that the individual brings his or her own wants and needs to any situation. The therapist focuses on the **here-and-now**, rather than the client's past. Various techniques are employed, such as the 'empty chair', where the client is encouraged to talk to whoever s/he sees in the chair. Perls believes that the unresolved traumas of the past affect new relationships, but that these should be acted out in the present. Clients are coerced, if necessary, into an awareness of what is happening, and urged to take direct action. The aim is to help people to become '**whole**' by acknowledging all facets of themselves.

(d) **Transactional Analysis**. Eric Berne (1968) sees personality as consisting of **three ego-states**: parent, adult and child. These states are identified in role play, when the client and the therapist act out personal transactions or interactions with others. Each person is capable of communicating using either their child, adult or parent state. If this state is not recognised by the partner, underlying misunderstandings occur (because of course we do not only communicate in words). Berne identified a number of ways in which individuals use these strategies and interactions destructively; once understood, they can be changed and utilised to give greater control over the individual's life.

### Evaluation of Humanistic Therapies

Rogers was largely instrumental in encouraging evaluative studies of insight therapies, but there are methodological difficulties in doing so, as controlled research into this area is somewhat difficult. Rogers used a technique called 'Q sorts' devised by Stephenson (1953), which aims to aid the client to make an objective assessment about self-perceptions, whether there is a mismatch between the 'perceived self' and the 'ideal self' (what I think I am and what I think I should be). This technique can be used in order to measure improvement during and after therapy. There are doubts as to how objective any form of self-assessment can be.

It was suggested that the warmth and personality of the therapist actually effected the 'cure', rather than any specific technique used. Parloff *et al.* (1978) found that a positive outcome is not necessarily related to the therapist's genuineness and empathy, as had been previously believed.

Many group therapies derived from humanistic therapies not only save on the therapist's time, but clients can learn from one another's opinions; also if a therapist draws a conclusion about you, you can reject this, but if several people in your group come to the same conclusion, it is not so easily rejected.

### Self-assessment Questions

1. What factors are common to all humanistic therapies?
2. Describe Rogers's therapy.
3. How does this differ from any one of the other therapies?
4. Discuss the strengths and weaknesses of the humanistic therapies.

## SECTION VI   TREATMENT EFFECTIVENESS

So, which is the best treatment to effect a cure? the lay reader might ask. Treatment of mental disorders is not that clear-cut; for example, one might state categorically that penicillin is the best treatment for a throat infection and a plaster cast for a broken leg; it is obviously useless to reverse the two treatments. The same therapy, is sometimes effective and sometimes ineffective for seemingly the same mental disorder, because no two cases are identical.

## Concept of Cure

The other problem posed by the above question is the idea of 'cure'. How does one determine that a client is 'cured' of a mental disorder? As mentioned earlier, does the patient decide s/he is cured? Does the therapist decide? Should an independent therapist be called in to make an assessment? If so, should the second therapist be of the same theoretical persuasion as the first?

First one has to decide what constitutes a cure. Behaviourists would say removal of the aberrant behavour, **removal of the symptom** is seen as a cure for the disorder. If the social phobic can now mix in society, if the snake phobic no longer runs away screaming on seeing a snake, then the behaviourist counts them as cured. Overt behaviour can be seen and measured. But for how long does this constitute a cure – for life?

If the patient re-enters treatment a year or two later, with symptoms which could be related to their earlier problem, this could be called **symptom substitution**. It could be argued that they were not really cured initially, but their problems simply driven underground, merely to resurface at the next troubled period in life. **Beech (1972)** reports that symptom substitution is relatively uncommon.

Psychoanalytic therapies aim to find the **underlying problem**, and in recognising this, the patient will resolve the problem. How to be certain this has occurred, is exceedingly difficult. It is impossible to measure id–ego conflicts, even if we are willing to accept that these do in fact occur. Projective tests which aim to measure internal conflicts are, of course, open to the charge of being scored subjectively (e.g. Rorschach, see Chapter 3, Section III). Many of the insight therapies are dependent upon the client–therapist relationship, so can an objective view of 'cure' be reached? Rogers himself suggests that insight therapy is not suitable for patients with severe mental disorders, who have no insight. Somatic treatments, like behaviour therapies, tend to use symptom removal, or changes in overt behaviour, as signs of a 'cure'.

One confounding variable in evaluation of any research is the 'hello/goodbye' effect. When a patient or client first commences treatment, they tend to exaggerate their problems and unhappinesss to show their need for treatment. At the end of therapy, they may exaggerate their feelings of well-being, in order to show the therapist their appreciation, or to convince themselves they had not wasted time and money. In addition is the phenomenon of **spontaneous remission**; Bergin and Lambert (1978) reported that between 30 and 60 per cent of patients 'get better' without treatment. Schizophrenia, particularly, is said to fall into the 'rule of thirds'. One third get better on their own, one third get better with treatment, the final third will never show improvement. Patients or clients who are in therapy, but would have exhibited spontaneous remission are therefore included in statistics showing the number of patients discharged or 'cured'.

## Comparing Therapies

A number of studies have been conducted comparing behavioural therapies with insight-type therapies. Little difference in effectiveness was reported by researchers (Sloane *et al.*, 1975; Berman *et al.*, 1985). This may be because specific therapies are usually selected for specific disorders, thereby gaining the optimum chance of success. For example, modelling and systematic desensitisation are frequently successful for phobics, whereas psychoanalytic therapies are not; the latter are more useful in problems that require self-understanding. Behaviour therapies and cognitive behaviour therapies are more useful in helping to change a specific aspects of one's behaviour. None of the therapies are successful alone in treating schizophrenia or manic-depression; however, used in conjunction with chemotherapy they help very effectively with problems of day-to-day living.

## Outcome-Research Studies

**Eysenck (1952)** reviewed five studies of the effectiveness of psychoanalysis and 19 studies of eclectic therapies (mixed therapies, such as behaviour modification plus other treatments). He concluded that only 44 per cent of the psychoanalysis patients showed improvement compared to 64 per cent of the eclectic treatment groups. However, **Bergin (1971)** re-reviewed these studies and found that if different criteria were used for 'improvement', the psychoanalysis success rate was raised to 83 per cent. As was noted earlier, it all depends on how one defines 'cure'.

**Smith and Glass (1977)** reviewed 400 studies of a variety of therapies, and found that any therapy produced a more favourable outcome than no therapy at all. Smith *et al.* (1980) did a **meta-analysis** of 475 studies, each of which compared a therapy group with an untreated control group. They concluded that the average patient receiving any therapy showed greater improvement on outcome measures than 80 per cent of the untreated controls. One can only assume that patients in compared groups were equally matched. One of the methodological problems of meta-analysis is that different researchers use a variety of criteria.

**Shapiro (1983)** suggests that outcome studies may all show similar results, not only because appropriate therapies are selected for particular client groups, but also that all therapies have two important factors in common: the warm and supportive relationship between therapist and client, and the expectation that things will improve.

### Evaluation

It is still a matter for discussion how 'cure' is defined in mental disorders. If the aim of therapy is to make the client more comfortable with himself or herself, then the client can give self-ratings; if the aim is to make society comfortable with the client, other criteria must be used.

No one therapy has proved superior for all mental disorders; therapy must be chosen that seems to be the 'best fit' with the client's problem. In addition, if the client–therapist relationship is seen to be of paramount importance to success, these two individuals must have a 'mutual respect and understanding' (Rogers).

### Self-assessment Questions

1. What are the problems of deciding whether a patient is cured of a mental disorder?

2. Why is it difficult to make a direct comparison of treatment effectiveness?
3. Which treatments have been found to be most effective for which disorders?


## SECTION VII   INSTITUTIONALISATION OR DEINSTITUTIONALISATION?

### Introduction

Whether an individual should remain at home (if they have a home) or enter an institution or hospital for treatment, is an important subject for discussion. Until comparatively recently institutionalisation was seen as the obvious choice for most mental disorders, including mental handicap. It was seen as 'best' – but best for whom, the patient, their family, society? Nowadays there is a strong move to keep patients in their own homes. This section aims to briefly examine some of the factors involved in these decisions.

### Homecare

The majority of patients with mental illnesses or mental retardation, live at home. Some need to be hospitalised for a short time, to receive specific treatments or to give carers a rest, but the aim is to return people to their own homes as soon as possible, to resume their atmosphere of normality. However, this is not always possible: if people have disrupted their family ties to such an extent that reparation would only cause greater problems, or if the problem was precipitated by the family in the first place, then other plans have to be made.

### Asylum

The word asylum means refuge: early asylums of the Middle Ages were more like a prison than a refuge, with inmates left in chains. Early treatments, such as tranquillising chairs or cribs, designed to physically restrain the patient and restrict·sensory input, were used in the absence of any drug treatments, in order to calm the person's rages. In fact, cold bath treatment was used until the beginning of this century. By 1792, **Philippe Pinel**, in France, had pioneered the removal of chains and the provision of more humanitarian surroundings. From this model, more humanitarian housing and treatment was provided. In looking back at the asylums of the Middle Ages, one has to remember that housing for the vast majority of the population of that time would be deemed unacceptable today.

## Institutions

Victorian times saw the building of large institutions for the mentally ill and mentally retarded. Initially both were housed together, but gradually differentiation occurred, after diagnosis and classification was introduced.

The old institutions housed hundreds of patients, usually well away from towns and cities so that they would not offend the sensitivities of 'normal' people. The effect was that the 'norm' of accepted behaviour for each of these institutions was defined by the inmates of each institution. This set a ceiling which many could have exceeded, had they been aware it was desirable or even possible. Many institutions acted as whole communities and were self-supporting in many ways, growing their own food, with the help of the patients. In this way, one might argue, there was good as well as bad in the old institutions. There was also always companionship, even if it could not be called 'friendship', there was always someone else there.

## Deinstitutionalisation and New Provision

New treatment methods, for example control of long-term disorders with chemotherapy, meant that many patients were confined to institutions when they could have been living outside in the community. Unless they had friends or family willing to assist in their rehabilitation, this was not possible. Gradually the idea of sheltered accommodation or community care homes was pioneered, and patients are being moved out of the big, old institutions into smaller, **'family group' homes** or **sheltered housing**. Sometimes these are run entirely by a group of ex-patients, often with resident or day-time care assistants.

## Problems with Deinstitutionalisation

This move of course is not without its problems. Although everyone agrees that people should not be made to live in institutions when they could live in houses, there is frequently opposition to where these should be sited (subject to the '**not in my backyard**' syndrome).

**Ignorance** on the part of the general public about what constitutes mental disorder provides fuel for opposition. Until people realise that these individuals are not going to steal from them, harm or frighten their children or lower the tone of the neighbourhood, then prejudice will persist. Much public relations work still needs to be done.

**Preparation** work also needs to be done with the patients themselves. Providing a house and taking previously institutionalised patients straight from hospital to the house, is not the way to success. **Education** or re-education on matters such as shopping, cooking, cleaning and maintaining personal hygiene has to be undertaken. **Behaviour therapy** may be necessary, to make the quantum leap from acceptable institutional behaviour to acceptable behaviour in the outside world. **Facilities** such as day centres, sheltered workshops or jobs need to be provided, to avoid the cases of the 'bed and breakfast' ex-patient, who aimlessly wanders the streets all day until allowed back into the accommodation in the evening. Externalising patients, health authorities are now realising, is not the cheap option it first appeared. If homes in the community are to benefit patients, then many factors must be considered and many self-help facilities provided, otherwise we shall simply resurrect the 'revolving door' – patients having to return to hospital for further treatment.

## Responses

Health authorities have responded differentially to the provision of housing, and at different speeds. By 1987, for example, Southampton Health Authority had provided 250 homes which appeared to be running successfully, with inhabitants participating in local facilities. Nearby Portsmouth, on the other hand, with a similar size township, had only provided 50 homes and appeared to lack day-facilities.

According to statistics supplied by the Department of Health, in Great Britain in 1985, there were 74,837 available beds for the mentally ill, with staffing care, compared to 55,000 in 1990/1. The provisional number of mentally ill in-patients in 1990/1 was 48,700, plus 12,487 places in local authority, private and residential homes, compared with 8355 of the latter in 1985.

The Department of Health states that 'Although the number of long-term illness beds is falling steadily at an average rate of 2500 a year, this reduction is offset by a substantial increase in community services.' The numerate reader will have already observed that from the figures above, there was an overall number of **83,172 beds** available in **1985**, but only **62,487** available from all sources in **1990/1**. One can only assume that either there has been a large increase in the number of mentally ill now living in their own homes, or a large decrease in the incidence of mental disorder – or perhaps the increasing number of inhabitants in 'cardboard-box cities' may account for some of the shortfall.

Statistics for the mentally handicapped are not available from the same source, because of the complexity of the problem. There may be incomplete records, for example, of people who have always lived at home and never required housing provision by the state.

## Summary

Whether patients are treated at home or as in-patients depends partly on the severity of their problem, partly on the treatment recommended and partly upon whether they have family support. The movement to deinstitutionalise those suffering from mental disorders is a welcome step, provided it is not regarded solely as a cheap alternative to hospitalisation. The careful provision of small-group homes and adequate day-care may well prove just as **expensive** as the old institutions, but provide **increased self-esteem** and **individualisation** required by ex-patients, which is after all the object of the exercise. Sales of the old institutions can be expected to offset some capital costs. Careful monitoring is necessary in this freer situation to ensure that those who need care are not denied it, or counted as outside certain boundaries.

There will always be the need for in-patient accommodation, for acute problems and those who may need temporary removal from their usual place of habitation.

## Self-assessment Questions

1. What forms of accommodation are available today for people suffering from mental disorders?
2. What else is needed besides somewhere to live?
3. What are the advantages and problems of deinstitutionalisation?
4. How would it be possible to tell if an individual was in the right placement?

## FURTHER READING

V. Axline, *Dibs: in Search of Self* (Harmondsworth: Penguin, 1964).

A. T. Beck and G. Emery, *Anxiety Disorders and Phobias: A Cognitive Perspective* (New York: Basic Books, 1985).

C. Rogers, *On Becoming a Person* (Boston: Houghton Mifflin, 1961).

# Bibliography

Abrams, R. (1975) 'What's new in convulsive therapy?', in Arieti, S. and Chrzanowski, G. (eds), *New Dimensions in Psychiatry* (New York: Wiley).

Agras, S., Sylvester, D. and Oliveau, D. (1969) 'The epidemology of common fears and phobias', unpublished manuscript.

Allen, M.G. (1976) 'Twin studies of affective illness', *Archives of General Psychiatry*, **33**, 1476–8.

Allport, G.W. (1937) *Personality: A Psychological Interpretation* (New York: Holt, Rinehart and Winston)

Allport, G.W. (1965) *Letters from Jenny* (New York: Harcourt, Brace and World).

Allport, G.W. and Odbert, H.S. (1936) 'Trait names: a psycho-lexical study', *Psychological Monographs: General and Applied*, **47** (whole no. 211).

American Psychiatric Association (1987) *Diagnostic and Statistical Manual of Mental Disorders* (3rd edn revised) (Washington, DC: American Psychiatric Association).

Anastasi, A. (1958) in R.M. Lerner (1986) *Concepts and Theories in Human Development*, 2nd edn (New York: Random House).

Atkinson, J.W. and Feather, N.T. (1966) *A Theory of Achievement Motivation* (New York: Wiley).

Bailey, C.L. (1979) 'Mental illness – a logical misrepresentation', *Nursing Times*, May, 761–2.

Bandura, A. (1965) 'Influence of model's reinforcement contingencies on the acquisition of imitative responses', *Journal of Personality and Social Psychology*, **1**, 589–95.

Bandura, A. (1969) *Principles of Behaviour Modification* (London: Holt, Rinehart and Winston).

Bandura, A., Blanchard, E.B. and Ritter, B. (1969) 'Relative efficacy of desensitization and modelling approaches for inducing behavioural, affective and attitudinal changes', *Journal of Personality and Social Psychology*, **13**, 173–99.

Bannister, D., Salmon, P. and Lieberman, D. (1964) 'Diagnosis–treatment relationships in psychiatry: a statistical analysis', *British Journal of Psychiatry*, **110**, 726–32.

Barahal, H. (1958) '1000 prefrontal lobotomies: five to ten year follow-up study', *Psychiatric Quarterly*, **32**, 653–78.

Barratt, C. L. (1969) 'Systematic desensitisation versus implosive therapy', *Journal of Abnormal Psychology*, **74**, 587–92.

Barrett, P.T. and Kline, P. (1982) 'The itemetric properties of the Eysenck personality questionnaire: a reply to Helmes', *Personality and Individual Differences*, **3**, 73–80.

Basmajian, J.V. (1977) 'Learned control of single motor units', in Schwartz, G.E. and Beatty, J. (eds) *Biofeedback: Theory and Research* (New York: Academic Press).

Bayley, N. 'Development of mental abilities' in Mussen, P.H. (ed.) *Carmichael's Manuel of Child Psychology*, vol. 1, 3rd edn (New York: Witley), 163–209.

Beck, S.J. (1952) *Rorschach's Test, vol. 3: Advances in Interpretation* (New York: Grune and Stratton).

Beck, A.T., Ward, C., Mendelson, M., Mock, J. and Erbaugh, J. (1962) 'Reliability of psychiatric diagnosis: II. A study of consistency of clinical judgements and ratings', *American Journal of Psychiatry*, **119**, 351–7.

Beck, A. and Emery, G. (1985) *Anxiety Disorders and Phobias: A Cognitive Perspective* (New York: Basic Books).

Bee, H. (1989) *The Developing Child* (New York: Harper and Row).

Beech, H.R., Watts, Frazer and Desmond Poole (1972) 'Classical conditioning of sexual deviation: a preliminary note', *Behaviour Therapy*, **2**, 233–9.

Bem, D.J. (1983) 'Constructing a theory of the triple typology: some (second) thoughts on nomothetic and idiographic approaches to personality', *Journal of Personality*, **51**, 566–77.

Bem, D.J. and Allen, A. (1974) 'On predicting some of the people some of the time: the search for cross-situational consistencies in behaviour', *Psychological Review*, **81**, 506–20.

Bergin, A. (1971) 'The evaluation of therapeutic outcomes', in Garfield, S.L. and Bergin, A. (eds), *Handbook of Psychotherapy and Behaviour Change: An Empirical Analysis* (New York: Wiley).

Bergin, A. and Lambert, M. (1978) 'The evaluation of therapeutic outcomes', in Garfield, S.L. and Bergin, A. (eds), *Handbook of Psychotherapy and Behaviour Change: An Empirical Analysis* (2nd edn) (New York: Wiley).

Berne, E. (1968) *Games People Play* (Harmondsworth: Penguin).

Bernstein, D. and Nietzel, M. (1980) *Introduction to Clinical Psychology* (New York: McGraw-Hill).

Binet, A. and Simon, T. (1905) 'Méthodes nouvelles pour le diagnostic du niveau intellectuel des anormaux', *L'Année Psychologique*, **11**, 191–244.

Birch, A. and Malim, A. (1988) *Developmental Psychology: from Infancy to Adulthood* (Basingstoke: Macmillan).

Blaney, P. (1975) 'Implications of the medical model and its alternatives', *American Journal of Psychiatry*, **132**, 911–14.

Blanchard, E.B., Miller, S.T., Abel, G., Haynes, M. and Wicker, R. (1979) 'Evaluation of biofeedback in the treatment of borderline essential hypertension', *Journal of Applied Behaviour Analysis*, **12**, 99–109.

Blinkhorn, S.F. and Hendrickson, D.E. (1982) 'Average evoked responses and psychometric intelligence', *Nature*, **295**, 596–7.

Bliss, E.L. (1980) 'Multiple personalities: a report of 14 cases with implications for schizophrenia and hysteria', *Archives of General Psychiatry*, **37**, 1388–97.

Block, J. (1961/78) *The Q-sort Method in Personality Assessment and Psychiatric Research* (Palo Alto: Consulting Psychologists Press).

Block, J. (1971) *Lives Through Time* (Berkeley, California: Bancroft Books).

Block, J. (1981) 'Some enduring and consequential structures of personality', in Rabin, A.I., Aronoff, J., Barclay A.M. and Zucker, R.A. (eds), *Further Explorations in Personality* (New York: Wiley).

Blum, G.S. (1949) 'A study of the psychoanalytic theory of psychosexual development', *Genet. Psychol. Monogr.*, **39**, 3–99.

Bodmer, W.F. (1972) 'Race and IQ: the genetic background', in Richardson, K. and Spears, D. (eds), *Race, Culture and Intelligence* (Harmondsworth, Middlesex: Penguin).

Booth, T. (1975) *Growing up in Society* (London: Methuen).

Bouchard, T.J. and McGue, M. (1981) 'Familial studies of intelligence: a review', *Science*, **22**, 1055–9.

Bowers, K.S. (1973) 'Situationism in psychology: an analysis and critique', *Psychological Review*, **80**, pp. 307–36.

Briggs, K.C. and Myers, I.B. (1962) *The Myers-Briggs Type Indicator* (Manual) (ETS Princeton).

Brown, G.W., Bone, M., Dalison, B. and Wing, J.K. (1966) *Schizophrenia and Social Care* (London: Oxford University Press).

Browne, J.A. and Howarth, E. (1977) 'A comprehensive factor analysis of personality questionnaire items: a test of twenty putative factor hypotheses', *Multivariate Behavioural Research*, **12**, 399–427.

Bruner, J.S. (1956) 'You are your constructs', *Contemporary Psychology*, **1**, 355–6.

Bruner, J. (1966) *Towards a Theory of Instruction* (Cambridge, Massachusetss: Harvard University Press).

Burks, B.S. (1928) 'The relative influence of nature and nurture upon mental development: A comparative study of foster parent–foster child resemblance and true parent–true child resemblance', *Yearbook of the National Society for the Study of Education*, **27**, 219–316.

Burt, C. (1955) 'The evidence for the concept of intelligence', *British Journal of Educational Psychology*, **25**, 158–77.

Burt, C. (1966) 'The genetic determination of intelligence: a study of monozygotic twins reared together and apart' *British Journal of Psychology*, **57**, 137–53.

Cattell, R.B. (1947) 'Confirmation and clarification of primary personality factors', *Psychometrika*, **12**, 197–220.

Cattell, R.B. (1965) *The Scientific Analysis of Personality* (Harmondsworth, Penguin).

Cattell, R.B. (1973) *Personality and Mood by Questionnaire* (San Francisco: Jossey-Bass).

Cattell, R.B., Eber, H.W. and Tatsnoka, M. (1970) *Handbook for Sixteen Personality Factor Questionnaire* (Champaign, Ill., Institute for Personality and Ability Testing).

Cattell, R.B. and Kline, P. (1977) *The Scientific Analysis of Personality and Motivation* (New York: Academic Press).

Chaplin, W.F. and Goldberg, L.R. (1984) 'A failure to replicate the Bem and Allen study of individual differences in cross-situational consistency', *Journal of Personality and Social Psychology*, **47**, 1074–90.

Chickering, A.W. (1976) 'The double-bind of field dependence/independence in program alternatives for educational development', in Messick, S., *Individuality in Learning* (San Francisco: Jossey-Bass).

Child, I.L. (1968) 'Personality in culture', in Borgatta, E.F. and Lambert, W.W. (eds), *Handbook of Personality Theory and Research* (Chicago: Rand McNally).

Chipeur, H.M., Rovine, M.J. and Plomin, R. (1989, June) 'Lisrel Modeling: genetic and environmental influences on IQ revisited'. Presented at the Annual Meeting of the Behavior Genetics Association, Charlottesville, VA.

Clare, A. (1980) *Psychiatry in Dissent* (London: Tavistock).

Cleckley, J. (1976) *The Mask of Sanity* (5th edn) (St Louis: Mosby).

Cochrane, R. (1974) 'Crime and personality: theory and evidence', *Bulletin of the British Psychological Society*, **27**, 19–22.

Cooper, J.E., Kendall, R., Gurland, B., Sharple, L., Copeland, J. and Simon, R. (1972) 'Psychiatric diagnosis in New York and London', *Maudsley Monograph no. 20* (London: Oxford University Press).

Coyle, J., Price, D. and Delong, M. (1983) 'Alzheimer's disease: a disorder of cortical cholinergic innervation', *Science*, **219**, 1184–90.

Cronbach, L.J. and Snow, R.E. (1977) *Aptitudes and Instructional Methods: A Handbook for Research on Interactions* (New York: Irvinton).

Cummings, J. and Benson, D. (1983) *Dementia: a Clinical Approach* (Woburn, Mass.: Butterworth).

Darlington, R.B. (1986) 'Long-term effects of preschool programs', in U. Neisser (ed.), *The School Achievement of Minority Children* (Hillsdale, NJ: Erlbaum).

Davidson, J.E. and Sternberg, R.J. (1984) 'The role of insight in intellectual giftedness', *Gifted Child Quarterly*, **28**, 58–64.

DeMyer, M. (1975) 'The nature of the neuropsychological disability of autistic children', *Journal of Autism and childhood Schizophrenia*, **5**, 109–27.

Diament, C. and Wilson, G.T. (1975) 'An experimental investigation of the effects of covert sensitisation in an analogue eating situation', *Behaviour Therapy*, **6**, 499–509.

Digman, J.M. and Inouye, J. (1986) 'Further specification of the five robust factors of personality', *Journal of Personality and Social Psychology*, vol. 50, pp. 116–23.

Drake, R.D. and Soderer, L.I. (1986), 'The adverse effects of intensive treatment of chronic schizophrenia', *Comprehensive Psychiatry*, **27**, 313–26.

Edmunds, G. and Kendrick, D.C. (1980) *The Measurement of Human Aggressiveness* (Chichester: Ellis Horwood).

Egeland, J.A., Gerhard, D., Pauls, D., Sussex, J., Kidd, K., Allen, C., Hostetter, A. and Housman, D. (1987) 'Bipolar affective disorders linked to DNA markers on chromosome 11', *Nature*, **325**, 783–7.

Elliott, C., Murray, D.J. and Pearson, L.S. (1983) *The British Ability Scales* (rev. edn) (Windsor: Nelson-NFER).

Ellis, A. (1984) 'Rational-emotive therapy', in R.J. Corsini (ed.), *Current Psychotherapies* (3rd edn) (Itasca, Ill: Peacock Press).

Emmelkamp, P. and Wessels, H. (1975) 'Flooding in imagination versus flooding in vivo: a comparison with agoraphobics', *Behaviour Research and Therapy*, **13**, 7–15.

Endicott, J., Nea, J., Fleiss, J., Cohen, J., Williams, J.B. and Simon, R. (1982) 'Diagnostic criteria for schizophrenia: reliability and agreement between systems', *Archives of General Psychiatry*, **39**, 884–9.

Endicott, J. and Spitzer, R.L. (1978) 'A diagnostic interview: the Schedule for Affective Disorders and Schizophrenia', *Archives of General Psychiatry*, **35**, 837–44.

Erikson, E. (1963) *Childhood and Society* (New York: Norton).

Ertl, J.P. (1971) 'Fourier analysis of evoked potentials and human intelligence', *Nature*, **230**, 525–6.

Ertl, J.P. and Schafer, E.W.P. (1969) 'Brain response correlates of psychometric intelligence', *Nature*, **223**, 421–2.

Estes, W.K. (1982) 'Learning, memory and intelligence', in Sternberg, R.J., *Handbook of Human Intelligence* (Cambridge: Cambridge University Press).

Eysenck, H.J. (1947) *Dimensions of Personality* (London: Routledge and Kegan Paul).

Eysenck, H.J. (1952) 'The effects of psychotherapy: an evaluation', *Journal of Consulting Psychology*, **16**, 319–24.

Eysenck, H.J. (1959) 'The Rorschach Test', in Buros, O.K. (ed.), *The V Mental Measurement Year Book* (New Jersey: Gryphon Press).

Eysenck, H.J. (1964) *Crime and Personality* (London: Routledge and Kegan Paul).

Eysenck, H.J. (1986) 'The theory of intelligence and the psychophysiology of cognition', in Sternberg, R.J. (ed.) *Advances in the Psychology of Human Intelligence*, vol. 3, 1–34 (Hillsdale, NJ: Erlbaum).

Eysenck, H.J. and Eysenck, M.W. (1985) *Personality and Individual Differences: a Natural Science Approach* (New York: Plenum Press).

Eysenck, H.J. and Eysenck, S.B.G. (1964) *Manual of the Eysenck Personality Inventory* (London: ULP).

Eysenck, H.J. and Eysenck, S.B.G. (1969) *Personality Structure and Measurement* (London: Routledge and Kegan Paul).

Eysenck, H.J. and Eysenck, S.B.G. (1975) *Manual for the Eysenck Personality Questionnaire* (London: Hodder and Stoughton).

Eysenck, H.J. and Eysenck, S.B.G. (1976) *Psychoticism as a Dimension of Personality* (London: Hodder and Stoughton).

Eysenck, H.J. and Kamin, L.J. (1981) *Intelligence: the Battle for the Mind* (London: Macmillan).

Eysenck, H.J. and Wilson, G.D. (1973) *Experimental Studies of Freudian Theories* (London: Methuen).

Eysenck, S.B.G. and Eysenck, H.J. (1970) 'Crime and personality: an empirical study of the three-factor theory', *British Journal of Criminology*, **10**, 225–39.

Falek, A. and Moser, H.M. (1975) 'Classification in schizophrenia', *Archives of General Psychiatry*, **32**, 59–67.

Farrington, D.P., Biron, L. and Le Blanc, M. (1982) 'Personality and delinquency in London and Montreal', in Gunn, J.C. and Farrington, D.P. (eds), *Advances in Forensic Psychiatry and Psychology* (Chichester: Wiley).

Fisher, S. and Greenberg, R. (1977) *The Scientific Credibility of Freud's Theories and Therapy* (Brighton: Harvester Press).

Fonagy, P. (1981) 'Experimental research in psychoanalytic theory', in Fransella, F. (ed.) *Personality* (London: Methuen).

Fonagy, P. and Higgitt, A. (1984) *Personality Theory and Clinical Practice* (London: Methuen).

Fontana, D. (1988) *Psychology for Teachers* (2nd edn) (Leicester/Basingstoke: British Psychological Society/Macmillan).

Frank, B.M. and Noble, J.P. (1984) 'Field independence–dependence and cognitive restructuring', *Journal of Personality and Social Psychology*, **47**, 1129–1135.

Franks, C.M. (1956) 'Conditioning and personality: a study of normal and neurotic subjects', *Journal of Abnormal Social Psychology*, **52**, pp. 143–50.

Franks, C.M. (1957) 'Personality factors and the rate of conditioning', *British Journal of Psychology*, **48**, 119–26.

Franks, C.M. (1984) 'Behaviour therapy with children and adolescents', in Wilson, G.T., Franks, C.M., Brownell, K.D. and Kendall, P.C. (eds) *Annual Review of Behaviour Therapy: Theory and Practice* (vol.9) (New York: Guilford).

Fransella, F. (1975) *Need to Change?* (London: Methuen).

Fransella, F. (1984) 'Personal Construct Therapy', in Dryden, W. (ed.), *Individual Therapy in Britain* (London: Harper and Row).

Fraser, E.D. (1959) *Home Environment and the School* (London: University of London Press).

Freeman, F.S. (1962) *Theory and Practice of Psychological Testing* (3rd edn) (New York: Holt).

Freud, A. (1936) *The Ego and the Mechanisms of Defence* (London: Chatto and Windus).

Freud, S. (1923) 'The ego and the id', in *Standard Edition of the Complete Psychological Works of Sigmund Freud*, **19** (London: Hogarth Press).

Friedman, M. and Rosenman, R.H. (1974) *Type A Behaviour and Your Heart* (New York: Knopf).

Furnham, A. (1981) 'Personality and activity preference', *British Journal of Social Psychology*, **20**, 57–68.

Furnham, A. (1982) 'Psychoticism, social desirability and situation selection', *Personality and Individual Differences*, **3**, 43–51.

Gale, A. (1973) 'Individual differences: studies of extraversion and EEG', in Kline, P. (ed.), *New Approaches in Psychological Measurement*.

Gale, A. (1981) 'EEG studies of extraversion–introversion: what's the next step' in Gibson, H.B. (ed.) *Hans Eysenck: the Man and his Work* (London: Peter Owen).

Galin, D. and Ornstein, R. (1972) 'Lateral specialization or cognitive mode: an EEG study', *Psychophysiology*, **9**, 412–18.

Galton, F. (1869) *Heredity Genius: an inquiry into its Laws and Consequences*, 2nd edn, reprinted 1978 (London: Julian Friedmann).

Gardner, H. (1983) *Frames of Mind: the Theory of Multiple Intelligences* (London: Heinemann).

Gardner, H. and Feldman, D. (1985) 'Project Spectrum', Annual Report submitted to the Spencer Foundation. Unpublished.

Gardner, R.W., Jackson, D.N. and Messick, S.J. (1960) 'Personality organisation in cognitive controls and intellectual abilities', *Psychological Issues*, **2** (Monograph 8).

Garfield, S.L., Praner, R.A. and Bergin, A.E. (1971) 'Evaluation of outcome in psychotherapy', *Journal of Consulting and Clinical Psychology*, **37**, 307–13.

Gazzaniga, M.S. (1985) *The Social Brain: Discovering the Networks of the Mind* (New York: Basic).

Ginsburg, H. (1972) *The Myth of the Deprived Child: Poor Children's Intellect and Education* (Engelwood Cliffs, New Jersey: Prentice-Hall).

Gittleman-Klein, R., Klein, D., Abikoff, H., Katz, S., Gloisten, A. and Kates, W. (1976) 'Relative efficacy of methylphenidate and behaviour modification in hyperkinetic children: an interim report', *Journal of Abnormal Child Psychology*, **4**, 361–79.

Goldberg, L.R. (1981) 'Language and individual differences: the search for universals in personality lexicons', in Wheeler, L. (ed.) *Review of Personality and Social Psychology*, vol. 2, pp. 141–65 (Beverly Hills: Sage).

Goldberg, E. and Morrison, S. (1963) 'Schizophrenia and social class', *British Journal of Psychiatry*, **109**, 785–802.

Goldman-Eisler, F. (1948) 'Breast feeding and character formation', *Journal of Personality*, **17**, 83–103.

Gottesman, I. and Shields, J. (1972) *Schizophrenia and Genetics: A Twin Study Vantage Point* (New York: Academic Press).

Gottesman, I. and Shields, J. (1982) *Schizophrenia: the Epigenetic Puzzle* (New York: Cambridge University Press).

Gould, S.J. (1981) *The Mismeasure of Man* (London: Penguin).

Gove, W.R. (1970) 'Societal reaction as an explanation of mental illness: an evaluation', *American Sociological Review*, **35**, 873–84.

Gruen, A. (1957) 'A critique and re-evaluation of Witkin's perception and perception–personality work', *Journal of General Psychology*, **56**, 73–93.

Hall, C.S. and Lindzey, G. (1978) *Theories of Personality*, 3rd edn (New York: Wiley).

Hampson, S. (1988) *The Construction of Personality: an Introduction*, 2nd edn (London: Routledge).

Hampson, S. and Kline, P. (1977) 'Personality dimensions differentiating certain groups of abnormal offenders from non-offenders', *British Journal of Criminology*, **17**, 310–31.

Haney, C., Banks, C. and Zimbardo, P. (1973) 'Interpersonal dynamics in a simulated prison', *International Journal of Criminology and Penology*, **1**, 69–97.

Haracz, J. (1982) 'The dopamine hypothesis: an overview of studies with schizophrenic patients', *Schizophrenia Bulletin*, **8**, 438–69.

Hare, R.D. (1980) 'A research scale for the assessment of psychopathy in criminal populations', *Personality and Individual Differences*, **1**, 111–19.

Hartshorne, H. and May, M.A. (1928) *Studies in the Nature of Character, Vol. 1, Studies in Deceit* (New York: Macmillan).

Heather, N. (1976) *Radical Perspectives in Psychology* (London: Methuen).

Hebb, D.O. (1949) *The Organization of Behavior* (New York: Wiley).

Heim, A. (1970a) *Intelligence and Personality – their Assessment and Relationship* (Harmondsworth: Penguin).

Heim, A. (1970b) *The AH6 Group Tests of High Level Intelligence* (Windsor: NFER-Nelson).

Hendrickson, D.E. and Hendrickson, A.E. (1980) 'The biological basis of individual differences in intelligence', *Personality and Individual Differences*, **1**, 3–33.

Herman, R. (1984) 'The genetic relationship between identical twins', *Early Child Development*, **16**, 265–75.

Hibbert,G. (1984) 'Hyperventilation as a cause of panic attacks', *British Medical Journal*, **288**, 263–64.

Hill, A.B. (1976) 'Methodological problems in the use of factor analysis: a critical review of the experimental evidence for the anal character', *British Journal of Medical Psychology*, **49**, 145–59.

Hirshberg, N. (1978) 'A correct treatment of traits', in London, H. (ed.), *Personality: a New Look at Metatheories* (New York: Macmillan).

Holley, J.W. (1973) 'Rorschach Analysis', in Kline, P. (ed.) *New Approaches in Psychological Measurement* (Chichester: Wiley).

Hollingshead, A.B. and Redlich, F.C. (1958) *Social Class and Mental Illness : A Community Study* (New York: Wiley).

Holmes, D.S. (1974) 'Investigations of repression: differential recall of material experimentally or naturally associated with ego threat', *Psychological Bulletin*, **81**, 632–53.

Horn, J.M., Loehlin, J.L. and Willerman, L. (1979) 'Intellectual resemblance among adoptive and biological relatives: the Texas adoption project', *Behaviour Genetics*, **9**, 177–207.

Howarth, E. (1982) 'Factor analytical examination of Kline's scales for psychoanalytic concepts', *Personality and Individual Differences*, **3**, 89–92.

Hyman, B.T., Van Hoesen, G. Damasio, A. and Barnes, C.L. (1984) 'Alzheimer's disease: cell-specific pathology isolates the Hippocampal formation', *Science*, **225**, 1168–70.

Inglis, J. (1969) 'Electrode placement and the effect of ECT on mood and memory in depression', *Canadian Psychiatric Association Journal*, **14**, 463–471.

Insell, T., Murphy, D., Cohen, R., Alterman, I., Itts, C. and Linnoila, M. (1983) 'Obsessive compulsive disorders. A double-blind trial of clomipramine and clorgyline', *Archives of General Psychiatry*, **40**, 605–12.

Irvine, S.H. (1966) 'Towards a rationale for testing attainments and abilities in Africa', *British Journal of Educational Psychology*, **36**, 24–32.

Jahoda,M. (1958) *Current Concepts of Positive Mental Health* (New York: Basic Books).

Jensen, A.R. (1969) 'How much can we boost IQ and scholastic achievement?', *Harvard Educational Review*, **39**, 1–123.

Jensen, A.R. (1981) 'The chronometry of intelligence', in Sternberg, R.J. (ed.) *Advances in Research on Intelligence*, **1** (Hillsdale, New Jersey: Lawrence Erlbaum).

Jung, C.G. (1923) *Psychological Types* (London: Routledge and Kegan Paul).

Kahn, S., Zimmerman, G., Csikszentmihaly, M. and Getzels, J.W. (1985) 'Relations between identity in young adulthood and intimacy at midlife', *Journal of Personality and Social Psychology*, **49**, 1316–22.

Kamin, L.J. (1974) *The Science and Politics of IQ* (Potomac, MD: Lawrence Erlbaum Associates).

Kamin, L.J. (1977) *The Science and Politics of IQ* (Harmondsworth: Penguin).

Kanner, L. (1943) 'Autistic disturbances of affective contact', *Nervous Child*, **2**, 217–250.

Kelly, G.A. (1955) *The Psychology of Personal Constructs* (New York: Norton).

Kendrick, D.C. (1981) 'Neuroticism and extraversion as explanatory concepts in clinical psychology', in Gibson, H.B. (ed.), *Hans Eysenck, the Man and his Work* (London: Peter Owen).

Kenrick, D.T. and Stringfield, D.O. (1980) 'Personality traits and the eye of the beholder: crossing some traditional philosophical boundaries in the search for consistency in all of the people', *Psychological Review*, **87**, 88–104.

Kety, S.S., Rosenthal, D., Wender, P. and Schulsinger, F. (1968) 'The types and prevalence of mental illness in the biological and adoptive families of adopted schizophrenics', in Rosenthal, D. and Kety, S.S. (eds), *The Transmission of Schizophrenia* (Elmsford, NY: Pergamon).

Kety, S.S., Rosenthal, D., Wender, P., Schulsinger, F. and Jacobson, B. (1975) 'Mental illness in the biological and adoptive families of adopted individuals who have become schizophrenic: a preliminary report based on psychiatric interviews', in Fieve, R.R., Rosenthal, D. and Brill, H. (eds) *Genetic Research in Psychiatry* (Baltimore: Johns Hopkins University Press).

Kirby, R. and Radford, J. (1976) *Individual Differences* (London: Methuen).

Klerman, G. (1972) 'Drug therapy of clinical depression', *Journal of Psychiatric Research*, **9**, 253–270.

Klerman, G. (1975) 'Drug therapy of clinical depressions – current status and implications for research on neuropharmacology of the affective disorders', in Klein, D. and Gittleman-Klein, R. (eds), *Progress in Psychiatric Drug Treatment* (New York: Bruner/Mazel).

Klerman, G. (1988) 'Depression and related disorders of mood (affective disorders)', in Nicholi, A. M. Jnr (ed.), *The New Harvard Guide to Psychiatry* (Cambridge, Mass: Harvard University Press).

Kline, P. (1972) *Fact and Fantasy in Freudian Theory* (London: Methuen).

Kline, P. (1981a) *Fact and Fantasy in Freudian theory*, 2nd edn (London: Methuen).

Kline, P. (1981b) 'Recent research into the factor analysis of personality', in Fransella, F. (ed.) *Personality* (London: Methuen).

Kline, P. (1983) *Personality: Measurement and Theory* (London: Hutchinson).

Kline, P. (1984) *Psychology and Freudian Theory: an Introduction* (London: Methuen).

Kline, P. and Storey, R. (1977) 'A factor analytical study of the oral character,' *British Journal of Social and Clinical Psychology*, **16**, 317–28.

Klopfer, B. *et al.* (1956) *Developments in the Rorschach Technique, vol. 2, Fields of Application* (New York: Harcourt Brace).

Kohn, M.L. (1968) 'Social class and schizophrenia: A critical review', in Rosenthal, D. and Kety, S.S. (eds) *The Transmission of Schizophrenia* (Elmsford, NY: Pergamon).

Kraepelin, E. (1913) *Psychiatry* (8th edn) (Leipzig: Thieme).

Lader, M. (1975) *The Psychophysiology of Mental Illness* (London: Routledge and Kegan Paul).

Laing, R. (1967) *The Politics of Experience and the Bird of Paradise* (Harmondsworth: Penguin).

Lamiell, J.T. (1981) 'Toward an idiothetic psychology of personality', *American Psychologist*, **36**, (3), 276–89.

Laing, R.D. (1964) 'Is schizophrenia a disease?', *International Journal of Social Psychiatry*, **10**, 184–93.

Laing, R.D. (1965) *The Divided Self* (Harmondsworth, Middlesex: Penguin).

Lang, P.J. and Melamed, B.G. (1969) 'Case report: avoidance conditioning therapy of an infant with chronic ruminative vomiting', *Journal of Abnormal Psychology*, **74**, 1–8.

Lanyon, R.I. (1984) 'Personality assessment', *Annual Review of Psychology*, **35**, 667–701.

LaRue, A., Dessonville, C. and Jarvik, L.F. (1985) 'Aging and mental disorders', in Birren, J.E. and Schaie, K.W. (eds) *Handbook of Psychology of Aging* (2nd edn) (New York: Van Nostrand-Reinhold).

Lazare, A., Klerman, G.I. and Armor, D.J. (1966) 'Oral, obsessive and hysterical personality patterns: an investigation of psychoanalytic concepts by means of factor analysis', *Archives of General Psychiatry*, **14**, 624–30.

Lazarus, A.A. (1971) *Behavior Therapy and Beyond* (New York: McGraw-Hill).

Leahy, A.M. (1935) 'Nature–nurture and intelligence', *Genetic Psychology Monograph*, **17**, 235–308.

Lee, V.E., Brooks-Gunn, J. and Schnur, E. (1988) 'Does Head Start work? A 1–year follow-up comparison of disadvantaged children attending

Head Start, no preschool, and other preschool programmes', *Developmental Psychology*, **24**, 210–22.

Levinger, G. and Clark, J. (1961) 'Emotional factors in the forgetting of word associations', *Journal of Abnormal and Social Psychology*, **62**, 99–105.

Lieberman, M.A., Yalom, J.D. and Miles, M.B. (1973) *Encounter Groups: First Facts* (New York: Basic Books).

Linton, H.B. (1955) 'Dependence on external influence: correlates in perception, attitudes and judgement', *Journal of Abnormal and Social Psychology*, **51**, 502–7.

London: H. and Exner, J.E. (eds) (1978) *Dimensions of Personality* (New York: Wiley).

Lovaas, O.I., Koegel, R., Simmons, J. and Long, J. (1973) 'Some generalisation and follow-up measures on autistic children in behaviour therapy', *Journal of Applied Behaviour Analysis*, **6**, 131–66.

Maccoby, E. and Jacklin, C. (1974) *The Psychology of Sex Differences* (Stanford, California: Stanford University Press).

Mackay, D. (1975) *Clinical Psychology – Theory and Therapy* (London: Methuen).

Mackenzie, B. (1984) 'Explaining the race difference in IQ: the logic, the methodology, and the evaluation', *Journal of American Psychologist*, **39**, 1214–33.

Magenis, R., Overton, K., Chamberlin, J.,Brady, T. and Lovrein, E. (1977) 'Paternal origin of the extra chromosome in Down's syndrome', *Human Genetics*, **37**, 7–16.

Malim, A., Birch, A. and Wadeley, A. (1992) *Perspectives in Psychology* (Basingstoke: Macmillan).

Marks, I.M. (1981) 'Review of behavioral psychotherapy: I. Obsessive-compulsive disorders', *American Journal of Psychiatry*, **138**, 584–92.

Marx, M.H. (1976) *Introduction to Psychology: Problems, Procedures and Principles* (New York and London: Macmillan).

Maslow, A.H. (1968) *Towards a Psychology of Being* (New York: Van Nostrand Reinhold).

Mattes, J. and Gittleman, R. (1983) 'Growth of hyperactive children on maintenance regimen of methylphenidate', *Archives of General Psychiatry*, **40**, 317–21.

May, P. (1968) *Treatment of Schizophrenia: A Comparative Study of Five Treatment Methods* (New York: Science House).

May, P. (1974) 'Psychotherapy research in schizophrenia – another view of present reality', *Schizophrenia Bulletin*, **1**, 126–32.

May, P., Tuma, A.H., Yale, C., Potepan, P. and Dixon, W.J. (1976) 'Schizophrenia: a follow-up study of results of treatment II. Hospital stay over two to five years', *Psychiatry*, **33**, 481–6.

McClelland, D.C., Atkinson, J.W., Clark, R.A. and Lowell, E.L. (1953) *The Achievement Motive* (New York: Appleton-Century-Croft).

McCord, R.R. and Wakefield, J.A. Jr (1981) 'Arithmetic achievement as a function of introversion–extraversion and teacher presented reward and punishment', *Personality and Individual Differences*, **2**, 142–52.

McCrae, R.R. and Costa, P.T. (1985) 'Updating Norman's "adequate taxonomy": intelligence and personality dimensions in natural language and in questionnaires', *Journal of Personality and Social Psychology*, **49**, 710–21.

McCrae, R.R. and Costa, P.T., Jnr (1987) 'Validation of the five-factor model of personality across instruments and observers', *Journal of Personality and Social Psychology*, **52**, 81–90.

Melamed, B., Hawes, R., Heiby, E. and Glick, J. (1975) 'Use of filmed modelling to reduce uncooperative behaviour of children during dental treatment', *Journal of Dental Research*, **54**, 797–801.

Messick, S. and Associates (1976) *Individuality in Learning* (San Francisco, Jossey-Bass).

Minuchin, S., Baker, L., Rosman, B., Liebman, R., Milman, L. and Todd,T. (1975) 'A conceptual model of psychosomatic illness in children: family organisation and family therapy', *Archives of General Psychiatry*, **32**, 1031–38.

Mischel, W. (1968) *Personality and Assessment* (New York: Wiley).

Mischel, W. (1981) *Introduction to Personality*, 3rd edn (New York: Holt, Rinehart and Winston).

Moniz, E. (1936) *Tentatives Operatories dans le traitement des certaines psychoses* (Paris: Masson).

Moos, R.H. (1969) 'Sources of variance in responses to questionnaires and behaviour', *Journal of Abnormal Psychology*, **74**, 405–12.

Murphy, J. (1976) 'Psychiatric labelling in cross-cultural perspective', *Science*, **191**, 1019–28.

Murray, H.A. (1938) *Explorations in Personality* (New York: Oxford University Press).

Nelson, R.O. (1977) 'Assessment and therapeutic functions of self-monitoring', in Hersen, M., Eisler, R. and Miller, P.M. (eds) *Progress in Behavior Modification* (New York: Academic Press).

Newman, H.H., Freeman, F.N. and Holzinger, K. (1937) *Twins: a Study of Heredity and Environment* (Chicago, University of Chicago Press).

Norman, W.T. (1963) 'Toward an adequate taxonomy of personality attributes: replicated factor structure in peer nomination personality ratings', *Journal of Abnormal Social Psychology*, **66**, 574–88.

Noyes, R., Anderson, D., Clancy, J., Crowe, R.R., Slyman, D.J., Ghoneim, M. and Hinrichs, J.V. (1984) 'Diazepam and propanol in panic disorder and agoraphobia', *Archives of General Psychiatry*, **41**, 287–92.

Nurnberg, H., Prudic, J., Fiori, M. and Freedman, E. (1984) 'Psycho-pathology complicating acquired immune deficiency syndrome (AIDS)', *American Journal of Psychiatry*, **141**, 95–6.

Olweus, D. (1977) 'A critical analysis of the "modern" interactionist position', in Magnusson, D. and Endler, N.S. (eds), *Personality at the Crossroads: Current Issues in Interactional Psychology* (Hillsdale, New Jersey: Lawrence Erlbaum Associates).

Parkin, A.J., Lewinsohn, J. and Folkard, S. (1982) 'The influence of emotion on immediate and delayed retention: Levinger and Clark reconsidered', *British Journal of Psychology*, **73**, 389–93.

Parloff, M., Waskow, I., and Wolfe, B. (1978) 'Research of therapist variables in relation to process and outcome', in Garfield, S.L. and Bergin, A.E. (eds) *Handbook of Psychotherapy and Behavior Change: An Empirical Analysis* (2nd edn) (New York: Wiley).

Paton, D. (1990) 'Assessing the impact of disasters on helpers', *Counselling Psychology Quarterly*, 3, 149–52.

Paul, G. (1966) *Insight versus Desensitization in Psychotherapy* (Stanford, Calif.: Stanford University Press).

Paul, G.L. and Lentz, R. (1977) *Psychosocial Treatment of Chronic Mental Patients: Milieu versus Social Learning Programs* (Cambridge, Mass.: Harvard University Press).

Peck, D. and Whitlow, D. (1975) *Approaches to Personality Theory* (London: Methuen).

Perls, F.S. (1969) *Gestalt Therapy Verbatim* (Moab, Utah: Real People Press).

Pervin, L.A. (1983) 'The stasis and flow of behavior: toward a theory of goals', in Page, M.M. (ed.), *Personality: Current Theory and Research, 1982 Nebraska Symposium on Motivation*, vol. 30, pp. 1–53 (Lincoln, Nebraska: University of Nebraska Press).

Pervin, L.A. and Lewis, M. (eds) (1978) *Perspectives in Interactional Psychology* (New York: Plenum Press).

Piaget, J. (1954) *The Construction of Reality in the Child* (New York: Basic Books).

Plummer, S., Baer, D. and LeBlanc, J. (1977) 'Functional consideration in the use of time-out and an effective alternative', *Journal of Applied Behaviour Analysis*, 10, 689–706.

Pollak, J.M. (1979) 'Obsessive-compulsive personality: a review', *Psychological Bulletin*, 86, 225–41.

Popper, K. (1959) *The Logic of Scientific Discovery* (London: Hutchinson).

Popper, K. (1972) *Conjectures and Refutations: the Growth of Scientific Knowledge*, 4th edn (London: Routledge and Kegan Paul).

Prien, R., Kupfer, D., Mansky, P., Small, J.,Tuason, V., Voss, C. and Johnson, W. (1984) 'Drug therapy in the prevention of recurrences in unipolar and bipolar affective disorders', *Archives of General Psychiatry*, 41, 1096–104.

Quinlan, D.M. and Blatt, S.J. (1973) 'Field articulation and performance under stress: differential prediction in surgical and psychiatric nursing training', *Journal of Consulting and Clinical Psychology*, 39, p. 517.

Rheta Schreiber,F. (1973) *Sybil* (Harmondsworth: Penguin).

Rieder, R., Mann, L., Weinerger,D., Kammen, D. van and Post, R. (1983) 'Computer tomographic scans in patients with schizophrenia, schizoaffective and bipolar affective disorder', *Archives of General Psychiatry*, 40, 735–9.

Robbin, A. (1958) 'A controlled study of the effects of leucotomy', *Journal of Neurology, Neurosurgery and Psychiatry*, 21, 262–9.

Robbin, A. (1959) 'The value of leucotomy in relation to diagnosis', *Journal of Neurology, Neurosurgery and Psychiatry*, 22, 132–6.

Robins, L.N. (1966) *Deviant Children Grown Up* (Baltimore: Williams and Wilkins).

Rogers, C.R. (1951) *Client-centred Therapy* (Boston, Mass.: Houghton).

Rogers, C.R. (1959) 'A theory of therapy, personality and interpersonal relationships as developed in the client-centred framework', in Koch, S. (ed.), *Psychology: A Study of a Science: Formations of the Person in the Social Context*, 3 (New York: McGraw-Hill).

Rogers, C. R. (1970) *Encounter Groups* (Harmondsworth: Penguin).

Rogers, C. R. (1961) *On Becoming a Person: A Therapist's View of Psychotherapy* (Boston: Houghton Mifflin).

Rorschach, H. (1921) *Psychodiagnostics: A Diagnostic Test Based on Perception* (2nd edn, 1942) (Bern: Huber).

Rosenhan, D. (1973) 'On being sane in insane places', *Science*, **179**, 250–58.

Rosenthal, R. (1966) *Experimenter Effects in Behavioural Research* (New York: Appleton-Century-Croft).

Rosenthal, R. and Jacobson, L. (1968) *Pygmalion in the Classroom: Teacher Expectation and Pupils' Intellectual Development* (New York: Holt, Rinehart and Winston).

Ross, A.O. (1981) *Psychological Disorders of Childhood: A Behavioral Approach to Theory, Research and Practice* (2nd edn) (New York: McGraw-Hill).

Rotter, J.B. (1954) *Social Learning and Clinical Psychology* (Englewood Cliffs, Prentice-Hall).

Ruble, D.N. and Nakamura, C.Y. (1972) 'Task orientation versus social orientation in young children and their attention to relevant stimuli', *Child Development*, **43**, 471–80.

Rush, A., Beck, A., Kovacs, M. and Hollon, S. (1977) 'Comparative efficacy of cognitive therapy and pharmacotherapy in the treatment of depressed outpatients', *Cognitive Therapy and Research*, **1**, 17–39.

Rushton, J.P. and Chrisjohn, R.D. (1981) 'Extraversion, neuroticism, psychoticism and self-reported deliquency: evidence from eight separate samples', *Personality and Individual Differences*, **2**, 11–20.

Rutter, M. (1966) 'Prognosis: psychotic children adolescence and early adult life', in Wing, J.K. (ed.), *Childhood Autism: Clinical, Educational, and Social Aspects* (Elmsford, NY: Pergamon).

Rutter, M. and Lockyer, L. (1967) 'A five to fifteen year follow-up of infantile psychosis: I. Description of sample', *British Journal of Psychiatry*, **113**, 1169–82.

Ryff, C.D. and Heinke, S.G. (1983) 'Subjective organisation of personality in adulthood and ageing', *Journal of Personality and Social Psychology*, **44**, 807–16.

Sacks, O. (1985) *The Man who Mistook His Wife for a Hat* (London: Picador).

Sakel, M. (1938) 'The pharmacological shock treatment of schizophrenia', *Nervous and Mental Diseases Monograph*, **62**.

Saville, P. and Blinkhorn, S. (1976) *Undergraduate Personality by Factored Scales* (Windsor: National Foundation for Educational Research).

Scarr, S. and Weinberg, R.A. (1977) 'Intellectual similarities within families of both adopted and biological children', *Intelligence*, **1**, 170–91.

Scarr-Salapatek, S. (1971) 'Social class and IQ', *Science*, **174**, 28–36.

Scheff,T.J. (1966) *Being Mentally Ill: a Sociological Theory* (Chicago: Aldine).

Schiff, M., Duyne, M. Dumaret, A., Stewart, J., Tomkiewicz, S. and Fenigold, J. (1978) 'Intellectual status of working-class children adopted early into upper-middle class families', *Science*, **200**, 1503–4.

Schneider, K. (1959) 'Primary and secondary symptoms in schizophrenia', in Hirsch, S.R. and Shepherd, M. (eds), (1974) *Themes and Variations in European Psychiatry* (New York: John Wright).

Scott, M.J. and Stradling, S.G. (1992) 'Post-traumatic stress disorder without the trauma', unpublished manuscript.

Seligman, M. (1974) 'Depression and learned helplessness', in Friedman, R.J. and Katz, M.M. (eds) *The Psychology of Depression: Contemporary Theory and Research* (Washington, DC: Winston-Wiley).

Semeonoff, B. (1981) 'Projective techniques', in Fransella, F. (ed.), *Personality: Theory, Measurement and Research* (London: Methuen).

Shackleton, V. and Fletcher, C. (1984) *Individual Differences: Theories and Applications* (London: Methuen).

Shapiro, D. A. and Shapiro, D. (1982) 'Meta-analysis of comparative therapy outcome studies: a replication and refinement', *Psychological Bulletin*, **92**, 581–604, 665.

Shapiro, D. A. and Shapiro, D. (1983) 'Comparative therapy outcome research: methodological implications of meta-analysis', *Journal of Consulting and Clinical Psychology*, **51**, 42–53.

Shapiro, D. and Surwit, R.S. (1979) 'Biofeedback', in Pomerleau, O.F. and Brady, J.P. (eds), *Behavioral Medicine: Theory and Practice* (Baltimore: Williams and Wilkins).

Sheldon, W. (1942) *The Varieties of Temperament: A Psychology of Constitutional Differences* (New York: Harper).

Shields, J. (1962) *Monozygotic Twins Brought up Apart and Brought up Together* (Oxford: Oxford University Press).

Shields, J. (1976) 'Heredity and environment', in Eysenck, H.J. and Wilson, G.D. (eds), *A Textbook of Human Psychology* (Baltimore: University Park Press).

Shopsin, B., Gershon,S., Thompson, H. and Collins, P. (1975) 'Psychoactive drugs in mania', *Archives of General Psychiatry*, **32**, 34–42.

Shostrum, E.L., Knapp, R.R. and Knapp, L. (1976) 'Validation of the personal orientation dimensions. An inventory for the dimensions of actualising', *Educational and Psychological Measurement*, **36** (2), pp. 491–4.

Shuey, A.M. (1966) *The Testing of Negro Intelligence* (3rd edn) (New York: Social Science Press).

Simon, B. (1971) *Intelligence, Psychology and Education – a Marxist Critique* (London: Lawrence and Wishart).

Skeels, H.M. (1966) 'Adult status of children with contrasting early life experiences', *Monographs of the Society for Research in Child Development, 31* (whole no. 3).

Skinner, B.F. (1974) *About Behaviourism* (London: Jonathan Cape).

Sloane, R., Staples, F., Cristol, A. Yorkston, N. and Whipple, K. (1975) *Psychoanalysis versus Behavior Therapy* (Cambridge, Mass.: Harvard University Press).

Smith, M.L. and Glass, G.V. (1977) 'Meta-analysis of psychotherapeutic outcome studies', *American Psychologist, 32*, 752–60.

Smith, M.L., Glass, G.V. and Miller, B.L. (1980) *The Benefits of Psychotherapy* (Baltimore, Maryland: Johns Hopkins University Press).

Spearman, C. (1904) 'General intelligence, objectively determined and measured', *American Journal of Psychology, 15*, 201–93.

Spitzer, R.L. (1976) 'More on pseudoscience and the case for psychiatric diagnosis', *Archives of General Psychiatry, 33*, 459–470.

Spitzer, R., Endicott, J. and Gibbon, M. (1979) 'Crossing the border into borderline personality and borderline schizophrenia', *Archives of General Psychiatry, 36*, 17–24.

Sprague, R. and Sleator, E. (1977) 'Methylphenidate in hyperkinetic children. Differences in dose effects on learning and social behaviour', *Science, 198*, 1274–76.

Stephenson, W. (1953) *The Study of Behavior* (Chicago, Ill.: University of Chicago Press).

Sterman, H.B. (1973) 'Neurophysiologic and clinical studies of sensorimotor EEG biofeedback training: some effects on epilepsy', *Seminars in Psychiatry, 5*, 507–25.

Stern, S., Rush, J. and Mendels, J. (1980) 'Toward a rational pharmacotherapy of depression', *American Journal of Psychiatry, 137*, 545–52.

Sternberg, R.J. (1984) 'What should intelligence tests test? Implications of a triarchic theory of intelligence for intelligence testing', *Educational Researcher, 13* (1), 5–15.

Sternberg, R.J. (1985) *Beyond IQ: a Triarchic Theory of Human Intelligence* (Cambridge University Press).

Sternberg, R.J. (1988) *The Triarchic Mind: a New Theory of Human Intelligence* (New York: Viking).

Sternberg, R.J. (1990) *Metaphors of Mind: Conceptions of the Nature of Intelligence* (Cambridge University Press).

Sternberg, R.J. (in press) *Sternberg Triarchic Abilities Test* (San Antonia, TX: The Psychological Corporation).

Stott, D.H. (1978) *Helping Children with Learning Difficulties* (London: Ward Lock).

Szasz, T. (1967) *The Myth of Mental Illness* (London: Paladin).

Szasz, T. (1973) *The Manufacture of Madness* (London: Paladin).

Tausch, R. (1978) 'Facilitative dimensions in interpersonal relations: verifying the theoretical assumptions of Carl Rogers in school, family, education, client-centred therapy', *College Student Journal, 12*, 2.

Terman, L.M. (1921) 'In symposium: intelligence and its measurement', *Journal of Educational Psychology, 12*, 127–33.

Terry, R.D. and Wisiniewski, H.M. (1977) Structural aspects of aging in the brain', in Eisdorfer, C. and Friedel, R.O. (eds), *Cognitive and Emotional Disturbances in the Elderly* (Chicago: Medical Yearbook Publishers).

Thomas, L. (1978) 'A personal construct approach to learning in education, training and therapy', in Fransella, F. (ed.), *Personal Construct Psychology, 1977* (London: Academic Press).

Thurstone, L.L. (1938) 'Primary mental abilities', *Psychometric Monograph*, 1.

Tobias, P. (1974) 'IQ and the nature–nurture controversy', *Journal of Behavioural Science*, **2**, 24.

Truax, C.B., Schuldt, W.J. and Wargo, D.G. (1968) 'Self-ideal concept congruence and improvement in group psychotherapy', *Journal of Consulting and Clinical Psychology*, **32**, 47–53.

Tupes, E.C. and Christal, R.E. (1961) 'Recurrent personality factors based on trait ratings', *USAF ASD Technical Report*, no. 61–97.

Ullman, L. and Krasner, L. (1975) *A Psychological Approach to Abnormal Behavior* (2nd edn) (Englewood Cliffs, NJ: Prentice-Hall).

Vagg, P.R. and Hammond, S.B. (1976) 'The number and kind of invariant personality Q factors: a partial replication of Eysenck and Eysenck', *British Journal of Social and Clinical Psychology*, **15**, 121–30.

Vaughn, C. and Leff, J. (1976) 'The influence of family and social factors on the course of psychiatric illness. A comparison of schizophrenic and depressed neurotic patients', *British Journal of Psychiatry*, **129**, 125–37.

Vegelius, J. (1976) 'On various G index generalisations and their applicability within the clinical domain' (Uppsala: Acta Univ, Uppsaliensis).

Vernon, P.E. (1950) *The Structure of Human Abilities* (London: Methuen).

Vernon, P.E. (1960) *Intelligence and Attainment Tests* (London: University of London Press).

Vernon, P.E. (1964) *Personality Assessment* (London: Methuen).

Vernon, P.E. (1969) *Intelligence and Cultural Environment* (London: Methuen).

Vernon, P.E. (1972) 'The distinctiveness of field dependence', *Journal of Personality*, **40**, 366–91.

Wade, T.C. and Baker, T.B. (1977) 'Opinions and use of psychological tests', *American Psychologist*, **32**, 874–82.

Walker, S. (1984) *Learning Theory and Behaviour Modification* (London: Methuen).

Walsh, B., Stewart, J., Roose, S., Gladis, M. and Glassman, A. (1984) 'Treatment of bulimia with phenelzine', *Archives of General Psychiatry*, **41**, 1105–9.

Wapner, S. (1976) 'Process and context in the conception of cognitive style', in Messick, S. and Associates, *Individuality in Learning* (San Francisco: Jossey-Bass).

Warburton, F.W. (1951) 'The ability of the Gurkha recruit', *British Journal of Psychology*, **42**, 123–33.

Ward, C., Beck, A.T., Mendelson, M., Mock, J. and Erbaugh, J. (1962) 'The psychiatric nomenclature: reasons for diagnostic disagreement', *Archives of General Psychiatry*, **7**, 198–205.

Wessler, R. L. (1986) 'Conceptualising cognitions in the cognitive-behavioural therapies', in Dryden, W. and Golden, W. (eds) *Cognitive Behavioural Approaches to Psychotherapy* (London: Harper & Row).

Wilkinson, F.R. and Carghill, D.W. (1955) 'Repression elicited by story material based on the Oedipus complex', *Journal of Social Psychology*, **42**, 209–14.

Williams, J.D., Dudley, H.K. and Overall, J.E. (1972) 'Validity of the 16 PF and the MMPI in a mental hospital setting', *Journal of Abnormal Psychology*, **80**, 261–70.

Williams, L. Martin, G., McDonald, S., Hardy, L. and Lambert, L. (snr) (1975) 'Effects of a backscratch contingency of reinforcement for table serving on social interaction with severely retarded girls', *Behaviour Therapy*, **6**, 220–29.

Wilson, G.T. and O'Leary, K.D. (1980) *Principles of Behavior Therapy* (Englewood Cliffs, NJ: Prentice-Hall).

Wiseman, S. (1964) *Education and Environment* (Manchester: Manchester University Press).

Witkin, H. (1950) 'Individual differences in ease of perception of embedded figures.' *Journal of Personality*, **19**, 1–15.

Witkin, H.A. (1976) 'Cognitive Style in Academic Performance and in Teacher-student Relations' in Messick, S. and Associates, *Individuality in Learning* (San Francisco: Jossey-Bass).

Witkin, H. (1977) 'Role of the field dependent and field independent cognitive style in academic evolution: a longitudinal study', *Journal of Educational Psychology*, **69** (3), 197–211.

Wolpe, J. (1958) *Psychotherapy by Reciprocal Inhibition* (Stanford, Calif.: Stanford University Press).

World Health Organisation (1988) *International Classification of Diseases* (10th revision) (Geneva: WHO).

Yarrow, L. (1973) 'The relationship between nutritive sucking experiences in infancy and non-nutritive sucking in childhood', in Eysenck, H.J. and Wison, G.D. (eds), *The Experimental Study of Freudian Theories* (London: Methuen).

Zarit, S. (1980) *Aging and Mental Disorders: Psychological Approaches to Assessment and Treatment* (New York: Free Press).

Zeigob, L., Arnold, S. and Forehand, R. (1975) 'An examination of observer effects in patient–child interactions', *Child development*, **46**, 509–12.

Zigler, E. and Berman, W. (1983) 'Discerning the future of early childhood intervention', *American Psychologist*, **38**, 894–906.

Zitrin, C., Klein, D., Woerner, M. and Ross, D. (1983) 'Treatment of phobias 1. Comparison of imipramine hydrochloride and placebo', *Archives of General Psychiatry*, **40**, 125–38.

Zubin, J., Eron, L.D. and Schumer, F. (1966) *An Experimental Approach to Projective Techniques* (London: Wiley).

# Index